Acclaim for Saul Bellow's *It All Adds Up*

"Compelling. . . . The portrait that emerges in this [collection] . . . is that of a self-made man . . . few writers can wax so gloriously honest about their love of art. Bellow's is heart-stirring . . . *It All Adds Up* [is] revealing as well as moving, for [it] introduces a part of Bellow—his faith, whether aesthetic or divine—that seems central to his bold and sometimes visionary fiction."
                                                    —*The Boston Sunday Globe*

"Bellow remains, pre-eminently, a writer, a man who finds his way into thought through his language, and one who can write a prose as lively with thought as any in our time. . . . And when delivers his criticism, he does so with a wonderfully witty novelist's eye."
                                                    —*San Francisco Chronicle*

"An uneven, brilliant, dismaying, essential collection . . . *It All Adds Up* records an extraordinary artist's self-preservation amid his own strikingly contradictory vision."   —*New York Newsday*

"This collection of essays is probably the closest thing to autobiography we will get from a writer whose pursuit of the moral in his novels helped make the novel a moral quest."   —*Forward*

"These are vivid, vibrant documents telling us how we have lived during the life of Bellow's memory and how we might yet perfect ourselves, how the world might become that place in which art reigns and thought becomes aesthetic pleasure."   —*Chicago Tribune*

PENGUIN BOOKS

IT ALL ADDS UP

Saul Bellow, author of more than twelve novels and two short-story collections, was awarded the 1976 Nobel Prize for Literature. He has also won the Pulitzer Prize, three National Book Awards, and the 1990 National Book Foundation Medal for distinguished contribution to American letters. A longtime resident of Chicago, he now lives in New England.

ALSO BY SAUL BELLOW

Something to Remember Me By

The Bellarosa Connection

A Theft

More Die of Heartbreak

Him with His Foot in His Mouth and Other Stories

The Dean's December

To Jerusalem and Back: A Personal Account

Humboldt's Gift

Mr. Sammler's Planet

Mosby's Memoirs and Other Stories

Herzog

Henderson the Rain King

Seize the Day

The Adventures of Augie March

The Victim

Dangling Man

SAUL
BELLOW

It All
Adds Up

From the Dim Past to the
Uncertain Future

A NONFICTION
COLLECTION

PENGUIN BOOKS

PENGUIN BOOKS
Published by the Penguin Group
Penguin Books USA Inc., 375 Hudson Street,
New York, New York 10014, U.S.A.
Penguin Books Ltd, 27 Wrights Lane, London W8 5TZ, England
Penguin Books Australia Ltd, Ringwood, Victoria, Australia
Penguin Books Canada Ltd, 10 Alcorn Avenue,
Toronto, Ontario, Canada M4V 3B2
Penguin Books (N.Z.) Ltd, 182–190 Wairau Road, Auckland 10, New Zealand

Penguin Books Ltd, Registered Offices: Harmondsworth, Middlesex, England

First published in the United States of America by Viking Penguin,
a division of Penguin Books USA Inc., 1994
Published in Penguin Books 1995

10 9 8 7 6 5 4 3 2 1

THE LIBRARY OF CONGRESS HAS CATALOGUED THE HARDCOVER AS FOLLOWS:
Bellow, Saul.
It All Adds Up: From the Dim Past to the Uncertain Future:
A Nonfiction Collection/Saul Bellow.
p.   cm.
ISBN 0-670-85331-3 (hc.)
ISBN 0 14 02.3365 2 (pbk.)
I. Title
PS3503.E4488023   1994
814'.52—dc20   93–25554

Printed in the United States of America
Set in Adobe Janson Text
Designed by Francesca Belanger

Acknowledgments

I want to thank my agent, Harriet Wasserman, for urging me to take the time to put together this collection.

To Marjorie Shain Horvitz, my copy editor, who attended so diligently to the minute particulars and who devoted so much time to the correction of these pieces, special thanks are due.

Contents

PART THREE: *The Distracted Public*

PART FOUR: *Thoughts in Transition*

PART FIVE: *A Few Farewells*

PART SIX: *Impressions and Notions*

PREFACE

*I*t is never altogether pleasant to read what you wrote decades ago. Here and there I found pieces that pleased me, and for a moment I could say, like little Jack Horner, "Oh, what a good boy was I!" The least gratifying of my discoveries was that I, too, had a King Charles head and that I had been doodling away like Mr. Dick in *David Copperfield*. I was obsessed or distracted by the subject of distraction. A second King Charles head, smaller but nearly as persistent, presently materialized: I kept mentioning Wyndham Lewis. Why was it that I invoked few other names?

I have been reading Lewis for half a century or longer. His political ideas repelled me (I still dislike them), but he had thought more deeply and written more intelligently about the lot of the artist in the twentieth century than any of his contemporaries. I cared little for *The Art of Being Ruled*, but I have gone back repeatedly to books like *Men Without Art, America and the Cosmic Man, The Writer and the Absolute*, and his literary autobiography, *Rude Assignment*. I have studied him closely, and I referred to him oftener than I had realized. He has been described and dismissed as a Nietzschean, and I was occasionally advised to go to the source. But a writer of genius like Lewis is more than the sum of his influences. William Blake is sometimes described as a Rousseauan, but it was not Rousseau who wrote the *Songs of Experience*. A writer often casts about for the support of a precedent, and when I needed one I found myself frequently recalling what Lewis had to say on matters of importance.

In reading these pieces again, I kept thinking about Robert Frost's poem to the effect that there had been promises to keep and miles to go before I could sleep. Not so. I had already been fast asleep and had to trust the little horse to bring me home. *He* knew the way (more or less).

I have been invited to print *all* the trifles I wrote to support myself, but I have decided to acknowledge no "historical responsibilities." This therefore is not a reliquary but a gathering of some of the more readable essays. If I were to write these pieces today, I think that I should say less about distraction and emphasize instead the importance of attention. Many years ago, reading Tolstoy's essay on Maupassant, I was struck by his short list of indispensable qualifications for good writing. These were: a perspicuous style (I have to accept the translator's adjective), a moral foundation—that is, a strong stand taken on the problem of good and evil—and lastly the faculty of attention. By attending closely, the writer was to breed attentiveness in his readers, replacing the world with *his* world. Single-mindedness and passion are interchangeable here. All that remains to be said on the subject is that a writer is educated mainly by his mistakes. And as Henry James grimly suggests in his story "The Middle Years," when you have completed your self-education and mastered your trade, you are likely to find that your time has run out.

When a writer says "My time is up," it's highly probable that he doesn't really mean it. What most saddens him is that his mistakes are indelibly recorded in what he once wrote. If I had it to do again I could do it so much better, he says, and he longs to correct himself publicly and to revise and retract. Some of my friends have been deeply skeptical about adult education. Prevailing opinion has been that it is no use to attempt in middle age what should have been done in the years of maximum receptivity. But some of us are stubborn learners, and my sixties and my seventies proved to be enlightening decades. I learned many things that I should have known earlier.

The bitterness of my dissatisfaction in rereading some of these pieces is due to basic revisions, radical changes in my point of view. I can see now where I went wrong. The "road not taken" *was* taken, taken a hundred times. By now I have gone many miles toward the promise of sleep, but I reach my destination blindingly wide awake.

My state therefore is something like a state of insomniac illumination. I failed to understand the things I wrote, the books I read, the lessons I was taught, but I find that I am a most persistent self-educator, that I long for correction. Very possibly I have not achieved my goals, but it gives great satisfaction nonetheless to have rid oneself of tenacious old errors. To enter an era of improved errors.

It All Adds Up

MOZART: AN OVERTURE

(1992)

*I*n preparing this essay, I have found myself sizing up Mozart as if I were thinking of writing a novel in which he might appear as a character. I was not aware at the outset that this was what I was doing. It was only after I had written half of it that I recognized what I had done.

Mozart is immediately accessible to the naive. Others obviously require preparation. It is no criticism of twelve-tone composers, to choose an obvious example, to note that they oblige us to give some thought to the formal assumptions they expect us to share. Mozart, however, can be loved freely and naturally by amateurs. It is because I am an amateur that I have been invited to discuss Mozart, and I intend to make the most of my amateur standing, bypassing the problems that intrigue and vex the learned specialists I have read in my efforts to get a handle of my own on this subject.

My best course is to convert ignorance to an advantage. What follows is a confession, supplemented by such tentative ideas as are bound to flutter out when any of us makes an open declaration of this sort. I shall begin by saying that there are corners of my existence which from the first were furnished by Mozart. It does not seem to me that any other musical tenant ever had to be moved out to make room for him. I had an older sister—much my senior—who played the piano. She did not play particularly well. She was a perfect metronome (metrognome) of a pianist, but she did familiarize me with Mozart.

Bostonia magazine, Spring 1992. Delivered at the Mozart Bicentennial, 5 December 1991, in Florence, Italy.

There was a manufacturer in Chicago by the name of Gulbrantsen, and in his advertisements, painted on brick walls, an infant was shown pressing the pedals of a piano. The legend was: "The richest child is poor without a musical education." This was a warning taken seriously by parents in the Midwest. I was given violin lessons at an early age. Many of the music teachers were refugees from revolutionary Russia. Mine was a stout gloomy man from Odessa seeking a prodigy, a second Heifetz or Menuhin or Elman, to make his reputation. Obviously I lacked the gifts he was looking for, and he would snatch the bow and whip my bottom with it. He was so peevish and futile that I was more amused than hurt. I did, somehow, learn to fiddle adequately, and until middle age I was on the lookout for amateur musicians like myself and had the pleasure occasionally of playing Mozart sonatas arranged for duets and trios. In my student years I was an unpaid usher at the Auditorium Theater; the Ballet Russe de Monte Carlo and the San Carlo Opera came regularly to Chicago. Samuel Insull, the utilities tycoon, gave the city an opera house (before he fled to Greece and had to be extradited). International celebrities were brought to Orchestra Hall by Hurok the impresario. There were excellent teachers of theory and music history and first-rate performers at the south end of the Loop. Although I was not trained in a conservatory, I absorbed a considerable amount of music, and while I preferred books to instruments, there were odd corners of my existence reserved for Handel, Mozart, Pergolesi, etc.

I have now explained my amateur standing and will go on to the confessions I promised. But what does one confess today, when the worst of the sins have become venial? It is the violation of orderly processes of thought as prescribed by the higher rationality that throws you into sin. To be unscientific is in our time a grave mental offense.

Some of my speculations on Mozart are notably unscientific. I often puzzle over the nature of his genius. How was it that it should appear so early and develop so swiftly and be so complete? Was it because his father was an educator of corresponding genius? Nobody ever suspected genius of any sort in Leopold. Neither do the educational or genetic contributions of his mother strike his biographers as exceptional. Mozart, to borrow a figure from William Blake, was a piece of ground already spaded and seeded. It looks, in other words, as if he had brought it all with him. And then I think of other prodigies born into mathematical or musical families. The mature forms assumed by these exceptional creatures are not to be accounted for by environmental or historical theories. They resemble the flowers or the insects, they have powers that astonish and physiological refinements or resources of intelligence too curious to be explained by probability theory or the ponderous slowness of time, or by trial and error. What they suggest is the intervention of invisible purposes. "To a certain extent," writes Alfred Einstein, "it is true that Mozart was only a visitor upon this earth. Mozart as a man was nowhere truly at home: neither in Salzburg, where he was born, nor in Vienna, where he died."

At the heart of my confession, therefore, is the hunch that with beings such as Mozart we are forced to speculate about transcendence, and this makes us very uncomfortable, since ideas of transcendence are associated with crankiness or faddism—even downright instability and mental feebleness. These are the charges and the guilts you open yourself to when you confess that you find it impossible to dismiss such speculations. To some reasonable minds this might lead to the limiting of art—art in which religious or other "undesirable" tendencies survive—to ceremonial or traditional observances. On occasions like the present one: occasions of cultural piety.

Music, I assume (amateurishly), is based on a tonal code containing, inevitably, expressions of the whole history of feeling, emotion, belief—of essences inseparable from what we call our "higher life." I suggest also that this is where we tend to go when we have gone as far as we can in the new positive orthodoxies that keep us within bounds—the assumptions which our education and the business of the world have trained us to accept as normal, practical, and indispensable: the founding postulates of our scientific and technological achievements.

From all this a Mozart gives us an orderly and also an emotional exit—an endlessly rich and exalted release.

I don't want to make too much of this notion of a profound originality coming from God knows what source. I invoke it as a corrective to the earthbound psychology that rules our minds in this century. It does no harm to be reminded that this psychology is painfully limiting to the intelligence and is often little more than a convenient way to dispose of troublesome intimations of a forbidden nature. The miracles that fascinate us are the scientific and technological ones. These have changed space, time, and nature. To positivists ours is an object world ruled by ideas. A contemporary environment is made up of such embodied ideas—ideas of residence, transportation, seeing and hearing at a distance, etc. By means of such ideas (and they are highly sophisticated) the earth itself has been humanized. This is simple enough to see, and externally self-explanatory. Press a switch and you will see people, you will hear them speak. Few of us, however, can explain the techniques by which this is accomplished.

Years ago I read a curious book by Ortega y Gasset called *The Revolt of the Masses*. In it Ortega explains what a Mass Man is: he is not invariably a proletarian—educated professionals may also be mass men. This is not the place to explain what Ortega was talking about. Only one of his arguments concerns me here: he says that the Mass Man is unable to distinguish between a natural object or process and an artifact, a second-nature object. He takes it for granted, as part of the order of things, that when he enters an elevator and presses the button he will go up. When mechanisms fail, when, for instance, elevators do not rise or buses do not arrive, the spirit in which he protests reveals that he understands elevators or buses to be free commodities like daylight or the universal availability of breathable air.

To congratulate ourselves, however, on our educated enlightenment is simply an evasion of the real truth. We the "educated" cannot even begin to explain the technologies of which we make daily use. We speak of electronics or cybernetics—but it is all in vain. Natural processes are beyond us too, and despite our talk of lipids or carbohydrate metabolism, we understand virtually nothing about the physiology of digesting or the transmission of nerve impulses. Face-to-face with the technological miracles without which we could not live our lives, we are as backward as any savage, though education helps us to conceal this from ourselves and others. Indeed, it would utterly paralyze us to ponder intricate circuits or minicomputers, or attempt to gain a clear understanding of the translation of the discoveries of particle physics into modern arms.

These, however, are the miracles for which we have a very deep respect and which, perhaps, dominate our understanding of what a miracle is. A miracle is what brings people to Australia in ten hours. And we owe this to the scientific revolution.

What I am calling to your attention is entirely transparent. No other generation in history has lived in a world miraculously transformed by readily available artifacts. Ortega y Gasset notwithstanding, we are by and large no better at distinguishing nature from artifice than his Mass Man. Worse, we have lost Ortega's old-fashioned confidence in our power to explain what nature is. Can we say that we comprehend the metabolic internal blizzard that converts matter into energy?

Our assignment, in one sense, is simply to man the artifacts that technology provides in ever more esoteric and miraculous variations. But what of the music of *Don Giovanni* or *Così Fan Tutte* considered as a miracle—as a comprehensive revelation of what Eros can be in two such different outpourings of sound?

I suppose almost everyone would feel that just as the principles behind a product of technology can be fully grasped if we determine to study the method laid down for us by intelligent beings whom basically we resemble, we will be able also to give a full account of these operas. But when we try to do that, the music brings us to a standstill. There is a dimension of music that prohibits final comprehension and parries or fends off the cognitive habits we respect and revere. We appear to feel that we are riding the crest of a wave of comprehension that has already overcome nature, and we are committed to the belief that there are no mysteries—there is only the not-yet-known. But I think I have made myself clear. We are as ignorant of fundamentals as human beings ever were. Self-respect demands that we appear to be "with it."

And perhaps what I have been saying is related to the growing importance of Mozart, for as the twentieth century concludes, his Romantic rivals seem less great than they did fifty or sixty years ago. The most accomplished of contemporary music historians, writers like the brilliant Wolfgang Hildesheimer, feel that he is the sort of man we find singularly familiar, and Peter Porter some time ago in an *Encounter* essay (June 1983) wrote that Mozart "seems a modern man," closer to ourselves than Bach, "a personality in sight and comprehensible to our temperament." He goes on to say that there is enough evidence (by which he means documentary evidence—correspondence, personal reminiscences, data brought to light by researchers) "to induce a great sadness when we consider Mozart's life. It will not look like a triumph, it refuses to allow us to escape an uncomfortable if anachronistic sense of guilt; no arrangement of facts or twisting of fiction, from the sugary distortions of Sacha Guitry to the demeaning simplifications of Peter Schaffer's *Amadeus*, will fit Mozart out in the garments of vindication or apotheosis. He is so very unlike Beethoven, a titan of a very different sort."

Now, "modern" is a curious term: it can be used to degrade as well as (or more often than) to elevate. It can mean decadent, degenerate, nihilistic, abysmal, at one end—or it can signify a capacity to overcome contemporary disorder, or to adumbrate a stage in the formation of a new superiority, or to begin to distill a new essence. It can mean that the best of contemporary minds show qualities of power, subtlety, scope, and resourcefulness, of infinite plasticity, adaptability, of the courage to cope with all that world history has dumped on the generations of this present age. "The human mind," E. M. Forster observed, "is not a dignified organ." And he called upon us to "exercise it sincerely."

In Mozart's case, "sincerity" is a marginal consideration, since he was not obliged to seek the truth in German, French, Italian, or English. His objective was not sincerity; it was bliss. But as we will all understand immediately, the view that the mind is not a dignified organ is modern. It is exactly what we expect. It is this casualness, irony, levity, that we seem in our time to take for granted. The starchiness of nineteenth-century ideals, the pompousness of twentieth-century dictators, are rejected and mocked as dangerous and false. Reading about Mozart's personal life, we recognize that he was informal, to say the least, *sans façon*. He struck no attitudes—the very idea of "genius" was alien to him. From his letters we see that as an observer he was singularly modern. Let me give a few examples of this. Here is his description of the Archduke Maximilian, a brother of the emperor and the new Archbishop of Cologne:

> When God gives man a sacred office, He generally gives him understanding; and so it is, I trust, in the case of the Archduke.

But before he became a priest, he was far more witty and intelligent and talked less, but more sensibly. You should see him now. Stupidity oozes out of his eyes. He talks and holds forth incessantly and always in falsetto—and he has started a goitre. In short, the fellow has changed completely.   (1781—*aetat.* 35)

And here is his description of a Dominican monk from Bologna:

. . . regarded as a holy man. For my part I do not believe it, for at breakfast, he often takes a cup of chocolate and immediately afterwards a good glass of strong Spanish wine; and I have myself had the honor of lunching with this saint who at table drank a whole decanter and finished up with a full glass of strong wine, two large slices of melon, some peaches, pears, five cups of coffee, a whole plate of cloves, and two full saucers of milk and lemon. He may of course be following some sort of diet, but I do not think so, for it would be too much; moreover, he takes several little snacks during the afternoon. . . .   (21 August 1770)

Mozart has the novelist's gift of characterizing by minute particulars. He is not respectful, neither is he severe—not even when he writes: "Stupidity oozes out of his eyes." His manner of seeing comes directly from his nature, perhaps from a source close to the source of his music. The two styles, the verbal and the musical, have something in common. He often comments on the voices of the people he describes. The archbishop holds forth in falsetto. The poet Wieland, whom he meets in Mannheim in 1777, "has a rather childish voice" and a defect of speech "that makes him speak very slowly," so that he "can't say half a dozen words without stopping." As for singers, he comments extensively on them: "A fine singer, a baritone, and forced when he sings falsetto, but not as much as Tibaldi in Vienna." "Bradamante, in love with Ruggiero . . . is sung by a poor Baroness. . . . She appears under an assumed name . . . has a passable voice, and her stage presence would not be bad, but she sings off pitch like the devil."

He has a keen modern appetite for personal impressions, Einstein notes. About landscape—though he is a great traveler—he rarely writes. "About art he did not express himself at all." Einstein adds a little further on that in Rome, "the most beautiful flowers did not interest him, for he was sitting at home covering paper with music." From Rome, Mozart had written to his sister jokingly that beautiful flowers were being carried past in the street—"so Papa has just told me."

To be modern is to be mobile, forever en route, with few local attachments anywhere, cosmopolitan, not particularly disturbed to be an outsider in temporary quarters. On his journeys Mozart composed in his head. He was mobile by temperament. Nissen, one of his early biographers, records that Mozart's sister-in-law remembered that in his last years "he looked at everyone with a piercing glance, giving balanced answers to everything, whether he was merry or sad, and yet he seemed at the same time to be lost in thought about something entirely different. Even when he washed his hands in the morning he walked up and down, never stood still, knocked one heel against the other and was always reflective. . . . He was always enthusiastic about new entertainments, riding and billiards, for example. . . . He was always moving his hands and feet, always playing with something, e.g., his hat, pockets, watch-chain, tables, chairs, as if they were pianos. . . ."

What *was* permanent, evidently, he carried within. In 1788, he writes from Vienna: "We are sleeping tonight, for the first time, in our new quarters [in Währing], where we shall remain both summer and winter. On the whole the change is all the same to me, in fact I prefer it. . . . I shall have more time to work."

Einstein tells us that Mozart and his wife changed their residence in Vienna eleven times within a period of ten years, "sometimes after so little as three months. Their life was a perpetual tour, changing from one hotel room to another, and the hotel rooms were soon forgotten. . . . He was ready at any time to change Vienna for another city or Austria for another country."

Nor was art a "project" for him, as it was to be for others in the nineteenth century. Nor did the thought of being a genius fortify him. He shed superfluous externals, and he appears early in life to have made his reckonings as to what could be dispensed with. This was done with intuitive rapidity and sureness—the clear signs of a pure and faultless freedom. To a modern, the posturing of Romantic geniuses has become hateful. It smells of public relations and imagemaking. In this line we think of Wagnerian megalomania, histrionics, cultism, and politics. Mozart has none of these defects or designs. He does not care about politics. "Power," in the classic modern sense, holds no appeal for him. Scheming is utterly alien to his character. And on the practical side he is utterly without foresight. His recent biographers agree that the management of his own affairs was disastrous. From these failures he withdrew into work. Among his Viennese contemporaries, says Peter Porter, summarizing the conclusions of Hildesheimer, he was judged to be unserious and improvident by nature. But this negligence or inability to foresee consequences (how could he fail to understand that *Figaro* would antagonize the Viennese aristocracy and that it would punish him by boycotting his concerts?) is something like the Roman flowers, the endless procession of carriages on tour, the landscapes he ignores, the many changes of residence. These transient experiences are a background or horizon. *The Marriage of Figaro had* to be written; the withdrawal of patronage consequently *had* to be endured. And so with other snubs, defeats, and disappointments. He fell in love with a woman who would not have him and made do with her sister. Of the lively interest he took in Constanze we know from the boisterous sexual candor of the letters he wrote her. Was he making the best of things, or are his fantasies about his genitalia and hers also on the transient horizon, a pleasant subject for correspondence—*not* after all the main thing?

We today have a particular fondness for Mozart's adolescent levity about sex (and what Porter speaks of as his "coprophilic fun and his . . . infantile sexuality"). But Mozart's own contemporaries were habitually freer in this regard than we are. His mother, too, used plain language. The nineteenth century gave us an interregnum of puritanism. I have often thought that "repression" and "inhibition" as described by Freud refer to a temporary shift of "moral" emphasis. Students of English literature are familiar with this move from the open sensuality of Fielding and Laurence Sterne to Victorian prudery ("propriety") in Dickens or Trollope. Rousseau's *Confessions* or Diderot's *Les Bijoux Indiscrets* confirms this. What the twentieth century has is a "liberation," with all the excesses and exaggeration the term connotes. It would be wrong to take Mozart as a herald of the "freedoms" we "conquered" at midcentury. He was not at all the pioneer "swinger" of Peter Schaffer's

Amadeus. Seventy years ago, my Russian immigrant uncles, aunts, and cousins were still speaking freely and colorfully about bodily functions and things sexual—"country matters," as Shakespeare called them in *Hamlet.* (Such lewd double entendres are common in his plays. Specialists in Tudor and Stuart literature have collected them.) Bawdry has a long pedigree. Conversation in the courts of Elizabeth and James I was not what we came later to call "respectable."

Mozart's lewdness in his letters to his "Bäsle"—a first cousin— might have been recorded, Mr. Porter says, for a textbook on infantile sexuality. But it is nothing like our modern street language, which is seldom funny and tends rather to become routine. The high-spirited obscenities of the eighteenth century disappear from the Romantic literature of the nineteenth—perhaps as a concession to the self-improving bourgeois reader with his peculiar ideas of gentility.

Yet it is no use pretending that Mozart was not curiously erratic. There is plenty of evidence that he acted up, that he clowned, performed tricks, made gags. He had a liking for low company too. A certain Frau Pichler, who wrote historical novels, observes that both Mozart and Haydn never "demonstrated in their personal intercourse any unusual intellectual power at all, and scarcely any learning or higher culture. In society they displayed only a common temperament, insipid jests, and [in the case of Mozart] a thoughtless way of life; and yet what depths, what worlds of fantasy, harmony, melody . . ." etc., she writes.

As this same lady once sat at the piano playing "Non più andrai" from *Figaro,* "Mozart, who happened to be present, came up behind me, and my playing must have pleased him, for he hummed the melody with me, and beat time on my shoulder; suddenly, however, he pulled up a chair, sat down, told me to keep playing the bass, and began to improvise variations so beautifully that everyone held his breath, listening to the music of the German Orpheus. But all at once he had had enough; he jumped up and, as he often did in his foolish moods, began to leap over table and chairs, miaowing like a cat and turning somersaults like an unruly boy." Hildesheimer speaks of such outbursts as "physical necessities, automatic compensation for a transcendent mind . . . they are the results, as well as the reflection, of mental distraction."

To think about Mozart's personality and the circumstances of his life is, to me, very pleasant—his boisterous humor is so very contemporary. Still, we can no more understand him than we can understand our contemporary selves. We come away from books like Hildesheimer's study of Mozart confessing that the riddle of his character is beyond us. It stands concealed behind his music, and we will never get to the bottom of it. When we say he is modern I suppose we mean that we recognize the signature of Enlightenment, of reason and universalism, in his music—we recognize also the limitations of Enlightenment. We have learned from history that enlightenment, liberation, and doom may go together. For every avenue liberation opens, two are closed. Within Mozart's cheerful daylight secularity there is always an otherworldly darkness. And the freedom he expresses is never without sadness, a deep submission to melancholy. We are endowed—so I interpret him—with comprehension, but what we are required to comprehend is too much for us.

Hildesheimer is persuaded that both Mozart and Beethoven carried what he calls "a metaphysical aura." Beethoven was aware of this, and he cultivated and exploited it. Mozart, not knowing that he had such an aura, "exaggerated his physical presence with continual diversionary tactics, which became routine." He was clownishly demonic. He was a "stranger" who never understood the nature of his strangeness. Beethoven asserts his greatness. Mozart does not. He is not concerned with himself; rather he is intent on what he was born to do. In him there are few indications of ordinary *amour propre* or common vanity, and no signs whatever of *grandezza*.

Now, all this talk of "metaphysical auras" can be irritating, I know. Still, when people who are clearly sensible insist on speaking of metaphysics and auras, we had better control our irritation prudently and ask ourselves why clear-minded, well-balanced people are obliged to forsake the positivist common sense on which we all rely. It is the music itself that drives them away from the rules of intellectual respectability. The music presses us to ask why it is so continually fertile, novel, ingenious, inexhaustible—why it is able to tell us so much more than other languages can tell us and why it is given so readily, easily, gratuitously. For it is not a product of effort. What it makes us see is that there are things which must be done easily. Easily or not at all— that is the truth about art. Concentration without effort is at the heart of the thing. Will and desire are silenced (as many mystics have understood), and work is transformed into play. And what we see in Mozart's earthly record is the preservation of what matters amid distractions and harassments—shall we make a sketchy list of these: lodgings, taverns, salons, cold and stupid aristocrats, unpaid debts, petty tyrants like the Bishop of Salzburg and his flunkies, endless travels, irrelevant landscapes, bad music, disappointments in love. Even the burden of a natural superiority, which breeds rancor in others and must therefore be dissembled.

Against this, there is the understanding that work should be transformed into play—perhaps as Wisdom puts it in the Book of Proverbs: "The Lord possessed me in the beginning of his ways, before he made anything from the beginning. I was set up from eternity, and of old, before the earth was made. . . . I was with him forming all things: and was delighted every day, playing before Him at all times; playing in the world. And my delights were to be with the children of men." (Proverbs 8:22–3, 30–1)

We can't speak of Mozart without wondering "where it all comes from," without touching on certain "eternal," "mysterious" questions. Many have credibly argued that he is "modern" ("one of us"), and yet it is the essence of the "modern" to demystify. How is it that our "modern Mozart" should *increase* mystery? We are inclined to think of mystery as woolly or amorphous, yet Mozart, working in the light, openly, is all coherence. Although he does not use a cognitive language, we can, up to a point, understand him fully. His sounds and rhythms correspond to states of feeling that we have all somehow learned to interpret. This musical mode of speech is different from the semantic one that allows us to specify or denote. We feel moved to go beyond such speech, either in the direction of the pure exactness of mathematics or in the direction of the higher affects of sound or sight. The latter, the affects, are all the more powerful because they go beyond the definitions of speech, of intelligible discourse. This music of Mozart is the speech of affects. What can we call it *but* mysterious. In it we hear; through it is expressed our sense of the radical mystery of our being. This is what we hear in *Così Fan Tutte* or in the G-minor Quintet. In the latter more than a few writers have told us that they hear "the prayer of a lonely man," "the Garden of Gethsemane"— "cutting pain," says Abert. I prefer the term "radical mystery" to these religious interpretations. Radical mystery leaves Mozart freer to go into the problematic regions of existence in his Mozartean way. And all we can say about it is that it is "from beyond."

A few remarks now about the conditions of those of our contemporaries who listen to music. They—or, rather, we—can't be taken for granted. They are not what they were in the eighteenth century. I have already referred to Mozart as modern and drawn the usual unflattering picture, distorted if you like, of man in the present age. A strange creature—cerebral but not too intelligent, he lives in a special realm of consciousness, but his consciousness is inadequate. Applied science and engineering have so transformed the external world that it affects him as something magical. We know of course that it isn't magical; it is highly rational—a kind of rationality that might as well be magical. Self-respect demands that he (the pronoun includes us all) make gestures of rationality to signify that he is capable, at any rate, of keeping up. But you would agree—I think we are all ready to confess—that this "keeping up" is very tiring.

Civilized man does not give himself a good press. I don't say that he deserves to hold a good opinion of himself. Philosophy and literature have been particularly hard on him from the beginning of the modern age, and by now "Eurocentrism" has become a terrible reproach. We reproach ourselves even for the few decencies, bourgeois relics, with which we cover our shame. We hear from all sides that we are "inauthentic" and that we are, every one of us, impostors.

All of this, I think, comes from *us*. It is *we* who set up and *we* who knock down. If we are impostors, we are also those who expose impostors. This "being human" is our very own show. All that mankind is said to be, pro and contra, comes from mankind itself. Everything that we can possibly conceive is made into fact, and it all comes out of bottomless reservoirs of our invention and fantasy. Everything has to be tried out. Funnily enough, the same mind that takes in "Dallas" or rap music is also accessible to Homer and Shakespeare.

These are not merely diverting speculations. The awful truth is visible behind them. In this century, although briefly, slavery reappeared in Europe—in the wartime factories of Germany and in Siberian mines and forests. Only a few decades later, the finest kitchens and bathrooms in history were produced in the West, a wide-scale consumer culture such as the world had never seen.

But there is no need to make an inventory of the times. It is demoralizing to describe ourselves to ourselves yet again. It is especially hard on us since we believe (as we have been educated to believe) that history has formed us and that we are all mini-summaries of the present age.

When I say, however, that the mind that takes in the "Dallas" melodrama is capable of absorbing Homer and Shakespeare—or Mozart, since he is the focus of our attention—I am saying also that we have transhistorical powers. The source of these powers is in our curious nature. We have concentrated with immense determination on what forms us externally but that need not actually govern us internally. It can do that only if we grant it the right.

But we as individuals, in inner freedom, need not grant any such thing. This is a good moment to remind ourselves of this—now that the great ideological machines of the century have stopped forever and are already covered with rust.

What is attractive about Mozart (against this background of rusting ideological machinery) is that he is an individual. He learned for himself (as in *Così Fan Tutte*) the taste of disappointment, betrayal, suffering, the weakness, foolishness, and vanity of flesh and blood, as well as the emptiness of cynicism. In him we see a person who has only himself to rely on. But what a self it is, and what an art it has generated. How deeply (beyond words) he speaks to us about the mysteries of our common human nature. And how unstrained and *easy* his greatness is.

PART ONE

Riding Off in All Directions

IN THE DAYS

OF MR. ROOSEVELT

(1983)

I
t was in Chicago that Roosevelt was nominated in 1932, when I was seventeen years of age, just getting out of high school. When he defeated Hoover in November of that year, he didn't become President, merely. He became *the* President, presiding over us for so long that in a movie of the early forties, Billie Burke—Silly Billie—said to a fat, flummoxed senator that she had just been to Washington to see the coronation.

Early in the Depression, my algebra teacher, an elderly lady whose white hair was piled in a cumulus formation over her square face and her blue-tinted square glasses, allowed herself a show of feeling and sang "Happy Days Are Here Again." Our astonishment was great. As a rule, Miss Scherbarth was all business. Teachers seldom sounded off on topics of the day. It's true that when Lindbergh flew to Paris, Mrs. Davis told the class, "I do hope, from my heart, that he is as good a young man as he is brave, and will never disappoint us." A revelation to the sixth grade. But that Miss Scherbarth should interrupt her equations to sing out for FDR showed that the country had indeed been shaken to its foundations. It wasn't until later that I understood that City Hall was busted and that Miss Scherbarth wasn't being paid. In the winter of '33, when I was a freshman at Crane College, the whole faculty went to the Loop to demonstrate at City Hall. Shopkeepers were taking their scrip (municipal funny money) at a discount. My English teacher, Miss Ferguson, said to us afterward, "We forced our way into the mayor's office and chased him round his desk."

Esquire, December 1983.

Miss Ferguson, a splendid, somewhat distorted, but vigorous old thing, believed in giving full particulars. To chant the rules of composition was part of her teaching method. She would dance before the blackboard and sing out, "Be! Specific!" to the tune of Handel's "Hallelujah Chorus." A charming woman, she had overlapping front teeth, like the new First Lady. As she flourished her arms while singing her messages, it was not difficult to imagine her in the crowd that burst through the mayor's doors. They cried, "Pay us!"

In 1931, Chicago had elected its first foreign-born mayor. He was a Bohemian—Anton Cermak—and a formidable politician, one of the builders of the Democratic machine, soon to be taken over by the Irish. Cermak, who had tried to block Roosevelt's nomination, went down to Florida to make peace with the President-elect. According to Len O'Connor, one of the most knowledgeable historians of Chicago, Pushcart Tony was urged by alderman Paddy Bauler, who bossed the German vote, to come to terms with FDR. "Cermak," Bauler later recalled, "said he didn't like the sonofabitch. I sez, 'Listen, for Cry sakes, you ain't got any money for the Chicago schoolteachers, and this Roosevelt is the only one who can get it for you. You better get over there and kiss his ass or whatever you got to do. Only you better get the goddamn money for them teachers, or we ain't goin' to have a city that's worth runnin'.' So he goes over and, Christ Almighty, next thing I hear on the radio is that Cermak's got shot."

The assassin, Zangara, had supposedly aimed at Roosevelt, although there were those in Chicago who asserted that Cermak was his real target. Lots of people were in a position to benefit from Cermak's death. As he was rushed to the hospital, Cermak supposedly whispered to Roosevelt, "I'm glad it was me instead of you." This legend was the invention of a Hearst reporter, John Dienhart, who was a drinking pal of the mayor, as well as his public relations man. Dienhart's last word on this subject, as quoted in O'Connor's *Clout*, was: "I couldn't very well have put out a story that Tony would have wanted it the other way around."

Years later, the *Chicago Tribune* reported that in a letter of thanks to Mrs. W. F. Cross, the Florida woman who had struck away Zangara's arm as he was pulling the trigger, the White House had written: "By your quick thinking a far greater tragedy was averted." Colonel

McCormick's files collected anti-Roosevelt facts as Atlantic beaches gather stones. The Colonel's heart never softened toward the Roosevelts. But the writer of the White House letter, perhaps Roosevelt himself, had it right. Alas for Pushcart Tony Cermak, the tragedy *would* have been far greater.

The Roosevelt era began, therefore, with the unwilling martyrdom of a commonplace Chicago politician who had gone to make a deal—an old deal—with the new guy, an Eastern swell, old money from an estate on the Hudson, snooty people, governor of New York (so what!), a president with pince-nez and a long cigarette holder. How was Pushcart Tony to know that he had been killed by a bullet aimed at the very greatest of American politicians? Jefferson (himself no mean manipulator) and Madison had had eighteenth-century class. Jackson had had fire. Lincoln was our great-souled man. Wilson was the best America had to show in the way of professorial WASPdom. But FDR was a genius in politics. He was not an intellectual. He browsed in books of naval history, preferring those that were handsomely illustrated, and he pored over his stamp albums like many another patrician. Great politicians are seldom readers or scholars. When he needed brainy men, he sent to Columbia University for them. Following the traditions of monarchy, he created a privy council of brain trusters, who had more influence, more money to spend, than the members of his cabinet. Experts now tell us that Roosevelt was an ignoramus in economic matters, and the experts are probably right. But it wasn't the brain trusters who saved the U.S.A. from disintegration; it was—oddity of oddities—a country squire from Dutchess County, a man described by a shrewd foreign observer as the Clubman Caesar and by the witty if dangerous Huey Long as Franklin De La *No*. The unemployed masses, working stiffs, mechanics, laid-off streetcar conductors, file clerks, shoe salesmen, pants pressers, egg candlers, truckdrivers, the residents of huge, drab neighborhoods of "furriners," the greenhorns today described as ethnics—all these swore by him. They trusted only Roosevelt, a Groton boy, a Social Register nob, a rich gentleman from Harvard and Hyde Park. They did not call for a proletarian president.

There are many for whom it was bliss then to be alive. For older citizens it was a grim time—for the educated and professional classes the Depression was grievously humiliating—but for the young this faltering of order and authority made possible an escape from family and routine. As a friend of mine observed during the complacent Eisenhower period: "The cost of being poor has gone so high. You have to have a couple of hundred bucks a month. Back in the thirties we were doing it on peanuts." He was dead right. Weekly rent in a rooming house was seldom more than three dollars. Breakfast at a drugstore counter cost fifteen cents. The blue-plate-special dinner of, say, fried liver and onions, shoestring potatoes, and coleslaw, with a dessert of Kosto pudding, appeared on the hectographed menu for thirty-five cents. Young hustlers could get by on something like eight or ten dollars a week, with a bit of scrounging. The National Youth Administration paid you a few bucks for nominal assistance to a teacher, you picked up a few more at Goldblatt's department store as a stockroom boy, you wore hand-me-downs, and you nevertheless had plenty of time to read the files of the old *Dial* at the Crerar Library or in the public library among harmless old men who took shelter from the cold in the reading room. At the Newberry, you became acquainted also with Anarchist-Wobbly theoreticians and other self-made intellectuals who lectured from soapboxes in Bughouse Square, weather permitting.

Between the twenties and the thirties, a change occurred in the country that was as much imaginative as it was economic. In the twenties, America's stability was guaranteed by big business, by industrialists and statesmen whose Anglo-Saxon names were as sound as the gold standard. On March 4, 1929, when Herbert Hoover was inaugurated, I was out of school with a sore throat and had the new Majestic radio in its absurd large cabinet all to myself. I turned the switch—and there was the new Chief Executive taking the oath of office before a great crowd. From the papers, I knew what he looked like. His hair was parted down the middle, he wore a high collar and a top hat and looked like Mr. Tomato on the College Inn juice bottle. Full and sedate, he was one of those balanced and solid engineering-and-money types who would maintain the secure Republican reign of Silent Cal, the successor of the unhappy Harding. Big Bill Thompson, Chicago's Republican mayor, was a crook—all the local politicians were grafters and boodlers, but nobody actually felt injured by them. Great men like Samuel Insull or General Dawes were very sharp, certainly, but on the whole they were probably OK. The gangsters, who did as they liked, murdered one another, seldom harming ordinary citizens. Chicago, a sprawling network of immigrant villages smelling of sauerkraut and home-brewed beer, of meat processing and soap manufacture, was at peace—a stale and queasy peace, the philistine repose apparently anticipated by the Federalists. The founders had foreseen that all would be well, life would be orderly; no great excesses, no sublimity.

The sun shone as well as it could through a haze of prosperous gases, the river moved slowly under a chemical iridescence, the streetcars rocked across the level and endless miles of the huge Chicago grid. The city greeter, Mr. Gaw, who manufactured envelopes, met all prominent visitors at the railroad stations with old-style pizzazz and comical bombast. Chicago belonged to the Boosters, to the real estate men and the utilities magnates, to William Randolph Hearst and Bertie McCormick, to Al Capone and Big Bill Thompson, and in the leafy back streets where we lived, all was well.

A seven-cent streetcar fare took us to the Loop. On Randolph Street, we found free entertainment at Bensinger's billiard salon and at Trafton's gymnasium, where boxers sparred. The street was filled with jazz musicians and City Hall types. My boyhood friend Fish, who was allowed to help himself to a quarter from the cash register in his father's poolroom, occasionally treated me to a hot dog and a stein of Hires root beer on Randolph Street. When we overspent, we came back from the Loop on foot—some five miles of freightyards and factories; joints that manufactured garden statuary, like gnomes, trolls, and undines; Klee Brothers, where you got a baseball bat with the purchase of a two-pants suit; Polish sausage shops; the Crown Theater at Division and Ashland, with its posters of Lon Chaney or Renée Adorée, its popcorn machine crackling; then the United Cigar Store; then Brown and Koppel's restaurant, with the nonstop poker game upstairs. It was a good dullness, this Hoover dullness. Higher activities were not prohibited, but you had to find them for yourself. If you subscribed to the *Literary Digest*, you might get the complete works of Flaubert as a bonus. Not that anybody read those red buckram-bound books.

Fish matured before the rest of us. At fourteen, he was being shaved by the barber, paying grandly with two bits from his papa's cash register. His virile Oriental face was massaged with witch hazel, his chin was powdered, he came on boldly with the girls. He spent money also on books, pamphlets, and magazines. What he wanted from them was no more than a few quick impressions—he was no scholar—and after he had read a few pages he passed the magazines and pamphlets on to me. Through him I became familiar with Karl Marx and V. I. Lenin; also with Marie Stopes, Havelock Ellis, V. F. Calverton, Max Eastman, and Edmund Wilson. The beginning of the Great Depression was also the beginning of my mental life. But suddenly the comedy of comfort stopped, the good-natured absurdities of the painted flivver, Pikes Peak or Bust, the Babbitt capers. There were no more quarters in the till.

The tale of America as told in the twenties by America's leaders was that this country had scored one of the most brilliant successes in history. Hoover boasted in a 1928 campaign speech that the conquest of poverty in the United States was a palpable reality. "The poorhouse is vanishing from among us . . . our industrial output has increased as never before, and our wages have grown steadily in buying power. Our workers, with their average weekly wages, can today buy two and often three times more bread and butter than any wage earner of Europe. At one time we demanded for our workers a full dinner pail. We have now gone far beyond that conception. Today we demand larger comfort and greater participation in life and leisure."

How bitterly Hoover must have regretted the full dinner pail. He had, after all, meant well. To postwar Europe he had been a benefactor. But now the big businessmen who boasted of the bread and butter they were stuffing us with (Silvercup, not European bread) became once more what Eleanor Roosevelt's uncle Teddy had called "malefactors of great wealth." Their factories closed and their banks failed.

Private misery could not be confined: it quickly overflowed into the streets. Foreclosures, evictions, Hooverville shanties, soup lines— old Dr. Townsend of Long Beach, California, was inspired with his plan for the aged when he saw elderly women rooting for food in garbage cans. Maggoty meat for Americans? Were Chicago and Los Angeles to become Oriental cities like Shanghai or Calcutta?

The great engineer had botched his job. What would his successor do? Reputable analysts, taking Roosevelt's measure, were not encouraged by their findings. Walter Lippmann wrote in 1932 that FDR was "an amiable man with many philanthropic impulses" but accused him of "carrying water on both shoulders," of hanging on to both right-wing and left-wing supporters, a politician lavish with "two-faced platitudes." Roosevelt was no crusader, no enemy of entrenched privilege, "no tribune of the people," and Lippmann saw in him no more than "a pleasant man who, without any important qualifications for the office, would like very much to be President."

But Lippmann had examined the wrong musician, studied a different score, for when Roosevelt sat down to play, he stormed over the executive keyboard, producing music no one had ever heard before. He was dazzling. And the secret of his political genius was that he knew exactly what the public needed to hear. It amounted to that, a personal declaration by the President that took into account the feelings of the people, and especially their fears. In his first inaugural address he told the great crowd before the Capitol: "This is preeminently the time to speak the truth, the whole truth, frankly and boldly. This great Nation will endure as it has endured, will revive and will prosper." And then: "We do not distrust the future of essential democracy. The people of the United States . . . have asked for discipline and direction under leadership. They have made me the present instrument of their wishes."

With this powerful statement the tale of the twenties concluded, and a new tale began. Against the boastfulness of the Coolidge-and-Hoover decade were set the humiliations and defeats of the Depression. It was generally agreed that the Depression was to be viewed as what insurance companies term an act of God, a natural disaster. Peter F. Drucker puts the matter correctly in his memoirs: "As after an earthquake, a flood, a hurricane, the community closed ranks and came to each other's rescue . . . the commitment to mutual help and the willingness to take chances on a person were peculiar to Depression America." Professor Drucker adds that there was nothing like this on the other side, in Europe, "where the Depression evoked only suspicion, surliness, fear, and envy." In the opinion of Europeans, the only choice was between communism and fascism. Among world leaders, Roosevelt alone spoke with assurance about "essential democracy." It is not too much to say that another America was imaginatively formed under his influence. Recovery programs were introduced with public noise and flourishes during his first hundred days, and although huge sums were spent, it presently became apparent that there would be no recovery. That he was nevertheless elected repeatedly proves that what the voters wanted was to live in a Rooseveltian America, which turned the square old U.S.A. of the Hoovers topsy-turvy. I can remember an autumnal Chicago street very early one morning when I heard clinking and ringing noises. The source of these sounds was hidden in a cloud, and when I entered the sphere of fog just beginning to be lighted by the sun, I saw a crowd of men with hammers chipping mortar from old paving bricks—fifty or sixty of the unemployed pretending to do a job, "picking them up and laying 'em down again," as people then were saying. Every day Colonel McCormick's *Tribune* denounced these boondoggles. In the center of the front page there was always a cartoon of moronic professors with donkey tails hanging from their academic mortarboards. They were killing little pigs, plowing under crops, and centupling the national debt, while genial FDR, presiding at the Mad Hatter's tea party, lightheartedly poured out money. The brick chippers, however, were grateful to him. These jobless bookkeepers, civil engineers, or tool-and-diemakers were glad to work on the streets for some twenty dollars a week. The national debt, which enraged the Colonel, that dotty patriot, meant nothing to them. They desperately needed the small wages the government paid them. The drama of professional dignity sacrificed also appealed to many of them.

Memorable days. In 1934, I took to the road with a pal. With three dollars between us, enough to keep us in cheese and crackers, we bummed the freights. We joined the multitude of men and boys that covered the boxcars like flocks of birds. In South Bend, Indiana, we passed the Studebaker plant and a crowd of sit-in strikers yelling and cheering from the rooftop and the open windows. We shouted and joked with them, rolling at about five miles an hour in summer warmth through the fresh June weeds, the Nickel Plate locomotive pulling us toward a horizon of white clouds. It now occurs to me that I didn't know how hard I was grieving for my mother, who had died just before Roosevelt was inaugurated. With her death and the remarriage of my father, the children scattered. I was turned loose—freed, in a sense: free but also stunned, like someone who survives an explosion but hasn't yet grasped what has happened. I didn't know anything. At the age of eighteen, I didn't even know that I was an adolescent. Words like that came later, in the forties and fifties.

Of course, I sympathized with the strikers. Thanks to Fish's pamphlets, I was able to call myself a socialist, and the socialist line was that FDR's attempted reforms were saving the country for capitalism, only the capitalists were too stupid to understand this. Radical orthodoxy in the thirties held that parliamentary European reformism had failed and that the real choice, on a world scale, was between the hateful dictatorships of the right and the temporary and therefore enlightened dictatorships of the left. American democracy would not in the long run prove an exception. So said the radicals. One of them, Edmund Wilson, had written in 1931 that if American radicals wished to accomplish something valuable, "they must take communism away from the communists and take it without ambiguities or reservations, asserting emphatically that their ultimate goal is the ownership of the means of production by the government." And in a weird panegyric of Lenin written after his pilgrimage to the tomb on Red Square, Wilson told his readers that in the Soviet Union you felt that you were "at the moral top of the world where the light never really goes out." He spoke of Lenin as one of the very highest products of humanity—"the superior man who has burst out of the classes and claimed all that man has done which is superior for the refinement of mankind as a whole."

I was an early reader of Edmund Wilson's *Axel's Castle*. By 1936, I had also read his *Travels in Two Democracies*. Wilson had opened my eyes to the high culture of modern Europe, and on that account I was in his debt. Besides, I had met him in Chicago when he was hauling a heavy gladstone bag on Fifty-seventh Street near the university, hot and almost angry, shining with sweat and bristling at his ears and nostrils with red hairs. A representative of all that was highest and best on the streets of Hyde Park—imagine that! His voice was hoarse and his manner huffy, but he was kindly and invited me to visit him. He was the greatest literary man I had ever met, and I was willing to agree with all his views, whether the subject was Dickens or Lenin. But despite my great admiration for him and my weakness for inspired utterances, I was not carried away by his Lenin worship. Perhaps because my parents were Russian Jews, I was as distrustful of Lenin and Stalin as Wilson was of American politicians. I didn't *believe* in Roosevelt as Wilson apparently believed in Lenin. I seem to have sensed, however, that Roosevelt was holding the country together, and in my obstinate heart I resisted the Wilsonian program for American radicals. I couldn't believe, anyway, that liberal graduates of Harvard and Princeton were going to abduct Marxism from the Marxists and save the U.S.A. by taking charge of the dictatorship of the American proletariat. I secretly believed that America *would* in the end prove an exception. America and I, *both* exceptional, would together elude prediction and defy determinism.

You didn't have to approve Roosevelt's policies to be a Rooseveltian. Myself, I liked his policies less and less as time went by. I can recall the marks I gave him (in my helplessness). For recognizing Hitler as a great evildoer he rated an A. His support of England moved me deeply (high marks). In his judgment of the Russians he fell to a D. With Joe Kennedy in London and Joseph Davies in Moscow, one of the most disgraceful appointments in diplomatic history, he flunked out. For opinions on his dealings with Stalin I refer the reader to the Poles, the Czechs, the Romanians, etc. He did nothing to prevent the murder of millions in Hitler's death factories, but of that we were then ignorant.

His most dazzling successes were domestic and psychological. For millions of Americans the crisis of the old order was a release, a godsend. A great gap opened, and a fresh impulse of the imagination rushed in. The multitudes were more mobile, diverse, psychologically flexible; they manifested new moods and colors; they were more urbane under FDR's influence. What was most important, for those who had the capacity for it, was the emotional catharsis of making a new start, of falling and rising again. The thirties were more sociable, more accepting of weakness, less rigid, less idolatrous, and less snobbish.

The Roosevelt influence was especially gratifying to the foreign-born. Millions of them passionately hoped to be *included*, to be counted at last as true Americans. Certain of the immigrants were parochial. Poles and Ukrainians, for instance, preferred to keep to their own communities and customs. Others, catching the American fever, changed their names, made up new personalities, and, energized by these distortions, threw themselves into the life of the country. Who knows how many people became somebody else, turned themselves into jazz singers, blackface comedians, sportsmen, tycoons, antebellum Southern ladies, Presbyterian vestrymen, Texas ranchers, Ivy

Leaguers, high government officials. It is not too much to say that these self-created people, people with false credentials, actors invisibly consumed by guilt and fear of exposure, were often empire builders. There's nothing like a shameful secret to fire a man up. If Hawthorne had not understood this, *The Scarlet Letter* would never have been written.

For these fertile and productive impostors, it was bliss to hear FDR say that in this country we were all of us aliens. An actor himself, he put on the most successful act of all. He even had a secret: he could not walk. Behind this secret much deeper secrets were concealed.

Consider briefly, for the purpose of contrast, the career of Fitzgerald's Jay Gatsby, a pretender who could not forgive himself. Born James Gatz, he was remade (should we say twice born?). Boy Scout motives of self-improvement and naive love-idealism kept him pure in heart and gullible. What Americans learned from Roosevelt's example was that *amour propre* (vanity, secrecy, ambition, pride) need not give anyone a bad conscience. You could, as Yeats suggested, "measure the lot, forgive myself the lot." Roosevelt, who, with his democratic charm, his gaiety, the dramatic nobility of his head, *looked* the great man, sent Americans the message that beyond pretending and theatricality there was a further range, in which one's deeper nature could continue to live, its truth undamaged. We may pretend, he seemed to be saying, as long as we are not taken in by our own pretenses. That way schizophrenia lies. From memoirs written by members of his inner circle we have learned that he loved spoofing, he was a gifted comedian who made fun of himself, a practical joker. He was well acquainted with Lear's *Nonsense Rhymes* and with *The Hunting of the Snark*. The irrational has its legitimate place by the side of the rational. OK. Life is real and earnest, but it is also decidedly goofy. With Roosevelt this was always clear. Others were more nebulous and more difficult. Compare, for instance, Roosevelt's Fala with the little dog of Richard Nixon in his "sincere" Checkers speech.

In domestic politics FDR's victorious intuition was that a president must discuss crises with the public in the plainest terms. Democracy cannot thrive if leaders are unable to teach or to console. A certain amount of deception is inevitable, of course. So many of society's institutions stand upon a foundation of fraud that you cannot expect a president to "tell all." Telling all is the function of intellectuals, supposedly. For Roosevelt it was sufficient to attack big business and expose malefactors of great wealth. He was not a philosopher. For his relations with the public he might, however, have taken his text from Isaiah: "Comfort ye." Among his successors in the White House, only Truman, in his different, "Give 'em hell," style, took a personal line with the voters. Some of our recent presidents, sophisticated technicians, instinctively resisted the personal line with the public. To Johnson and to Nixon this was an abomination. They were not leaders; they were professional behind-the-scenes operators. The very thought of taking the public into their confidence was horrifying to them. Forced to make a show of candor and an appeal for confidence, they averted their faces, their eyes filmed, their voices flattened. Frightful for a man like LBJ, stuffed with powers and with secrets, to abase himself before the cameras. He was not a Coriolanus but a democratic technician. Under such technicians decay was inevitable.

A civilized man, FDR gave the U.S.A. a civilized government. I suppose that he was what Alexander Hamilton would have called an "elective king," and if he was in some respects a demagogue, he was a demagogue without ideological violence. He was not a führer but a statesman. Hitler and he came to power in the same year. Both made superb use of the radio. Those of us who heard Hitler's broadcasts will never forget the raucous sounds of menace, the great crowds howling as he made his death threats. Roosevelt's chats with his "Fellow Americans" are memorable for other reasons. As an undergraduate I was fully armored in skepticism, for Roosevelt was very smooth and one couldn't be careful enough. But under the armor I was nonetheless vulnerable. I can recall walking eastward on the Chicago Midway on a summer evening. The light held long after nine o'clock, and the ground was covered with clover, more than a mile of green between Cottage Grove and Stony Island. The blight hadn't yet carried off the elms, and under them drivers had pulled over, parking bumper to bumper, and turned on their radios to hear Roosevelt. They had rolled down the windows and opened the car doors. Everywhere the same voice, its odd Eastern accent, which in anyone else would have irritated Midwesterners. You could follow without missing a single word as you strolled by. You felt joined to these unknown drivers, men and women smoking their cigarettes in silence, not so much considering the President's words as affirming the rightness of his tone and taking assurance from it. You had some sense of the weight of troubles that made them so attentive, and of the ponderable fact, the one common element (Roosevelt), on which so many unknowns could agree. Just as memorable to me, perhaps, was to learn how long clover flowers could hold their color in the dusk.

LITERARY NOTES ON

KHRUSHCHEV

(1961)

Khrushchev, the heir of Lenin and Stalin, Malenkov's successor, and the evident head of the Russian oligarchy, has stamped his image on the world and compels us to think about him. It is hard, of course, to believe that this bald, round, gesticulating, loud man may be capable of overcoming, of ruining, perhaps of destroying us.

"It's him, Khrushchev, dat nut," a garage attendant on Third Avenue said to me last September as the fleet of Russian Cadillacs rushed by. This time Khrushchev was a self-invited visitor. He did not arrive with our blessings, and he did not have our love, but that didn't seem to matter greatly to him. He was able, nevertheless, to dominate the headlines, the television screens, the UN Assembly, and the midtown streets. An American in his position, feeling himself unwanted and, even worse, unloved, would have been self-effacing. Not Khrushchev. He poured it on, holding press conferences in the street and trading insults from his balcony with the crowd, singing snatches of the "Internationale," giving a pantomime uppercut to an imaginary assassin. He played up to the crowd and luxuriated in its attention, behaving like a comic artist in a show written and directed by himself. And at the UN, roaring with anger, interrupting Mr. Macmillan, landing his fists on the desk, waving a shoe in the air, hugging his allies and bugging his opponents, surging up from his seat to pump the hand of the elegant black Nkrumah in his gilt crimson toga or interrupting his own blasts at the West to plug Soviet mineral water, suddenly win-

Esquire, March 1961.

some, Khrushchev the charmer, not once did he give up the center of the stage. And no one seemed able to take it from him.

Balzac once described the statesman as a "monster of self-possession." He referred, of course, to the bourgeois statesman. Khrushchev is another sort of fish altogether. And since his debut on the world scene shortly after Stalin died and Malenkov "retired," Khrushchev—running always a little ahead of Bulganin—has astonished, perplexed, bamboozled, and appalled the world. If the traditional statesman is a prodigy of self-possession, Khrushchev seems instead to give himself away. He seems to be a man of candor, just as Russia seems to be a union of socialist republics. Other statesmen are satisfied to represent their countries. Not so Khrushchev. He wishes to personify Russia and the communist cause.

Timidity will get us nowhere. If we want to understand him we must give the imagination its freedom and let it, in gambler's language, go for broke. Anyway, he *compels* us to think of him. We have him continually under our eyes. He is in China, he is in Paris and Berlin and San Francisco, and he performs everywhere. In Austria he inspects a piece of abstract sculpture and, with an astonished air, he asks the artist to tell him what the devil it stands for. Listening or pretending to listen, he observes that the sculptor will have to hang around forever to explain his incomprehensible work. He arrives in Finland in time to attend the birthday celebration of its president; he pushes the poor man aside and frolics before the cameras, eats, drinks, fulminates, and lets himself be taken home. In America, on his first visit, his progress across the land was nothing less than spectacular. And no fifteenth-century king could have been more *himself*, whether with the press, with Mr. Garst on the farm, with the dazzling dolls of Hollywood, or with the trade union leaders in San Francisco. "You are like a nightingale," he said to Walter Reuther. "It closes its eyes when it sings, and sees nothing and hears nobody but itself." In Hollywood with Spyros Skouras, he matched success stories, each protagonist trying to prove that he rose from greater depths. "I was a poor immigrant." "I began working when I learned to walk—I was a shepherd boy, a factory laborer, I worked in the coal pits, and now I am prime minister of the great Soviet state." Neither of them mentioned the cost of his rise to the public at large: Skouras said nothing of the effects of Hollywood on the brains of Americans, nor did Khrushchev mention deportations and purges. We who had this greatness thrust upon us had no spokesman in the debate. But then, people in show business have always enjoyed a peculiar monopoly of patriotism. The mixture of ideology and entertainment on both sides brought about an emotional crisis on the West Coast, and it was here that Khrushchev was provoked into disclosing some of his deeper feelings. "When we were in Hollywood, they danced the cancan for us," he told the meeting of the trade union leaders in San Francisco. "The girls who dance it have to pull up their skirts and show their backsides. They are good, honest actresses but have to perform that dance. They are compelled to adapt themselves to the tastes of depraved people. People in your country will go to see it, but Soviet people would scorn such a spectacle. It is pornographic. It is the culture of surfeited and depraved people. Showing that sort of film is called freedom in this country. Such 'freedom' doesn't suit us. You seem to like the 'freedom' of looking at backsides. But we prefer freedom to think, to exercise our mental faculties, the freedom of creative progress." I take these words from a semiofficial Russian-sponsored publication. It does not add what some American reports added, namely, that the Premier here raised his coattails and exposed his rear to the entire gathering as he swooped into a parody of the cancan.

This, friends, is art. It is also an entirely new mode of historical interpretation, by the world leader of Marxist thought who bodily, by the use of his own person, delivers a critique of Western civilization. It is, moreover, theater. And we are its enthralled and partly captive audience. Khrushchev's performance is, in the term used by James Joyce, an epiphany, a manifestation that summarizes or expresses a whole universe of meanings. "We will bury you," Khrushchev has told the capitalist world, and though it has since been said over and over that this is merely a Ukrainian figure of speech, meaning "We will exceed you in production," I think that in watching this dance we might all feel the itching of the nose which, according to superstition, means that someone is walking on our graves. We would not be far out in seeing auguries of death in this cancan. The "culture of surfeited and depraved people" is doomed. That is the meaning of his brutal and angry comedy. It is also what he means when he plays villain and buffoon to the New York public. To him this is the slack, shallow, undisciplined, and cultureless mob of a decadent capitalist city. Still, life is very complicated, for if the Hollywood cancan is poor stuff, what can we say of the products of socialist realism with their pure and loyal worker heroes and their sweet and hokey maidens? Khrushchev himself is far above such junk. It is possible to conclude from this that in a dictatorship the tyrant may suck into himself all the resources of creativity and leave the art of his country impoverished.

It may, in fact, take not only Russia but the entire world to feed the needs of a single individual. For it can't be ideology alone that produces such outbursts; it must be character. "I have often thought," wrote William James, "that the best way to define a man's character would be to seek out the particular mental or moral attitude in which, when it came upon him, he felt himself most intensely active and alive. At such moments there is a voice inside which speaks and says: '*This* is the real me!'" So perhaps Khrushchev feels himself, or attempts to reach himself, in these outbursts. And perhaps it is when the entire world is watching him soar and he is touching the limits of control that he feels most alive. He does not exhibit great range of feelings. When he takes off the rudimentary masks of bureaucratic composure or peasant dignity or affability, he is angry or jeering. But fear is not the best school for expressiveness, and no man could be an important party functionary under Stalin without the ability to live in fear. We cannot therefore expect him to be versatile. He had, however, what it took to finish the course: the nerves, the control, the patience, the piercing ambition, the strength to kill and to endure the threat of death. It would be premature to say that he has survived all that there is to survive in Russia, but it is a safe guess that in the relief of having reached first place he is whooping it up. Instead of having been punished for his crimes, he has become a great leader, which persuades him that life is inherently dramatic. And in his joy at having reversed the moral-accounting system of bourgeois civilization, he plays his role with ever greater spirit.

Our ablest political commentators have used theatrical metaphors to describe Khrushchev's behavior. Mr. Sulzberger in the *New York Times* speaks of the "fierce illogic of a Brendan Behan play." Others have been reminded of the Leningrad circus, and a British psychologist has suggested that Khrushchev may have made a study of Pavlov's conditioned reflex. After Pavlov had rewarded his dogs for responding to given signals, he scrambled the pattern, and the animals suffered a hysterical breakdown. Our leaders, amid flowers and smiles and exchanges of charm, made appointments to meet Khrushchev at the summit, only to find that he had turned into Ibsen's Great Boyg of the northern snows, who deafened them with snarls and stunned them with ice. If Khrushchev had needed instruction in the technique of blowing hot and cold, he could have gotten it from Hitler, who made a great deal of noise in the world, rather than from Pavlov, who made very little. From Hitler he might have learned that angry demonstrations unnerve well-conducted people and that in statesmanship the advantage always lies with the unprincipled, the brutal, and the insane. Hitler could at will convulse himself with rage and, when he had gained his ends, be coolly correct to his staff, all in a matter of moments. Khrushchev does not seem to have this combination of derangement and cold political technique that threatens the end of the world in fire and ice. But does he need lessons from Professor Pavlov in psychological techniques? Teach your granny to suck an egg.

No, the dramatic metaphor is the best one, and in trying to place his style, even before I had seen Khrushchev in action during his recent American visit—a short, buoyant, ruddy, compact, gesturing, tough man—it struck me that Marcel Marceau, another mime, appearing in The Overcoat at a New York theater, and Khrushchev, at the other side of town, had both been inspired by the Russian comic tradition. The masterpiece of that tradition is Gogol's Dead Souls. From Gogol's landlords and peasants, grotesquely thickheaded or just as grotesquely shrewd, provincial autocrats, creeps, misers, officials, gluttons, gamblers, and drunkards, Khrushchev seems to have taken many of the elements of his comic style. He is one of Gogol's stout men who "know better than thin men how to manage their affairs. The thin ones are more often employed on special missions, or are merely 'on the staff,' scurrying hither and thither; their existence is somehow too slight, airy and altogether insubstantial. The stout ones are never to be found filling ambiguous posts, but only straightforward ones; if they sit down anywhere, they do so solidly and firmly, so that, though their position may creak and bend beneath them, they never fall off."

When the occasion demands more earnestness, he plays the Marxist. Speaking at the UN, he made me think, when he called for colonial liberation, of Trotsky in the first years of the Russian Revolution and in particular of Trotsky's conduct during the signing of the Treaty of Brest-Litovsk. There, to the amazement of the German generals, he delayed the negotiations in order to make speeches calling on the world proletariat to support and extend the revolution. Those days are gone forever, of course. They were gone even before Lenin died. And there is a great difference between the fresh revolutionary ardor of Trotsky and the stale agitational technique of an old party hack. Still, when it suits him, Khrushchev is a Marxist. Defending the poor working girls of Hollywood, he delivered the judgment of Marxian orthodoxy on their wriggling and kicking (more of the alienating labor imposed by capitalism on humanity).

There are certain similarities between Khrushchev's Marxism and the liberal ideology of Western businessmen. They make use of it at their convenience. Khrushchev, however, enjoys a considerable advantage in that the needs of Russian history and those of his own personality have coincided so that he is able at times to follow his instincts without restraint. He has besides a great contempt for the representatives of the West, who are unable to do without the brittle, soiled, and compromised conventions of civilized diplomacy. Those conventions figure as the great coma, the deep sleep, and Khrushchev despises the sleepers and takes advantage of them. The pictures taken at the summit reveal the extent of his success. General de Gaulle's mouth is drawn very small in a pucker of foreboding and distaste. Mr. Macmillan seems deeply hurt. Former President Eisenhower looks sad but also opinionated. Things have gone wrong again, but it is certainly no fault of his. Together, all three must have seemed to Khrushchev like Keats's "still unravished bride of quietness." And it is not hard to guess what he, the descendant of serfs, risen to a position of such might, must have experienced. Confronting the leaders of the bourgeois West, so long feared and hated, he saw himself to be tougher, deeper, and more intelligent than any of them. And, in expressing his feelings, more free.

It's hard to know whether the Khrushchev we saw banging with his shoe at the UN Assembly is the "real" Khrushchev. But one of the privileges of power seems to be the privilege of direct emotional self-expression. It is not a privilege exercised by many people in the West, so far as I can see.

"Men who have arrived can do what they like," declared our own

Daily News recently in one of its snappy ads. "There was a guy who liked spaghetti and beer, but when he became a junior executive, he thought it more fitting to order steak and asparagus. It was only when he became president of his company that he felt assured enough to go back to spaghetti and beer."

Such are the privileges of power, but bafflingly enough, apart from artists and tyrants, few people, even among company presidents, feel strong enough to tell the world how they feel. New York's Police Commissioner Kennedy, a man who has apparently arrived, could not, some time ago, express his honest views as to the religious convictions of the Jewish members of the force. Everyone knows that the commissioner is not anti-Semitic. Yet the New York Rabbinate felt compelled, as did Mayor Wagner, for formal reasons, to ask for a retraction. So it's not easy to speak one's mind. Even the artists have taken cover, disguising themselves as bank clerks and veiling their sayings. That leaves us with the tyrants. (Is it only a coincidence that Emily Post died during Khrushchev's visit?)

Masked in smiles and peasant charm, or in anger, the Russian Premier releases his deepest feelings, and if we are not shaken by them, it is because we are not in close touch with reality. In the West, the connections between opinion, feeling, and bodily motion have been broken. We have lost the expressive power. It is in the use of such power, falsely exploiting his Russian and peasant background, that Khrushchev has shown himself to be an adept. He has a passion always ready to exploit, and though he lies, he has the advantage. The principles of Western liberalism seem no longer to lend themselves to effective action. Deprived of the expressive power, we are awed by it, have a hunger for it, and are afraid of it. Thus we praise the gray dignity of our soft-spoken leaders, but in our hearts we are suckers for passionate outbursts, even when those passionate outbursts are hypocritical and falsely motivated. "The best lack all conviction, while the worst/Are full of passionate intensity."

At times Khrushchev goes beyond Gogolian comedy; this is no longer the amiable chiseler who stuffs himself with fish or pancakes dipped in butter. Gogol's Chichikov, to congratulate himself when he has pulled a fast one, dances in the privacy of his room. But Khrushchev goes into his cancan before the world public with a deep and gnomish joy. Here is a man whom all the twisted currents of human purpose have brought within reach of world power. At a time when public figures show only secondary or tertiary personal characteristics, he appears to show only primary ones. He wears his instincts on his sleeve, or like Dostoyevsky's Father Karamazov, that corrupt and deep old man, he feigns simplicity.

When the charm and irony wear thin, he shows himself to be a harsh, arbitrary, and complicated man. It was a simple enough matter for him to have joked contemptuously with Spyros Skouras; in debate with well-informed men who press him closely, he becomes abusive, showing that the habit of authority has made him inflexible. He seems unable to discuss any matter except on his own terms. Nature, history, Russian Marxism, and, perhaps most of all, the fact that he has survived under Stalin make it impossible for him to entertain other views. What amounted in Paris to ex-President Eisenhower's admission of a blunder must have seemed to him incredible. He lives under an iron necessity to be right. What he perhaps remembers best about men who were not right is their funerals. For him the line between the impossible and the possible is drawn with blood, and foreigners who do not see the blood must appear preposterous to him.

THE FRENCH AS

DOSTOYEVSKY SAW THEM

(1955)

*R*enting an apartment in Paris was not a simple matter in 1948, but Nicolaus, a good friend of mine, had found one for my family on the Right Bank in a fussy building. From the U.S. I had brought a new Remington portable typewriter, which the landlady absolutely demanded as a gift. She had to have the rent in dollars, too. Francs would not do. The rental was steep. Nicolaus, however, said the apartment was worth the money. He knew Paris, and I took his word for it. Nicolaus spoke French perfectly. People from Indianapolis take to French quite naturally; I met several of them in Paris, and they were all fluent. My old pal was a consummate Frenchman, carried a pair of gloves and drove a French car. He was annoyed with me when I asked my landlady what one did about the garbage here. "In France," he said to me severely, detaining me in his chilly dining room, "no man would ask such a question. Garbage is not your concern. You are not supposed to know that garbage exists. Besides, *ordures* is not a nice word."

I said that I was sorry and that I shouldn't have asked.

The landlady now brought forth her *inventaire*. An amazing document! A catalogue of every object in the house, from the Chippendale chair to the meanest cup, fully and marvelously described in stiff, upright, copious characters. We started to go through the list, and moved from Madame's room, a flapper's boudoir of the twenties, backward to the kitchen. Madame read the description and displayed each article. "Dining room table, *Style Empire*. Condition excellent. Trian-

Foreword to Fyodor M. Dostoyevsky, *Winter Notes on Summer Impressions* (New York: Criterion, 1955). First published in *New Republic*, 23 May 1955.

gular scratch on left side. No other defect." We finished in the kitchen with three lousy tin spoons.

"Ah," said Nicolaus. "What a sense of detail the French have!"

I was less impressed, but one must respect respect itself, and I did not openly disagree.

As soon as Madame left, I turned a somersault over the Chippendale chair and landed thunderously on the floor. This lightened my heart for a time, but in subsequent dealings with Madame and others in France, I could not always recover my lightness of heart by such means.

Depressed and sunk in spirit, I dwelt among Madame's works of art that cold winter. The city lay under perpetual fog, and the smoke could not rise and flowed in the streets in brown and gray currents. An unnatural smell emanated from the Seine. Many people suffered from the *grippe Espagnole* (all diseases are apt to be of foreign origin) and many more from melancholy and bad temper. Paris is the seat of a highly developed humanity, and one thus witnesses highly developed forms of suffering there. Witnesses and, sometimes, experiences. Sadness is a daily levy that civilization imposes in Paris. *Gay* Paris? Gay, my foot! Mere advertising. Paris is one of the grimmest cities in the world. I do not ask you to take my word for it. Go to Balzac and Stendhal, to Zola, to Strindberg—to Paris itself. Nicolaus said the Parisians were celebrated for their tartness of character. He declared that it would be better for me to feel my way into it than to criticize it. Himself, he was a connoisseur of the Parisian temperament. I was lacking in detachment, he said. To this accusation I pleaded guilty. I was a poor visitor and, by any standard, an inferior tourist.

Once, I tried to show a lady from Chicago the view of the Forum from the Tarpeian Rock, but she had just arrived from Florence and would not stop talking of its wonders, even when we were standing before so famous a sight. She annoyed me greatly, and I said to myself, "Damn her! I *know* she's been in Florence. But now she's on the Tarpeian Rock." And I said to her, "Do you know what used to happen here?" She seemed not to hear but answered with a remark about the Signoria, which, for a split second, made me want to throw her down like one of the ancient criminals. But I wronged her. How could she react to the Tarpeian Rock when she had not yet absorbed the Signoria?

But I was going to tell the story of my first reading of *Winter Notes on Summer Impressions*.

My young son came down with the measles. Our lanky doctor observed that the apartment was not nearly warm enough. "You must heat the boy's room," he said, and filled out a requisition for an emergency coal ration. I put on my coat and took the paper to the *Mairie* of our arrondissement, as instructed. There I sat and waited, as one waits in government offices the world over.

A large stained room. Shadows of chicken wire. Blinding lights. Several ladies at an official table, each of them the spit and image of Colette, their cheeks autumnally red, their heads bushy, small brown cigarette butts between their lips—no French civil servant who lacks a *mégot* can be an authentic officer of the state.

For an hour or two I waited my turn, and when it came I stated my case simply and presented the doctor's note; I confidently expected to receive a coal order.

"*Ah, non!*" Colette number one told me. The doctor's order was written upon one of his regular prescription blanks, whereas a special blank was provided for coal orders, very similar to but not identical with the prescription sort of blank. The real thing had perforations on the *left* side.

Didn't the Mesdames believe that my order bore the doctor's signature? Did they think that I had forged it? Not necessarily, said Colette number two. Nevertheless they could do nothing that was not in proper form. They could issue emergency coal rations solely upon presentation of the perforated *fiche*. The *rougeole* did not impress them, though I prided myself on having pronounced the word creditably. From the look on the face of Colette number three I knew that the coal ration was a dead issue. I made my way back to the dripping street, telling myself in French that I was going to get my coal on the black market. *Je vais acheter*, etc. I was determined not to allow the natives to talk me down.

It was on the same day that I found on the stand of a *bouquiniste* near the Châtelet a book by Dostoyevsky called *Le Bourgeois de Paris*— the French title of *Winter Notes*—and I sat in the illegally heated room, in the odor of the paste my son was using on his paper dolls, and eagerly and sometimes wildly read it. Its prejudices ought to have offended me;

instead I was unable to suppress certain utterances of satisfaction and agreement. I, too, was a foreigner and a barbarian from a vast and backward land. And one is more foreign in France than in other countries. Americans find it hard to believe that foreigners are unalterably foreign, for they have seen generations of immigrants who became Americans. But old cultures are impermeable and exclusive—none more so than the French. I should like to make it clear that I had not heaped blame irrationally upon France. I said to myself often, "Because you have paid the price of admission and have come with your awkward affections in your breast and dollars in your pocket, do you expect these people to take you to their hearts and into their homes? You must try to appreciate the fact that they have other and more important things to think about. Food, for one. Only three years ago, Hitler was deporting thousands, shooting hostages. A war has been fought here, probably the most atrocious in history. And now the communists are trying to drag France into Russia. America presses from the other side. Armies of tourists are beginning to pour in. And do you have to interject your irrelevant self?"

Yet as I read *Winter Notes*, I realized that to foreign eyes the French in 1862 were not substantially different from those of 1948. The great wars had not made too many changes here. If the lessons of war could be learned, wouldn't we all be very different? If death and suffering had the power to teach us . . . Et cetera. Hard, stubborn man, alas, does not easily correct himself, forgets what he has felt and seen . . . (being very sententious with myself).

Some of Dostoyevsky's strictures repelled me by their harshness. He is disagreeable as only a great radical can be. Recalling how evasive he had been when the czar's soldiers killed Polish patriots, I disliked his Slavophile notions. And then, too, a Jewish reader can seldom forget Dostoyevsky's anti-Semitism.

It is, however, essential to remember that it was for his participation in the Petrashevsky "conspiracy" that Dostoyevsky had been sent into exile. The idols of this immature and probably harmless group of young men were the French radicals—Saint-Simon, Fourier, and Sebastian Cabet among others. The Petrashevsky group had given a banquet honoring Fourier's birthday. Dostoyevsky was therefore no ordinary Russian tourist in Paris. He had been condemned to death for his adherence to French and Western ideas. Reprieved, he had been severely punished. He had only just returned from Siberia, and he now proceeded, understandably enough, to examine the European right to teach and lead young Russians.

It would be naive not to assume that he had already judged Europe. It's not for his fairness that he is famous. Besides, it is not easy to blame him. But he had certainly formed his views of Europe beforehand; he was already under Slavophile influence, and in London he went to visit Herzen, the greatest of the Russian exiles in Europe. Some of Herzen's views are reflected in these articles. Unfortunately for the betterment of mankind, it's not always the fair-minded who are clearly in possession of the truth. In France, England, and Germany, Dostoyevsky found what he needed to support his biases. Bourgeois France aroused his profoundest hatred. There is not a nation anywhere that does not contradict its highest principles in daily practice, but the French contradiction was in his eyes the very worst because France presumed to offer the world political and intellectual instruction and leadership.

Examining the great slogans of the French Revolution, Dostoyevsky declared that liberty in France was the possession of those who had a million francs:

> Equality before the law as it is now put into practice, each Frenchman can and ought to consider a personal insult. What is left of the formula? Fraternity. Now, this is a very curious item and, it must be admitted, still forms the chief stumbling block for the West.
>
> The Westerner speaks of fraternity as of a great motivating force of humankind and does not understand that it is impossible to obtain fraternity if it does not exist in reality. . . . But in French nature, and in Occidental nature in general, it is not present; you find there instead a principle of individualism, a principle of isolation, of intense self-preservation; of personal gain, of self-determination of *I*, of opposing this *I* to all nature and the rest of mankind as an independent, autonomous principle entirely equal and equivalent to all that exists outside itself.

It is the Western form of individualism that offends Dostoyevsky. He invokes a higher individualism, to which the desire for fraternal love is natural, an individualism that is self-effacing and sacrificial:

Understand me: voluntary, fully conscious self-sacrifice utterly free of outside constraint, sacrifice of one's entire self for the benefit of all, is in my opinion a sign of the supreme development of individuality, of its supreme power, absolute self-mastery and freedom of will.

Elsewhere, and especially in *The Brothers Karamazov*, Dostoyevsky asks the question that inevitably arises from this attitude: How Christian can a civilization—any civilization—be? And as an artist must, he answers with ever more profound questions. But his severity toward the French never relaxes. In the French bourgeois character he sees a betrayal of the greatest hopes of the modern age.

It is in *Winter Notes* that his antagonism toward France first appears. It culminates in his wild satire of *Bribri and Mabiche*, a funny and also rather ugly affair. Poets (and novelists) wish to see a poetic principle in human action, but they are not always gratified at the effects of literature on social behavior. Dostoyevsky abhors "literary" bourgeois motives and the idolatry of culture.

What happens when literature becomes part of the life of a nation?

I myself did not know whether to cheer or weep when I saw posted in a station in Paris the announcement of a discussion of Racine by the police of the district. *Flics!* Cops! you see. And Racine! I must admit that I derived a curious ironic satisfaction from this. Wonderful France, where even the bulls are educated for sensibility. The pervasiveness of literary culture in Paris was not always pleasant. I had to submit when my dentist carried on about a dull play of Camus called *Les Justes*, and Sartre's latest novel. On the boulevard Saint-Germain, a fashionable shop displayed silk scarves inscribed romantically with the names of Jean-Paul and Simone. Often Parisians struck me as behaving exactly like a huge cast of characters. Baudelaire complained in *Mon Coeur Mis à Nu* that everyone in France looked like Voltaire.

A great civilization always distinguishes, frames, sets apart, places an imprint of value, upon its members. The Parisian face is thus framed, individually distinguished. The historic task of a civilization is to remake the world in its own image. To a Frenchman, the French world *is* the world. In no other form is it conceivable. Do you want to see an Eskimo? Turn to the *Encyclopédie Larousse*. There you may see him *as he is*. He cannot be otherwise. On a fiercely hot day in Paris, a storekeeper told me, *"La chaleur est plus brutale chez vous."* He had never been *chez moi*, but he had no need to leave Paris in order to know this.

But now the stable heavens have been torn asunder. Above is a chaos that French order cannot bear to see. The world has been expanded, horribly. Walls have fallen. The old stability has turned to bitter dust, and the Parisian countenance is filled with irony and with anger.

These are circumstances that bring out the deepest characteristics of a culture. Although we give exclusiveness as one of the criteria of culture, not all cultures are equally exclusive. Everywhere there are natural and human recognitions that supersede the cultural. It is the greater culture that allows the greatest latitude to certain natural human needs and simplicities.

Let it be remembered that it was as a journalist that Dostoyevsky wrote these *Winter Notes*. The articles were published in a review called *Vremya* and were read by most educated Russians. Our American journalism today is quite different. Vast organizations prepare for us their version of things as they are abroad. For this purpose they employ numbers of quite ordinary reporters. And when the stuff gathered by these reporters comes in, it is processed editorially. And then we are fed a homogeneous substance called information, created by experts (or ideologists) well and thoroughly indoctrinated in the views of the management. Rarely are talented and educated writers permitted to convey in their own words their own sense of reality. No. If an activity is not, in our bureaucratic times, corporate, vetted by "responsible" people, it is suspect. What we read in our national papers and magazines is an artificial mixture concocted to appease our desire to be informed.

Winter Notes is often intemperate, worse than unfair, and even frivolous. With his usual comic and cruel candor, Dostoyevsky concedes that his observations are sometimes sour and jaundiced, and it is characteristic of him that he does not conceal his prejudices. For him the revelation of bias is a step toward the truth. "Good" principles tempt us to conceal ill feeling and to lie. Liberalism, whether it is Eastern or Western, is habitually deceitful. "Let us come forward as we are," Dostoyevsky is forever saying, "in our native crudity. No disguises."

This is one of his important principles, and he holds to it with fanatical consistency. You may study his views on many topics in the huge, crazy, foaming, vengeful, fulminating book called *A Writer's Diary*. In this collection of his journalistic writings, he records repeatedly his ever mounting bitterness toward Europe. Europeans cannot understand Russia, he says. Even those who attempt "to grasp our Russian essence" do so in vain; they "will long fail to comprehend . . ."

Yet Dostoyevsky considered himself a most practical Christian. The literary historian D. S. Mirsky speaks of "the rational and pragmatic nature of his Christianity." A statement of this sort about a man who freely confessed his hatred of Frenchmen, Germans, and Poles gives one pause. We are explicitly commanded by Christianity not to do this. Non-Christians have long understood the difficulty—no, the impossibility—of following this injunction. It is almost unnecessary to add that Christians have too. If I employ the word "almost," it is because the mixture of nationalism and Christianity is not easy to comprehend. Was Dostoyevsky able to love Russians more because he detested Germans? Is it perhaps necessary to fix a limit to the number of people one can try to love? It does not surprise modern readers, acquainted with twentieth-century psychology, that the power to hate increases the power to love also. The Duc de Saint-Simon said long ago that love and hate were fed by a single nerve. The same thought is expressed clearly enough by William Blake, and Dostoyevsky was not ignorant of it. But his personal opinions were not rational. As an artist, he was both rational and wise.

An odd thing: When Dostoyevsky was toward the end of his career, corresponding with his friend the infamous reactionary Pobedonostyev, he referred once to a problem he was facing in the composition of *The Brothers Karamazov*. Dostoyevsky had just concluded the section of *The Brothers* in which Ivan had declared that he doubted the existence of God—had offered to return his "ticket" to the Creator. Having made a powerful case for atheism, Dostoyevsky now prepared the answer of faith. For this he turned to Father Zosima. He hoped, he told Pobedonostyev, to avoid polemics. These he considered "inartistic." To answer artistically is to do full justice, to respect propositions and harmonies with which journalists and polemicists do not have to bother their heads. In the novel, Dostoyevsky cannot permit himself to yield to cruel, intemperate, and arbitrary personal judgments. The writer's convictions, perhaps fanatically held, must be tamed by truth.

The degree to which you challenge your own beliefs and expose them to destruction is a test of your worth as a novelist.

A TALK WITH THE YELLOW KID

(1956)

"*I* have always affected a pearl stickpin upon my neckwear," says Yellow Kid Weil. The Kid, who is now in his eighties, is an elegant and old-fashioned gentleman; he likes round phrases and leisurely speech. One of the greatest confidence men of his day, he has publicly forsworn crime and announced his retirement. A daughter of his in Florida urges him to pass his remaining years with her, but he prefers Chicago. He will tell you that he knows of no better place, and he has lived in many places. Chicago is his city.

As we stood talking in the lobby of the Sun-Times Building not long ago, a young photographer came running up to the famous criminal, threw an arm about his narrow old shoulders, and said affectionately, "Hi ya, Kid. Kid, how's it goin'?" At such moments his bearded old face is lit with a smile of deepest pleasure, and looks of modesty and of slyness also steal over it. Bartenders, waitresses, reporters, know him. The vanishing race of old intellectuals in the neighborhood of Bughouse Square respects him. Real estate men, lawyers, even judges and bankers, will sometimes greet him. Why should he live elsewhere? He was born in Chicago, his career began there.

It was Bathhouse John Coughlin, Chicago's primitive alderman and illustrious boss, who named him the Yellow Kid. Bathhouse had started out in life as a masseur in the old Brevoort Hotel. When he attained great power he was not too proud to talk to a young fellow like Joe Weil, as the Kid was then known. Weil came often to Coughlin's saloon. An early comic strip called "Hogan's Alley and the Yellow Kid" was then appearing in the *New York Journal*, to which Coughlin subscribed. Weil followed it passionately, and Bathhouse John saved the papers for him. "Why, you're the Kid himself," Coughlin said one day, and so Weil acquired the name.

The Kid is now very frail, and it becomes him. His beard very much resembles the one that the late Senator James Hamilton Lewis, a great dandy, used to wear. It is short, parted in the middle, and combed into two rounded portions, white and stiff. Beneath the whiskers, the Kid's chin is visible, an old man's chin. You think you have met with a happy old quack, a small-time charlatan who likes to reminisce about the wickedness of his past, until you become aware of the thin, forceful, sharp mouth under the trembling hairs of old age. It is the mouth of a masterful man.

He must once have been very imposing. Now there is a sort of fallen nattiness about him. His shoes are beautifully shined, though not in top condition. His suit is made of a bold material; it has gone too often to the cleaner, but it is in excellent press. His shirt must belong to the days of his prosperity, for his neck has shrunk and the collar fits loosely. The cloth has a green pattern of squares within squares. Tie and pocket handkerchief are of a matching green. His little face is clear and animated. Long practice in insincerity gives him an advantage; it is not always easy to know where he is coming from.

By his swindles he made millions of dollars, but he lost as many fortunes as he made, and he lost them always in legitimate enterprises. This is one of his favorite ironies, and he often returns to it. His wife was forever urging him to go straight. He loved her—he still speaks touchingly of her—and for her sake he wanted to reform. It never worked. There was a curse on any honest business that he tried, whether it was giving pianos away as a coffee premium or leasing the Hagenbeck-Wallace circus. An inner voice seemed to warn him to stay crooked, and he did not ignore it.

The years have not softened his heart toward the victims of his confidence schemes. Of course he was a crook, but the "marks" whom he and his associates trimmed were not honest men. "I have never cheated any honest men," he says, "only rascals. They may have been respectable, but they were never any good." And this is how he sums the matter up: "They wanted something for nothing. I gave them nothing for something." He says it clearly and sternly; he is not a pity-ing man. To be sure, he wants to justify his crimes, but quite apart from this he believes that honest men do not exist. He presents him-self as a Diogenes whose lifelong daylight quest for absolute honesty has ended in disappointment. Actually, he never expected to find it.

He is a thinker, the Kid is, and a reader. His favorite authors seem to be Nietzsche and Herbert Spencer. Spencer has always been the favorite of autodidactic Midwestern philosophers, that vanishing species. During the 1920s, the Kid belonged to a bohemian discussion group on the Near North Side called the Dill Pickle Club. Its brainy and colorful fleet of eccentrics—poets, painters, and cranks—have long been dispersed by vulgar winds. Once, Chicago promised to be-come a second London, but it was not to be; bowling alleys and bars increased, bookshops did not. New York and Hollywood took away the artists. Death did the rest. Herbert Spencer also was destined for the dustbin.

But the Kid is still faithful to him; he spends his evenings at his books—so at least he says—meditating upon the laws of society, the sanctioned and the unsanctioned, power and weakness, justice and his-tory. I do not think the Kid loves the weak, and he dislikes many of the strong, especially politicians and bankers. Against bankers he has a strong prejudice. "They are almost always shady," he says. "Their ac-tivities are usually only just within the law."

The twilight borderlands of legality attract the Kid's subtle mind. Not long ago he was picked up in the lobby of the Bismarck Hotel on suspicion. He had merely been chatting with one of the guests, he told me, but the manager was worried and phoned the confidence squad. The Kid is used to these small injustices, and they do not offend him or disturb his tranquillity. In court he listened attentively to the case preceding his own, that of a bookie.

"Why should this man be fined and punished?" said the Kid when his turn came at the bar. "Why should he be punished for betting when betting is permitted within the confines of the track itself?" The judge, to hear the Kid tell it, was very uneasy. He answered that the state derived revenues from the track. "I would gladly pay revenues to the state," the Kid said, "if I could rent a building within which confi-dence games would be legal. Suppose the state were to license me.

Then confidence men operating outside my building could be arrested and imprisoned. Inside the door, licensed operatives would be safe. It makes the same kind of sense, Your Honor." According to the Kid, the judge offered "no cogent reply."

Perhaps the Kid's antagonism toward bankers rests on an undivulged belief that he would have made a more impressive banker than any of them. In his swindles, he often enough pretended to be one. With phony Wall Street credentials, he would take in the president of some country bank who would be only too eager to give him permission to make use of his premises. Often the Kid would find a pretext to sit in the president's own office. Entering, his victims would see him seated behind the great mahogany desk and take him for the president.

At one time the Kid was actually the legitimate officer of a bank, the American State Bank on South La Salle Street in Chicago. He and Big John Worthington, a confidence man who closely resembled J. Pierpont Morgan, together paid some seventy thousand dollars and obtained a controlling interest. The Kid became a vice president. He started a racket in phony letters of credit by which he made about three hundred thousand dollars. He was not caught. On another occasion the Kid rented an empty bank building and filled it with his stooges. The stooges made it look busy; they arrived with bogus currency for deposit, and bags full of lead slugs. Taken in by this activity, the mark was swindled easily by the Kid. Once, he took a suite of offices in the heart of Chicago's financial district. Girls from secretarial schools were hired to look busy. They typed names from the telephone directory.

Sometimes the Kid posed as a doctor, sometimes as a mining engineer or as a professor or a geologist. Or, during World War I, as a financial representative of the Central Powers. He put magazines and books into circulation from which original photographs were removed and pictures of himself inserted. All his life long he sold nonexistent property, concessions he did not own, and air-spun schemes to greedy men.

The Kid's activities landed him in jail now and then—he has served time in Atlanta and Leavenworth—but he says, and not unbelievably, that there were not many dull days in his life. His total gains are estimated by the "police and the daily press" at about eight millions. Most of this money he lost in bad investments or squandered in high living. He loved wild parties, showgirls, champagne suppers, European trips. He had his clothes made in Bond Street or Jermyn Street. This English wardrobe is still good; real quality doesn't go out of fashion. But almost everything else is gone.

"Before I reached the years of maturity," the Kid said, "I fell in love with a young woman of the most extraordinary pulchritude. I brought her home one night to dinner. My mother," he said with a bluster of his whiskers and looking gravely at me with the thin diffused blue of his eyes, "was renowned for her perfection in the culinary art. We had a splendid meal, and later my mother said to me, 'Joseph, that is a most beautiful young woman. She is so lovely that she cannot be meant for you. She must have been meant for some millionaire.' From that moment I determined that I, too, would be a millionaire. And I was." The sexual incentive to be rich, the Kid told me, was always very powerful with him.

"I was of a very fragile constitution, unfit for the heavier sort of manual labor. I knew I could not toil like other men. How was I to live? My power lay in words. In words I became a commander. Moreover, I could not lead a tame life of monotony. I needed excitement, variety, danger, intellectual stimulus.

"I was a psychologist," he went on. "My domain was the human mind. A Chinese scholar with whom I once studied told me, 'People always see themselves in you.' With this understanding I entered the lives of my dupes. The man who lives by an idea enjoys great superiority over those who live by none. To make money is not an idea; that doesn't count. I mean a real idea. It was very simple. My purpose was invisible. When they looked at me they saw themselves. I only showed them their own purpose."

There are no longer such operators, says the great confidence man, perhaps jealous of his eminence. Where are they to come from? The great mass of mankind breeds obedient types. They express their protests in acts of violence, not ingeniously. Moreover, your natural or talented confidence man is attracted to politics. Why be a robber, a fugitive, when you can get society to give you the key to the vaults where the greatest boodle lies? The United States government, according to the Kid, runs the greatest giveaway program in history.

The Kid at one time tried to found an independent little republic upon a small island made of fill, somewhere in Lake Michigan. His object was to make himself eligible for foreign-aid grants.

A prominent figure, something of a public man, a dandy and a philosopher, the Kid says that he now frequently does good works. But the confidence squad still keeps an eye on him. Not so long ago he was walking down the street with a certain monsignor, he tells me. They were discussing a fund drive in the parish. Presently the con squad drew alongside, and one of the detectives said, "What you up to, Kid?"

"I'm just helping out the monsignor here. It's on the level."

The monsignor assured him that this was true.

The detective turned on him. "Why, you so-and-so," he said. "Aren't you ashamed to be wearin' the cloth for a swindle?"

The thought so enraged him that he took them both to headquarters.

The Kid laughed quietly and long over the copper's error; wrinkled, bearded, wry, and delighted, he looked at this moment like one of the devil's party.

"They refuse to believe I have reformed," he said. The psychology of a policeman, according to the Kid, is strict, narrow, and primitive. It denies that character is capable of change.

So much for the police, incurably, hopelessly dumb. But what about the criminals? The Kid did not think much of criminal intelligence either. And how does the underworld see the confidence men? I asked. Gangsters and thieves greatly dislike them, he said. They never trust them, and in some cases they take a peculiar and moral view of the confidence swindler. He is too mental a type for them.

"The attitude of the baser sort of criminal toward me is very interesting," he said. "They have always either shunned or behaved with extreme coldness to me. I never will forget a discussion I once had with a second-story man about our respective relations to our victims. He thought me guilty of the highest immorality. Worst of all, in his eyes, was the fact that I openly showed myself to dupes in the light of day. 'Why,' he said to me with an indescribable demeanor, 'you go right up to them. *They see your face!*' This seemed to him the worst of all deceits. Such is their scheme of ethics," said the Kid. "In their view, you should sneak up on people to pick their pockets, or break and enter to burglarize their houses, but to look them in the eyes, gain their confidence, that is impure."

We parted on noisy Wacker Drive, near the Clark Street Bridge. No longer listening to the Kid, I heard the voice of the city. Chicago keeps changing, amazing its old-timers. The streetcars, for instance, are different. You no longer see the hard, wicked-looking, red, cumbrous, cowlike, trampling giant streetcars. The new ones are green and whir by like dragonflies. Glittering and making soft electrical sounds, one passed the Kid as he walked toward the Loop. Spruce and firm-footed, with his beard and wind-curled hat, he looked, beside the car, like the living figure of tradition in the city.

PART TWO

Writers, Intellectuals, Politics

THE SEALED TREASURE

(1960)

A few years ago, I traveled through the state of Illinois to gather material for an article. It was brilliant fall weather; the corn was high, and it was intersected by straight, flat roads over which it was impossible not to drive at top speed. I went from Chicago to Galena and then south through the center of the state to Cairo and Shawnee-town. Here and there, in some of the mining counties and in the de-populated towns along the Mississippi, there were signs of depression and poverty, but these had the flavor of the far away and long ago, for the rest of the state was dizzily affluent. "Pig Heaven," some people said to me. "Never nothing like it." The shops were filled with goods and buyers. In the fields were the newest harvesting machines; in the houses washers, dryers, freezers and refrigerators, air conditioners, vacuum cleaners, Mixmasters, Waring blenders, television and stereo-phonic hi-fi sets, electrical can openers, novels condensed by the *Read-ers' Digest*, and slick magazines. In the yards, glossy cars in giddy colors, like ships from outer space.

Down in Egypt, as the narrow southern end of the state is called, a Negro woman, her head wrapped in an old-fashioned bandanna, flashed by in her maroon Packard with a Boston bull terrier affection-ately seated on her shoulder. Here at least was some instinct for the blending of old and new. For the most part, everything was as new as possible. Churches and supermarkets had the same modern design. In the skies, the rich farmers piloted their own planes. The workers bowled in alleys of choice hardwood, where fouls were scored and pins reset by electrical devices. Fifty years ago, the Illinois poet Vachel Lindsay had visited these towns preaching the Gospel of Beauty and calling on the people to build the New Jerusalem.

Except for the main stem, the streets were boringly empty, and at night even the main stem was almost deserted. Restless adolescents gathered in the ice cream parlors or loitered before the chain saws, vibrating recliners, outboard motors, and garbage disposal units displayed in shop windows. These, like master spirits, ruled the night in silence.

Some important ingredients of life were conspicuously absent.

I had been asked to write about Illinois, but how was I to distinguish it from Indiana, Michigan, Iowa, or Missouri? The houses were built and furnished in the same style, the cows were milked by the same machines, the programs broadcast by CBS and NBC were alike in Rockford, Illinois, and Danbury, Connecticut, and Salt Lake City, Utah. The magazines, the hairstyles, the salad dressings, the film stars, were not merely American but international. What but slight differences in the menu and the cut of the clothes distinguished the comfortable life of middle-class Illinois from that of Cologne or Frankfurt?

I asked, "What do people do hereabouts?" "They work." "And when they don't work?" "They watch TV. They play a little poker or canasta or gin." "What else?" "They go to club meetings. Or to the drive-in movie. They pitch a little. They raise a little hell. They bowl. They drink some. They tinker around the place, fool with power tools. They teach the kids baseball in the Little League. They're den mothers over at the Cub Scouts." "Yes, but what do they *do*?" "Well, mister, I'm telling you what they do. What are you getting at?" "You see, I'm writing an article on life here." "Is *that* so! Gosh, you're barking up the wrong tree. There ain't nothing here to write about. There's nothing doing here, or anywhere in Ellenois. It's boring." "You can't have millions of people and nothing doing." "I tell you, you want to write about Hollywood or Las Vegas or New York or Paris. That's where they've got excitement."

I had a score of conversations like this one.

Was the vitality of these people entirely absorbed by the new things? Had a superior inventive and productive power taken them over, paralyzing all the faculties it did not need? Or had the old under-standing of reality been based on the threat of hunger and on the con-tinual necessity for hard labor? Was it possible that what people complained of as boredom might in fact be an unbearable excitement caused by the greatness of the change?

I went to the public libraries and was not surprised to learn that good books were very much in demand and that there were people in central Illinois who read Plato, Tocqueville, Proust, and Robert Frost. I had expected this. But what I did not understand was what use these isolated readers were making of the books they borrowed. With whom did they discuss them? At the country club, the bowling league, sort-ing mail at the post office, or in the factory, over the back fence, how did they bring up Plato's Justice or Proust's Memory? Ordinary life gave them little opportunity for such conversation. "You can't have millions of people and nothing doing." I was dead sure of that. But the intelligence or cultivation of a woman in Moline, Illinois, would nec-essarily be her secret, almost her private vice. Her friends at the bridge club would think it very odd of her to think such things. She might not reveal them to her sister, nor perhaps even to her husband. They would be her discovery, her treasure ten times sealed, her private source of power.

"The language, the dress, and the daily actions of men in democ-racies are repugnant to ideal conceptions," said Tocqueville. He said more, but this is text enough for the moment. Let us set beside it the fact that these men, or some of them, will read *The Divine Comedy*, *The Tempest*, and *Don Quixote*. What will they make of these works? They will, some of them, mix them up with television productions. Others will scale them down. Our understanding of them (it is time to drop the third person) will certainly be faulty. Nevertheless they move us. That is to say, human greatness can still be seen by us. And it is not a question of the gnat who sees the elephant. We are not members of a different species. Without a certain innate sympathy, we could not read Shakespeare and Cervantes. In our own contemporary novels, this power to understand the greatest human qualities appears to be dispersed, transformed, or altogether buried. A modern mass society has no open place for such qualities, no vocabulary for them, and no ceremony (except in the churches) that makes them public. So they remain private and are mingled with other private things that vex us or of which we feel ashamed. But they are not lost. The saleswoman in Moline, Illinois, *will* go to the library and borrow *Anna Karenina*. This society, with its titanic products, conditions but cannot absolutely denature us. It forces certain elements of the genius of our species to go into hiding. In America, these hidden elements take curiously personal, secret forms. Sometimes they corrupt people; sometimes they cause them to act with startling generosity. On the whole, they are not to be found in what we call our Culture.

They are not in the streets, in the stores, at the movies. They are the missing ingredients.

The greatest danger, Dostoyevsky warned in *The Brothers Karamazov*, was the universal anthill. D. H. Lawrence believed the common people of our industrial cities were like the great slave populations of the ancient empires. Joyce was apparently convinced that what happened to the ordinary modern man, his external life, was not interesting enough to chronicle. James Stephens in his preface to *Solitaria* by the Russian philosopher Rozanov said that novelists were trying to keep alive by artificial means feelings and states of being which had died out of the modern world, implying that we were only flattering the dwarfs by investing them with the passions of dead giants.

Mind manipulation, brainwashing, and social engineering are only the newest developments in an evolution long understood by writers of the civilized world. When we read the best nineteenth- and twentieth-century novelists, we soon realize that they are trying in a variety of ways to establish a definition of human nature, to justify the continuation of life as well as the writing of novels. Like it or not, says Dostoyevsky, it is our nature to be free and, under the sting of suffering, to choose between good and evil. And Tolstoy says of human nature that it contains a need for truth, which will never allow it to rest permanently in falsehood or unreality.

I think the novelists who take the bitterest view of our modern condition make the most of the art of the novel. "Do you think," Flaubert replies to a correspondent who has complained of *Madame Bovary*, "that this ignoble reality, so disgusting to you in reproduction, does not oppress my heart as it does yours? If you knew me better you would know that I abhor ordinary existence. Personally, I have always held myself as aloof from it as I could. But aesthetically I desired this once—and only once—to plumb its very depths."

The writer's art appears to seek a compensation for the hopelessness or meanness of existence. By some occult method, the writer has connected himself with the feelings and ideal conceptions of which few signs remain in ordinary existence. Some novelists, the naturalists, have staked everything on ordinary existence in their desire to keep their connection with the surrounding world. Many of these have turned themselves into recording instruments at best, and at worst they have sucked up to the crowd, disgustingly. But the majority of modern novelists have followed the standard of Flaubert, the aesthetic standard. The shock caused by the loss of faith, says Professor Heller in *The Disinherited Mind*, made Burckhardt adopt an aesthetic view of history. If he is right, a sharp sense of disappointment and aestheticism go together. Flaubert complained that the exterior world was "disgusting, enervating, corruptive, and brutalizing. . . . I am turning towards a kind of aesthetic mysticism," he wrote.

I am sticking to Flaubert because the connection between Yonville in Normandy and Galesburg in Illinois is constantly growing closer; because Flaubert believed that the writer by means of imagery and style must supply the human qualities that the exterior world lacked. And because we have all been schooled in his method, we are like the isolated lady in Moline whose sensitivity is her ten-times-sealed treasure.

Disappointment with its human material is built into the contemporary novel. It is assumed that society cannot give the novelist "suitable" themes and characters. Therefore the important humanity of the novel must be the writer's own. His force, his virtuosity, his powers of poetry, his reading of fate, are at the center of his book. The reader is invited to bring his sympathies to the writer rather than to the characters, and this makes him something of a novelist too.

The insistent aesthetic purpose in novelists like Flaubert and Henry James and Virginia Woolf and James Joyce is tyrannical at times. It overconditions the situation of the characters. We are greatly compensated with poetry and insight, but it often seems as though the writer were deprived of all power except the power to see and to despair. In reality, however, he has a very great power. Is it likely that Westerns, thrillers, movies, soap operas, and true confessions can usurp that power and permanently replace it? Not unless human nature is malleable without limits and can be conditioned to do without its ancient bread and meat.

A work of fiction consists of a series of moments during which we are willingly engrossed in the experiences of others. Or, as a recent article in the *Hudson Review* puts it, "the exuberant conviction that the individual life of *somebody else* holds all human truth and human potentiality" must be shared by the novelist and his reader. Let us say, putting it as mildly as possible, that modern society does not often inspire this exuberant conviction. We have learned to lie to ourselves about this. Americans, softly optimistic, do lie about the love they bear one another. My informant in Illinois was telling the truth when he said his life was boring, but he would have turned awfully pious if I had asked him whether he loved his neighbor. Then he would have stood on the creed and answered that he felt a boundless love for him.

The matter was put as strongly as possible by D. H. Lawrence. "The sympathetic heart is broken," he said. "We stink in each other's nostrils." That is, we cannot easily accept our own creaturely existence or that of others. And that is the fault of modern civilization, he tells us. We must in part agree, but the matter is so serious that we should be careful not to exaggerate. Our lives depend on it. Yes, there are good reasons for revulsion and fear. But revulsion and fear impair judgment. Anxiety destroys scale, and suffering makes us lose perspective.

One would have to be optimistic to the point of imbecility to raise the standard of pure Affirmation and cry, "Yea, Yea," shrilly against the deep background of "Nay"s. But the sympathetic heart is sometimes broken, sometimes not. It is reckless to say "broken"; it is nonsense to say "whole and unimpaired." On either side we have the black and white of paranoia.

As for the novelist, he must proceed with care and modesty. He should deplore no general evil on purely literary grounds. The world owes him nothing, and he has no business to be indignant with it on behalf of the novel. He must not expect life to bind itself to be stable for his sake or to accommodate his ambitions. If he must, let him, like Flaubert, "abhor ordinary existence." But he should not fall into despair over trifles. One of his legacies from Romanticism is a sensitivity to banality and ugliness, in which originates much of the small change of modern fiction—the teeth that are crooked, the soiled under-clothes, the clerk with carbuncles. From this comes a conventional un-earned wretchedness, a bitterness about existence, which is mere fashion.

The enormous increases in population seem to have dwarfed the individual. So have modern physics and astronomy. But we may be somewhere between a false greatness and a false insignificance. At least we can stop misrepresenting ourselves to ourselves and realize that the only thing we can be in this world is human. We are tem-porarily miracle-sodden and feeling faint.

FACTS THAT PUT FANCY

TO FLIGHT

(1962)

I have read somewhere that in the early days of the movies, a miner in Alaska rushed at the screen to batter down the villain with his shovel. Probably he was drunk, but his action was significant nevertheless. This man had considered it a practical thing to travel thousands of miles into a frozen wilderness to dig for buried treasure. Money, land, furs, jewels, champagne, cigars, silk hats, he must have accepted as legitimate objects of the imagination. Yet there was no place in his mind for this new sort of transaction. It evidently seemed to him that if the fellow had taken the trouble to tie the kicking heroine to the tracks, he must mean business. His imagination could conceive only of real objects. Thus with the selfsame shovel he dug for gold and swung at shadows.

Few people make this error in so primitive a form, but almost no one is altogether free from it. We understand, of course, that art does not copy experience but merely borrows it for its own peculiar purposes. Americans, however, do not find it always simple to maintain the distinction. For us the wonder of life is bound up with literal facts, and our greatest ingenuity is devoted to the real. This gives reality itself magical and even sacred properties and makes American realism very different from the European sort. With us the interest of the reader and often of the writer, as well, is always escaping toward facts.

The nonfactual imagination also returns to facts. Ask a woman to describe her son, and she is likely to tell you with pride that he is six feet two or three inches tall and weighs two hundred twenty pounds, that his shoes are size fourteen, and that he eats four eggs at breakfast and two pounds of steak at a sitting. Her love, in short, frequently takes a statistical form. Years ago, in Chicago, I used to listen to a Negro virtuoso, Facts-and-Figures Taylor, who entertained shouting crowds in Washington Park by reciting the statistics he had memorized in the public library. "You want to know what the steel industry exported in nineteen and twenty-one? You listen to this, now."

"You tell 'em, Facts-and-Figures. Give 'em hell!"

People who are not particularly friendly to art may be reconciled to it by factual interests—descriptions of the stretching or priming of the canvas and the method of applying the paints, the dollar value of the picture. One thinks more kindly of a painting valued at ten thousand dollars, the original factory colors dripped from a six-inch brush, than of one that has not applied to the prevailing form of the imagination for consideration. The theatergoer may be pleased to learn that behind the living room represented on the stage are fully furnished bathrooms or kitchens, which will never be seen but are there to give a reassuring sense of completeness or closure. The imitation will be absolutely genuine. Because we have a strong taste for the solid background, for documentation, for accuracy, for likeness, we are often confused about the borders between art and life, between social history and fiction, between gossip and satire, between the journalist's news and the artist's discovery.

The demands, editorial and public, for certified realities in fiction sometimes appear barbarous to the writer. Why this terrible insistence on factual accuracy? "Our readers will want to know," an editor will sometimes say, "whether your information is correct." The research department will then make inquiries. How many stories does the Ansonia Hotel really have, and can one see its television antenna from the corner of West End Avenue and Seventy-second Street? What do drugstores charge for Librium? What sort of mustard is used at Nedicks? Is it squeezed from a plastic bottle or applied with a wooden spoon?

These cranky questions will be asked by readers, compulsively. Publishers know they must expect their errors to be detected. They will hear not only from the lunatic fringe and from pedants but from specialists, from scholars, from people with experience "in the field," from protective organizations and public relations agencies, from persons who have taken upon themselves the protection of the purity of facts.

Archaeologists and historians are consulted by movie producers in the making of Roman spectaculars. As long as the chariots are faithful copies, the fire real Greek fire, it seems to make little difference that the dialogue makes you clutch your head, that the religious theme is trumped up with holy music and cunning lights. It presently becomes clear that the protagonist is not Ben-Hur, not Spartacus, but Know-How. Art based on simple illusion is art in one of its cruder forms, and it is this that Hollywood with its technical skill has brought to perfection.

The realistic method made it possible to write with seriousness and dignity about the ordinary, common situations of life. In Balzac and Flaubert and the great Russian masters, the realistic externals were intended to lead inward. I suppose that one might say that now the two elements, the inward and the external, have come apart.

In what we call the novel of sensibility, the intent of the writer is to pull us into an all-sufficient consciousness, which he, the writer, governs absolutely. In the realistic novel today, the writer is satisfied with an art of externals. Either he assumes that by describing a man's shoes he has told us all that we need to know about his soul, or he is more interested in the shoes than in the soul. Literalists who write to the editor are rather odd and amusing people who do not need to be taken too seriously, but the attitude of the writer himself toward externals is a serious matter.

The facts may excite a writer deeply, and in America we have a poetry of fact—the details of labor in Walt Whitman, the knowledge of navigation in Mark Twain, the descriptions of process in Hemingway's fishing stories. But in every case it is the writer's excitement that counts. Without this excitement, the facts are no more interesting than they would be in a manual of river navigation or a Sears Roebuck catalogue. What is happening now is that the intrinsic excitement of the facts themselves has become intense, and the literary imagination must rival the power of the real. In the U.S.A. today, the facts appear to have it all over the imagination.

The American desire for the real has created a journalistic sort of novel, which has a *thing* excitement, a glamour of *process;* it specializes in information. It resembles the naturalistic novel of Zola and the so-cial novel of Dreiser but is without the theoretical interests of the first and is unlike the second in that it has no concern with justice and no view of fate. It merely satisfies the readers' demand for information. It is literal. From this standpoint it may sometimes be called an improv-ing or a moral sort of book. However, it seldom has much indepen-dent human content, and it is more akin to popularized science or history than to the fiction of Balzac or Chekhov. It is not actively chal-lenged by the "novel of sensibility."

The living heirs of Henry James and Virginia Woolf do not do very well, and I'm afraid that they largely deserve their neglect. In their desire for mental independence and aesthetic sensibility, they have receded altogether too far from the externals. They give very lit-tle information; and after we have visited them in their tree houses once or twice, they lose their charm.

The novel in America has taken two forms, neither satisfactory. Those writers who wish to meet the demand for information have perhaps been successful as social historians, but they have neglected the higher forms of the imagination. The novel of sensibility has failed to represent society and has become totally uninteresting.

It seems hard for the American people to believe that anything could be more exciting than the times themselves. What we read daily and view on the TV has thrust imagined forms into the shadow. We are staggeringly rich in facts, in things, and perhaps, like the nouveau riche of other ages, we want our wealth faithfully reproduced by the artist.

By now it is misleading to speak of the facts as if they were solu-ble, washable, disposable, knowable. The facts themselves are not what they once were and perhaps present themselves to the imagina-tion of the artist in some new way. A. J. Liebling, in an uncommonly good article on Stephen Crane (*The New Yorker*, 5 August 1961), writes: "We have seen in our time that the best writers as they mature become journalists—Sartre, Camus, Mauriac, Hemingway." Are we to suppose, therefore, that the artistic imagination must be sent back into the world and its realities? Does the challenge of journalism in our time carry us higher than that of art?

Some of our novelists can scarcely help being better fact-bringers than artists. They are turning ground that has never been turned before—the army, the laboratory, the modern corporation, the anarchic sexual life of "free spirits": such phenomena in the raw state are not quickly assimilated into art. Moreover, it's hard for writers to get on with their work if they are convinced that they owe a concrete debt to experience and cannot allow themselves the privilege of ranging freely through social classes and professional specialties. A certain pride in their own experience, perhaps a sense of the property rights of others in *their* experience, holds them back.

The novelist, convinced that the novel is the result of his passionate will to know everything about the life of another human being, finds that he must get through the obstacles of the literal to come at his subject. Thus he is prevented from doing the essential thing. Hard knowledge is demanded of him; to acquire this knowledge, he must at least temporarily transform himself into some sort of specialist.

The greatest of the realists always believed that they owed a very special debt to truth. "The hero of my tale, whom I love with all the strength of my soul, whom I have tried to set forth in all his beauty, and who has always been, is, and always will be the most beautiful, is—the truth." So wrote Tolstoy at the conclusion of "Sevastopol in May." And Dostoyevsky, commenting on *Anna Karenina*, tells us that he found the book at times very monotonous and "confined to a certain caste only" and that as long as it was merely a description of life in society, it made no great claim to any deeper interest.

But later he says, "in the very center of that insolent and petty life there appeared a great and eternal living truth, at once illuminating everything. These petty, insignificant and deceitful beings suddenly became genuine and truthful people worthy of being called men."

That is, after all, what the novelist wants, isn't it?

WHITE HOUSE AND ARTISTS

(1962)

*O*ne of the editors of *The Noble Savage*, because the magazine has made so important a contribution to American culture, was invited to attend a White House dinner in honor of M. André Malraux, the French minister of culture, and to mingle with two hundred writers, painters, actors, musicians, and administrators and patrons of the arts. In this crowd *TNS*'s representative saw several novelists and poets at one time strongly alienated, ex-intransigents, former enemies of society, old grumblers, and lifelong manger dogs, all having a hell of a good time, their faces beaming, their wives in evening gowns (could they afford them?). Readers who remember H. G. Wells's *The Island of Dr. Moreau*, with its apes, dogs, and horses changed by the mad surgeon into approximately human forms, have only to think of these same creatures in formal dress (black tie) to get a bit of the flavor.

Casting back in history for a parallel, one wit spoke of the Jacksonian horde trampling the White House furniture (a proto-Beat occasion). A few old-time Washington matrons might have been ready to agree. But this was not in the least a Beat evening. It was square. Even the drunks were well behaved, though at the end of the evening the Schubert trio seemed to be getting to them, and some were tapping the time on their neighbors' knees. There was nothing Jacksonian about the planning and the protocol, the marines in braid, the butlers, the dance orchestra that played a sort of Catskill-intercourse music. Only Adlai Stevenson preserved a shade of intellectual irony. Everybody else seemed absurdly and deeply tickled. Mark Rothko whispered privately to me that of course all this was a lot of crap and meant nothing to him. "But my *sister!*" he said.

"Where is she?"

"Home with the kids. But absolutely beside herself with excitement. It's a great day for my sister."

What he really meant was "If Mama could only see me now."

Several old lions, accustomed to first honors always, spoke to no one but swept through the crowd with an extraordinary brazen fixity of expression, demanding recognition. At the other extreme were some humble souls who confessed a little brokenly that they were not worthy. A few writers, among them veterans of the Popular Front and believers in the upgrading of the masses, declared that a new era was beginning. The American presidency, for so many years sewed up in long johns, a rube presidency, was at last becoming modern. Henceforth the country would respect culture. Others, more skeptical, said that Mr. Kennedy was getting ready to exploit the eggheads. He could get them cheap, and they were falling all over themselves. The government could then show the world that it was an enlightened government, that it knew how to encourage the arts, and that American philistinism was a thing of the dead past. But the real truth, said the grumblers, was that Congress and the administration, though willing to fork over millions of dollars to oil companies in the form of depletion allowances or to cranberry growers to keep up their bogs, would not put up a cent to build a cultural center in Washington. All that dough for Billie Sol Estes and not a penny for singers and playwrights. But Congress has always taken a low view of the arts. Congress would have filled the White House with hog callers or stag shows. Now, grudgingly, it had given the land for a new cultural center but left the raising of funds to the benevolent rich. Finally, these critics declared, the Congress *is* representative—it *does* represent the mind, the spirit, and the feelings of the people. Why should painters and writers then lend themselves to schemes designed to conceal the true state of things?

My own feeling was that if the government really did intend to seduce and exploit American artists, it might do these artists little harm. The hand of the seducer obviously made their hearts beat faster and put a fine glow into their cheeks.

Mr. Kennedy's after-dinner speech was very witty, and a witty president is worth more to artists than a congressional pork barrel. M. Malraux, an impressive-looking man, spoke in greater earnest, saying that America had not sought imperial power and dominion. In private, Mr. Edmund Wilson exclaimed irascibly, in the tones of Mr. Magoo, "Hooey!" There *was* an American empire! I felt it would be a pity to waste Mr. Wilson's fine rumblings on a lousy republic and that his eccentricities deserved at least an imperial setting. But putting it all together again—the Philippines, Latin America, the failed Cuban invasion, the sins of Aramco, the haste with which Germany was reconstructed, the fascinating history of Chiang Kai-shek—I couldn't believe that we were ready to claim elevation to the rank of empire.

But this is the sort of quibble it takes a left-wing sectarian to appreciate. When Russia invaded Finland, the Trotskyites and the splinter Ohlerite faction suffered nearly as much as the Finns, but from another cause. They could not agree about the character of the Soviet state. Was this an imperialist invasion? Could a degenerated workers' state wage an imperialistic war? Can such questions of definition really matter much? Did Augustus Caesar have a stockpile of atomic bombs? Can an American name be worked into the list of imperial personalities—Augustus, Charles V, Napoleon, Gladstone even? Do we dare to add the name of Eisenhower? Kennedy?

Is it to be Emperor Kennedy, then? Well, that is a title to interest poets and artists and philosophers in a different fashion. Poor Descartes died because Queen Christina of Sweden, a Spartan bluestocking, had him up at dawn to give her lessons in mathematics. He was accustomed to lie abed until noon. There he had always done his best work. Pushkin complained about the czar, but then the czar took him seriously enough to oppress him, which is more than the American government cares to do for its writers. Voltaire quarreled with Frederick the Great, but it was perhaps to his credit that he could not make out with that militaristic Kraut. Ezra Pound suffered terrible miseries until he turned up his own dubious Caesar. If Mr. Wilson is right about the American empire, we must think through the whole thing again, and think more clearly. What is to be done? How shall we behave toward the mighty in Washington?

Boswell and Johnson throw some light on this matter. Johnson was honored by the king, who engaged him in private conversation in the library at the Queen's House. "His Majesty approached him, and

at once was courteously easy," says Boswell. When the king compli-
mented him handsomely, Johnson made no reply, explaining later: "It
was not for me to bandy civilities with my sovereign." To the king's
questions about one Dr. Hill, Johnson answered "that he was an ingenious man, but had no veracity." Urged to say more, he declined to
louse up Dr. Hill. "I now began to consider that I was depreciating
this man in the estimation of his Sovereign, and thought it was time
for me to say something that might be more favorable."

Boswell relates that Oliver Goldsmith was lying on the sofa during all the time in which Johnson was telling of his meeting with the
king, "fretting with chagrin and envy at the singular honor Dr. Johnson had lately enjoyed. At length the frankness and simplicity of his
natural character prevailed. He sprung from the sopha, advanced to
Johnson, and in a kind of flutter, from imagining himself in the situation which he had just been hearing described, exclaimed, 'Well, you
acquitted yourself in this conversation better than I should have done;
for I should have bowed and stammered through the whole of it.'"

This is the sort of thing that may happen in a fairly easygoing
monarchy tending toward the constitutional form. But what happens
in a large bureaucratic society? In the Han dynasty, men of letters became functionaries, and the state passed into the long torpor of orthodoxy and dogmatism. A better understanding between writers and the
imperial state has its dangers. I can foresee a bureaucratic situation,
partly created by men of letters, in which the very call girls (who owe
so many of their privileges to the federal tax structure) would be required to pass civil service examinations administered by poets!

One final outcome of this White House dinner should be noted.
One of the guests was Mr. David Rockefeller of the Chase Manhattan
Bank. With him President Kennedy had a long conversation about the
economy, which resulted in an exchange of letters between the two.
These letters were published by *Life*. So far as I know, there have been
no letters about the state of American culture. We can wait until the
other crises are over.

A MATTER OF THE SOUL

(1975)

*T*o accept the honor of opening these learned proceedings, I have come downtown at nine in the morning. I would not otherwise do this unless I were summoned by the police. It's not really my part of Chicago. This is the district dominated by banking, insurance, commodities speculation, and department stores, by the practice of law and the operations of politics, by steel, oil, chemicals, airlines, computers, and utilities. Culture is represented in these parts by the Public Library and the Art Institute.

Millions of people come to view the treasures of the Institute. Schoolchildren arriving in buses from the vast middle-class reaches of the city and from the slums are marched through the galleries. One of the curators has told me that sometimes the spittle of resentful kids has to be wiped from the glass. Compulsory veneration is bound to come out as rebellion, hatred, and blasphemy.

I remember these emotions from my own school days in Chicago, circa 1925, during the art-appreciation or the music period, when teachers showed us colored slides of *The Angelus* or Turner's *Téméraire* towed into the Thames sunset or, winding up the gramophone, played for us Chaliapin singing the "Song of the Flea" or Galli-Curci the "Bell Song" from *Lakmé* or Caruso or Tito Schipa or Madame Schumann-Heink. What did it signify to us? If we were sensitive, we responded to the piety of the teachers. If we were tough, we jeered, we razzed or cursed them in our hearts. But tough or sensitive, we somehow grasped the tacit Chicago assumption that this was a rough place, a city of labor and business, gangs and corrupt politics, ball games and prizefights. We were the children of groping, baffled immigrants who were trying to figure out what had become of them in America.

Crudity, disappointment, sickness, heartbreak, money, power, happiness, and love in rudimentary forms—this was what we were aware of. This was a place where matter ruled, a place where stone was value and value stone. If you were drawn toward a higher life—and you might well be, even in the city of stockyards, steel, and gangsters—you had to make your own way toward it. Conditions were vastly different in a city like Milan a century and a half ago, when Verdi arrived from his native village to study music and found there, and later in other cities, theaters, producers, musicians, and a public of exacting and responsive amateurs.

Not that one never heard of such things here. There was music in primordial Chicago. At the age of twelve, I myself performed Böhm's "Moto Perpetuo" on the violin in a student recital at Kimball Hall. And I had learned quite a lot about grand opera from Jeremiah, our roomer.

Jeremiah, whose hair was kinky and red, longed heart and soul to become a singer. A workingman, he operated a punch press in a factory. He sang for us in the kitchen. He rose on his toes, his octagonal glasses sweated, and when he brought his hands together I wondered whether his calluses might not be causing pain. Talentless and fervent, he made his friends smile. He had been an amateur boxer, and, at the YMCA, his nose was flattened. My private theory was that a punch in the nose had ruined his chances as a dramatic tenor. This gentle, hopeless man, my particular friend, studied singing with Alexander Nakutin in the Fine Arts Building. Chicago *has* a building of that name, and in those days it was filled with foreign professors of music. They had marvelous names like Borushek, Schneiderman, Treshansky, and their pupils were for the most part the sons and daughters of immigrants.

Chicago was a very different city in the days of open immigration. The quota laws of 1924 changed the character of urban America decisively. It stopped the flow of artisans, of cabinetmakers, skilled ironworkers, confectioners, bakers, cooks, instrument makers, and other craftsmen from Central Europe, Italy, and the Balkans. Internal population movements brought up unskilled workers from the South. Life took a different turn. The descendants of European artisans dropped their trades, many of which in any case would have become obsolete.

Chicago was merely an anticipation of what was to happen everywhere. A new world was quickly replacing the old one. Chicago and high culture—I say this with a certain surprise, as a Chicagoan—have drawn closer. Chicago now hears sophisticated concerts, while Milan has explosions in its banks. Italy's bourgeoisie closely resembles ours; in both cities, the young are increasingly similar. And intellectuals everywhere, alas, are more and more alike. The intellectuals, refined specialists in a hundred fields, are often as philistine as the masses from which they emerged. I hear a mathematician of high rank boast that he has yet to enter the "new" University of Chicago library, which opened five years ago. He needs nothing but papers in his own special field.

Intellectuals have not become a new class of art patrons. This means that the universities have failed painfully. They have not educated viewers, readers, and audiences as they should have done, and educated philistinism emerges as a new negative force here as in all countries. The learned are farther from art and taste than they were even a generation ago. If you believe in the truth of Stendhal's rule "*Le mauvais goût mène aux crimes*"—"Bad taste leads to crime"—you can foresee no end to crime waves to come. I am speaking of crimes against art. There is no sign that they are subsiding; they are multiplying madly.

I have not come here to lay a burden of discouragement on scholars devoted to the study of Verdi. I myself am not overcome by sadness when I speak of art in the modern world. I'm only trying to be clearheaded about what is happening. Millions, no, billions of human souls are riding into consciousness on a revolutionary storm. Over large parts of the earth, revolutions have produced police states and slave societies, where ideology replaces reality.

Max Weber had already told us early in the century that modernity is "disenchanted." Apparently the rise of consciousness is linked with certain kinds of privation. It is the bitterness of self-consciousness that we knowers know best. Critical of the illusions that sustained mankind in earlier times, this self-consciousness of ours does little to sustain us now. The question is: which is disenchanted, the world itself or the consciousness we have of it? The usual explanation is that the cause of our disenchantment lies in the rationality of the new social, economic, and technological order. No artist worth his salt will wish to concede this. He would rather argue that it is a false rationality that is to blame. But he hasn't an easy case to make.

Perhaps it is a mistake, though, to think always of the overall condition of art, or of an entire civilization, not portions of that civilization. Good performances still find discriminating audiences, and there still are readers waiting for books. They belong to a minority, but a fraction of a modern population can be numerically significant. A public numbering two or three hundred thousand would certainly satisfy the needs of most artists. There were of course in the nineteenth century national artists, like Dickens or Dostoyevsky or Verdi, who were strengthened and inspired by the interest and admiration and the vital support of an entire people. A Dickens who spoke to all of England, and in a measure for it, enjoyed an incomparable advantage, but with the possible exception of Russia—I am thinking here of Solzhenitsyn—this sort of position is not available to the artist of today. To have 250,000 readers is, however, nothing to complain of.

The number would be even larger if American education were not disabling, confusing, and alienating students. There must be 25,000,000 college graduates in the U.S., but one of the problems of the country is the silliness, instability, and philistinism of its educated people. I often think there is more hope for the young worker who picks up a paperback copy of Faulkner or Melville or Tolstoy from the rack in the drugstore than there is for the B.A. who has had the same writers "interpreted" for him by his teachers and can tell you, or thinks he can, what Ahab's harpoon symbolizes or what Christian symbols there are in *Light in August*. In colleges and universities, no passion for novels and poems is instilled. What people learn is how to conduct a cultured conversation for a few minutes without betraying ignorance or stupidity.

Still, the university is in some sense my patron—or was, when I still needed patronage. In the decades of prosperity after World War II, American universities gathered in poets, novelists, painters, and musicians and gave them sanctuary. Since private universities are supported by philanthropists, by the generosity of the rich, the rich were, indirectly, the patrons of these same poets, painters, and musicians. The very rich, however, seldom deal personally with artists. They let

institutions—foundations, universities, museums, and prize commit-
tees—set their standards for them in consultation with their tax lawyers or the trust departments of the big banks.

For patronage, as we all know well, is dominated by the tax policies of the federal government as interpreted by the Internal Revenue
Service. It is fair to say that many of the deepest human needs, those
we refer to when we use words like "art," are regulated by bodies and
individuals who have the least feeling for it.

I have in my time had the usual pipe dreams of ideal patronage—
sad daydreams about how nice it would have been to commune, as
writers did in the eighteenth century, with an aristocratic patron, himself a man of sensibility. How pleasant it was for Jonathan Swift to be
secretary to Sir William Temple. How useful Prince Esterházy was to
Haydn. And however cruel and capricious patrons might be—I think
of Mozart and his archbishop—one can't get over wishing that those
who dominated society with their money and their power had some
feeling for art, or at least some understanding of what a world *without*
art would be. For, quite simply, such a world would be a world corrupted—a condition far more desperate than any envisioned by the
most pessimistic ecologists.

My own situation is relatively simple. A novelist needs no instru-
mentalists, singers, choruses, theaters. I don't have to cope with patrons or trade unions, every year more painfully aware that opera is
being priced out of existence. I have paper and a typewriter and readers. My needs are easy to meet.

What novelists, composers, singers, have in common is the soul
to which their appeal is made, whether it is barren or fertile, empty
or full, whether the soul knows something, feels something, loves
something.

In our world it seems that as soon as a clear need appears, it is
met falsely. It becomes a new occasion for exploitation. We know this
to be true at all levels. To begin with trivial instances, we are not sold
real apples or real ice cream, we are sold the idea of an apple, the
memory of ice cream. Most people, for their fifteen cents, buy the idea
of a newspaper. On other levels still, they hear the idea of music in elevators. In politics they are presented with ideas of honor, patriotism;
in law, the shadows of justice. The media offer flimsy ideas of human
attachment, the films produce the spooks of passion and of love. Then

there are impresarios, performers, painters, and writers who offer in various packages the thinnest recollection, the phantom of art. Many contemporary artists appear to feel that it is sufficient to cast artificial pearls before real swine. This is how the modern world meets the deepest of human needs—by fraud, demagogy, opportunism, and profiteering.

The real thing will have to be preserved by tiny minorities until such abuses, probably inevitable in the present condition of our civilization, are driven out by an increase of stability and by the growth of taste and discrimination. I say "driven out," but I know that this wonderful improvement may never take place.

I am no prophet, only an observer. I observe, for instance, the hunger of huge audiences, which expresses itself in storms of applause the instant the last note of a concert has been played. On the radio one hears this. The crowd at the Mozarteum in Salzburg, or in London or New York, can hardly wait to burst into applause, shouting with primitive enthusiasm, following the harmony of the orchestra with a chaotic demonstration. This explosion, a great human release of everything at once, the performance of the crowd following the performance of the players, is a typhoon of collective release. They are yelling hoarsely, "Yes, *this* is the fine thing we all want!"

This howling and roaring is our gratitude for Aïda, a girl who never set foot on Michigan Boulevard. For Otello, a suffering black man dressed in brocaded robes and singing in Italian, utterly foreign to us except in music and humanity. The desire is there, and awe is moved in many thousands of people. The noise expresses a will to have such strange things, and to honor them. An Ethiopian maiden, a jealous Venetian general, interpreted by a nineteenth-century composer and presented by Italian singers, can have greater reality to people from Chicago's Ravenswood district than their own Chicago streets. And it is imperative that they should have a reality finer than those streets—something impractical, something gratuitous, something that does not defraud, exploit, or add more phantoms to a life already filled with phantoms, seductions, and cheats.

Perhaps the desire for such things will develop also into a responsibility toward them. Perhaps a society in which adolescents spend more than a billion dollars on Christmas gifts alone will come to understand that it is necessary for the public itself to ensure that its important needs will be met. Perhaps the public's role in patronage will increase. Perhaps even trade unions will wish to do something to sustain the arts and spend on music at least one percent of what they spend to put a president into the White House.

Utterly impossible ideas like this show me to be a genuine Chicagoan. Chicago's motto is "I will." I will what? Something different, I hope, from what it has willed in the past. Ladies and gentlemen, welcome to Chicago.

AN INTERVIEW WITH MYSELF

(1975)

*H*ow do you, a novelist from Chicago, fit yourself into American life? Is there a literary world to which you belong?

When I entered the Restaurant Voltaire in Paris with the novelist Louis Guilloux some years ago, the waiter addressed him as "Maître." I didn't know whether to envy him or to laugh up my sleeve. No one had ever treated me so reverentially. I knew how important literature was to the French. As a student I had sat (in Chicago) reading of *salons* and *cénacles*, of evenings at Magny's with Flaubert and Turgenev and Sainte-Beuve—reading and sighing: What glorious times! But Guilloux himself, a Breton and a former left-winger, seemed to flinch when he was called "Maître." It may be that even in Paris, literary culture is now publicly respected only by smarmy headwaiters. Here I am not altogether on firm ground. What is certain is that here nothing like this happens. In America we have no Maîtres, no literary world, no literary public. Many of us read, many love literature, but the traditions and institutions of literary culture are lacking. I do not say that this is bad. I only state it as a fact that ours is not a society that interests itself in such things. Any modern country that has not inherited these habits of deference simply does not have them.

American writers are not entirely neglected; they mingle occasionally with the great; they may even be asked to the White House, but no one there will talk literature to them. Mr. Nixon disliked writers and refused flatly to have them in, but Mr. Ford is as polite to them as he is to actors, musicians, television newscasters, and politicians. At

Ontario Review 4, 1975 (titled "Some Questions and Answers").

large receptions the East Room fills with celebrities who become ec-static at the sight of other celebrities. Secretary Kissinger and Danny Kaye fall into each other's arms. Cary Grant is surrounded by sena-tors' wives, who find him wonderfully preserved, as handsome in the flesh as on film. They can hardly bear the excitement of personal con-tact with greatness. As for culture, there are "few high topics" in nor-mal conversations. People speak of their diets, of their travels, of the vitamins they take and the problems of aging. Questions of language or style, the structure of novels, trends in painting, are not discussed.

The writer finds Mr. Ford's party a wonderful pop occasion. Sen-ator Fulbright seems almost to recognize his name and says, "You write essays, don't you? I think I can remember one of them." But the senator, as everyone knows, was once a Rhodes scholar. He *would* re-member an essay.

It is actually pleasant on such an evening for a writer to pass half disembodied and unmolested by small talk from room to room, look-ing and listening. He knows that active public men can't combine the duties of government with literature, art, and philosophy. Theirs is a world of high-tension wires, not of primroses on the river's brim. Ten years ago, Mayor Daley in a little City Hall ceremony gave me a five-hundred-dollar check, awarded by the Midland Authors' Society for my novel *Herzog*. "Mr. Mayor, have you read *Herzog*?" asked one of the reporters, needling him. "I've looked into it," said Daley, thick-skinned and staunch. Art is not the mayor's dish. Indeed, why should it be? I much prefer his neglect to the sort of interest Stalin took in poetry.

Are you saying that a modern industrial society dismisses art?

Not at all. Art is one of those good things which society encour-ages. It is quite receptive. But what Ruskin said about the English pub-lic in 1871 applies perfectly to us. "No reading is possible for a people with its mind in this state. No sentence of any great writer is intelligi-ble to them." For this Ruskin blamed avarice: ". . . so incapable of thought has it [the public] become in its insanity of avarice. Happily, our disease is, as yet, little worse than this incapacity of thought; it is not corruption of the inner nature; we ring true still, when anything strikes home to us . . . though the idea that everything should 'pay' has infected our every purpose so deeply."

You don't see avarice as the problem, do you?

No. "A people with its mind in this state" is where I lay the stress. We are in a peculiarly revolutionary state, a condition of crisis, a nervousness that never ends. Yesterday I came upon a description of a medical technique for bringing patients to themselves. They are exposed for some minutes to high-frequency sounds, until they become calm enough to think and to feel out their symptoms. To possess your soul in peace for a few minutes, you need the help of medical technology. It is easy to observe in bars, at dinner tables, everywhere, that from the flophouse to the White House, Americans are preoccupied by the same questions. Our own American life is our passion, the problems of our social and national life with the whole world as background, an immense spectacle presented daily by the papers and the television networks—our cities, our crime, our housing, our automobiles, our sports, our weather, our technology, our politics, our problems of sex and race and of international relations. These realities are real enough. But what of the formulae, the jargon, adopted by the mass media—the exciting fictions, the heightened and dramatized shadow events presented to the great public and believed by almost everyone to be real. Is reading possible for a people with its mind in this state?

Still, a book of good quality can find a hundred thousand readers. But you say that there is no literary public.

An influential book appears to create its own public. When *Herzog* was published, I became aware that there were some fifty thousand people in the United States who had evidently been waiting for something like it. Other writers have certainly had similar experiences. But such a public is a temporary one. There is no stable culture that permanently contains all these readers. Remarkably steady and intelligent people emerge somehow, like confident swimmers from the heaving waters, the wastes of the American educational system. They survive by strength, luck, and cunning.

What do they do while waiting for the next important event?

Yes. What can they read month in, month out? In what journals do they keep up with what matters in contemporary literature?

What about the universities? Haven't they done anything to train judgment and develop taste?

To most professors of English, a novel may be an object of the highest cultural importance. Its ideas, its symbolic structure, its position in the history of romanticism or realism or modernism, its higher relevance, require devout study. But what has this sort of cultural study to do with novelists and readers? What *they* want is the living moment; they want men and women alive in a circumambient world. The teaching of literature has been a disaster. Between the student and the book he reads lies a gloomy preparatory region, a perfect swamp. He must cross this cultural swamp before he is allowed to open his *Moby Dick* and read "Call me Ishmael." He is made to feel ignorant before masterpieces, unworthy; he is frightened and already repelled by the book he is meagerly qualified to begin. And if the method succeeds, it produces B.A.'s who can tell you why the *Pequod* leaves port on Christmas morning. What has been substituted for the novel itself is what can be said about the novel by the "educated." Some professors find educated discourse of this kind more interesting by far than novels. They take the attitude toward fiction that one of the church fathers took toward the Bible. Origen of Alexandria asked whether we were really to imagine that God walked in a garden while Adam and Eve hid under a bush. Scripture could not be taken literally. It must yield higher meanings.

Are you equating church fathers with professors of literature?

Not exactly. The fathers had sublime conceptions of God and man. If professors of humanities were moved by the sublimity of the poets and philosophers they teach, they would be the most powerful men in the university and the most fervent. But they are at the lower end of the hierarchy, at the bottom of the pile.

Then why are there so many writers at the universities?

A good question. Writers have no independent ground to stand on. They now belong to institutions. They can work for newsmagazines and publishing houses, for cultural foundations, advertising agencies, television networks. Or they can teach. There are only a few literary journals left, and those are academic quarterlies. The big national magazines don't want to publish fiction. Their editors want to discuss only the most significant national and international questions and concentrate on "relevant" cultural matters. By "relevant" they mean political. (And *I* mean grossly political.) The "real" questions facing us are questions of business and politics. There *are* questions of life and death at the heart of such important public matters. But these life-and-death questions are not what we discuss. What we hear and read is crisis chatter. The members of our intelligentsia *had* literature in their student days—they *did* it and are now well beyond it. At Harvard or Columbia, they read, studied, absorbed the classics, especially the modernist ones. These prepared them for the important, the essential, the incomparable tasks they were to perform as functionaries in business, in government, in the professions—above all, in the media. Sometimes I sense that they feel they have replaced writers. The "cultural" business they do is tinged by literature, or rather the memory of literature. I said before that our common life had become our most passionate concern. Can an individual, the subject of a novel, compete in interest with corporate destinies, with the rise of a new class, a cultural intelligentsia? The rise of a class is *truly* important.

Do you suggest that when we become so extremely politicized we lose interest in the individual?

Yes, if you confuse what is public, or before the attention of the public, with real politics. A liberal society so intensely political—as I have qualified the term—can't remain liberal for very long. I take it for granted that an attack on the novel is also an attack on liberal principles. I view "activist" art theories in the same way. The power of a work of art is such that it induces a temporary suspension of activities. It leads to contemplative states, to wonderful and, to my mind, sacred states of the soul. These are not, however, passive.

And what you call crisis chatter creates a contrary condition?

I should like to add that the truth is not loved because it is improving or progressive. We hunger and thirst for it—for its own sake.

To return for a moment to the subject of a literary world . . .

No tea at Gertrude Stein's, no Closerie de Lilas, no Bloomsbury evenings, no charming and wicked encounters between George Moore and W. B. Yeats. Reading of such things is very pleasant indeed. I can't say that I miss them, because I never knew anything like them. My knowledge of them is entirely bookish. That Molière put on the plays of Corneille, that Louis XIV himself may have appeared, disguised, in one of Molière's farces—such facts are lovely to read in a history of literature. I'd hardly expect Mayor Daley to take part in any farce of mine. I have, however, visited writers' clubs in communist countries and can't say that I'm sorry we have no such institutions here. When I was in Addis Ababa, I went to the emperor's zoo. As Selassie was the Lion of Judah, he was bound to keep a collection of lions. These poor animals lay in the filth of dim green cages too small for pacing, mere coops. Their marvelous eyes had turned dull yellow and blank, their heads were on their paws, and they were sighing. Bad as things are with us, they are not so bad as in the emperor's zoo or in writers' clubs behind the iron curtain.

Not so bad is not the same as good. What of the disadvantages of your condition?

There are moments of sorrow, I admit. George Sand wrote to Flaubert, in a collection of letters I looked into the other day, that she hoped he would bring his copy of her latest book on his next visit. "Put in it all the criticisms which occur to you," she said. "That will be very good for me. People ought to do that for each other, as Balzac and I used to do. That doesn't make one person alter the other; quite the contrary, for in general one gets more determined in one's *moi*, one completes it, explains it better, entirely develops it, and that is why friendship is good, even in literature, where the first condition of any worth is to be one's self." How nice it would be to hear this from a writer. But no such letters arrive. Friendships and a common purpose belong to a nineteenth-century French dream world. The physicist Heisenberg in a recent article in *Encounter* speaks of the kindly and even brotherly collaboration among scientists of the generation of Einstein and Bohr. Their personal letters were quoted in seminars and discussed by the entire scientific community. Heisenberg believes that in the musical world something of the same spirit appeared in the eighteenth century. Haydn's relations with Mozart were of this generous, affectionate kind. But when large creative opportunities are lacking, there is no generosity visible. Heisenberg says nothing about the malice and hostility of less lucky times. Writers today seldom wish other writers well.

What about the critics?

Edmund Wilson wouldn't read his contemporaries at all. He stopped with Eliot and Hemingway. The rest he dismissed. This lack of goodwill, to put it at its mildest, was much admired by his fans. That fact speaks for itself. Curious about Canadians, Indians, Haitians, Russians, studying Marxism and the Dead Sea scrolls, he was the Protestant majority's big literary figure. I have sometimes thought that he was challenged by Marxism or modernism in the same way that I have seen the descendants of Orthodox Jews challenged by oysters. A man like Wilson might have done much to strengthen literary culture, but he dismissed all that, he would have nothing to do with it. For temperamental reasons. Or Protestant majority reasons. Or perhaps the Heisenberg principle applies—men are generous when there are creative opportunities, and when such opportunities dwindle they are . . . something else. But it would have made little difference. At this moment in human evolution, so miraculous, atrocious, glorious, and hellish, the firmly established literary cultures of France and England, Italy and Germany, are not thriving. They look to us, to the "disadvantaged" Americans, and to the Russians. From America have come a number of great irrepressible solitaries, like Poe or Melville or Whitman, alcoholics, obscure government employees. In busy America there was no Weimar, there were no cultivated princes. There were only obstinate geniuses such as these writing. Why? For whom? There is a real *acte gratuit* for you. Very different from Gide's gratuitous murder of an utter stranger. Unthanked, these writers augmented life marvelously. They did not emerge from a literary culture, nor did they create any such thing. Irrepressible individuals or a similar type have lately begun to show themselves in Russia. There Stalinism destroyed a thriving literary culture and replaced it with a horrible bureaucracy. But in spite of this and in spite of forced labor and murder, the feeling for what is true and just has not died out. I don't see, in short, why we, here, should continue to dream of what we have never had. To have had it would not help us. Perhaps if we were to purge ourselves of nostalgia and stop longing for a literary world, we would see a fresh opportunity to extend the imagination and resume imaginative contact with nature and society.

Other people, scholars and scientists, know a great deal about nature and society. More than you know.

True. And I suppose I sound like a fool, but I nevertheless object that their knowledge is defective—something is lacking. That something is poetry. Huizinga, the Dutch historian, in his recently published book on America, says that the scholarly Americans he met in the twenties could speak fluently and stimulatingly, but he adds: "More than once I could not recognize in what he wrote the living man who had held my interest. Frequently repeated experience makes me hold the view that my personal reaction to American scholarly prose must not rest upon the qualities of the prose itself. I read it with the greatest difficulty; I have no sense of contact with it and cannot keep my attention fixed on it. It is for me as if I had to do with a deviant system of expression in which the concepts are not equivalent to mine or are arranged differently." That system has become even more deviant during the last fifty years. I want information and ideas, and I know that certain highly trained and intelligent people have it—economists, sociologists, lawyers, historians, natural scientists. But I read them with growing difficulty and exasperation. And I say to myself, "These writers are part of the educated public, your readers."

But whether or not a literary culture exists . . .

Excuse me for interrupting, but it occurs to me that Tolstoy would probably have approved of this and seen new opportunities in it. He had no use for literary culture and detested professionalism in the arts.

But should writers make their peace with the academic ivory tower?

In his essay "Bethink Yourselves," Tolstoy advises each man to begin at the point at which he finds himself. Better such towers than the cellar alternatives some writers choose. Besides, the university is no more an ivory tower than *Time* magazine, with its strangely artificial approach to the world, its remote-making managerial arrangements. There, too, you see an ivory tower, of a sort. Even more remote than Flaubert's *tour d'ivoire*. A writer is offered more money, bigger pensions, richer security plans by Luce enterprises than by any university. The ivory tower is one of those platitudes that haunt the uneasy minds of writers. Since we have none of the advantages of a literary world, we may as well free ourselves from its banalities. We need to think, and the university can be as good a place for thinking as any other. And you don't have to become an academic simply because you teach in a university.

Can you conveniently give a brief definition of academic?

I limit myself arbitrarily to a professorial type to be found in the humanities. The British pundit Owen Barfield refers in one of his books to "the everlasting professional device for substituting a plethora of talk" about what matters for what actually matters. He is sick of it, he says. Many of us are sick of it.

NOBEL LECTURE

(1976)

I was a very contrary undergraduate more than forty years ago. One semester I registered for a course in Money and Banking and then concentrated my reading in the novels of Joseph Conrad. I have never had reason to regret this. Perhaps Conrad appealed to me because he was like an American, speaking French and writing English with extraordinary power and beauty—he was an uprooted Pole sailing exotic seas. Nothing could seem more natural to me, the child of immigrants who grew up in one of Chicago's immigrant neighborhoods, than a Slav who was a British sea captain and knew his way around Marseilles. In England, he was wonderfully exotic. H. G. Wells warned Ford Madox Ford, with whom Conrad collaborated in the writing of several novels, not to spoil Conrad's "Oriental style." He was valued for his oddity. But Conrad's *real* life had little oddity in it. His themes were straightforward—fidelity, the traditions of the sea, hierarchy, command, the fragile rules sailors follow when they are struck by a typhoon. He believed in the strength of these fragile-seeming rules. He also believed in his art. He stated in the preface to *The Nigger of the "Narcissus"* that art was an attempt to render the highest justice to the visible universe: it tried to find in that universe, in matter as well as in the facts of life, what was fundamental, enduring, essential. The writer's method of attaining the essential was different from that of the thinker or the scientist, who knew the world by systematic examination. To begin with, the artist had only himself; he descended

Delivered in Stockholm on 12 December 1976. Published in *The Nobel Lecture* (New York: Targ Editions, 1979).

within himself, and in the lonely regions to which he descended he found "the terms of his appeal." He appealed, said Conrad, "to that part of our being which is a gift, not an acquisition, to the capacity for delight and wonder . . . our sense of pity and pain, to the latent feeling of fellowship with all creation—and to the subtle but invincible conviction of solidarity that knits together the loneliness of innumerable hearts . . . which binds together all humanity—the dead to the living and the living to the unborn."

This fervent statement was written some eighty years ago, and we may want to take it with a few grains of contemporary salt. I belong to a generation of readers who knew the long list of noble or noble-sounding words, words such as "invincible conviction" or "humanity," rejected by writers like Ernest Hemingway. Hemingway spoke for the soldiers who fought in the First World War under the inspiration of Woodrow Wilson and other orotund statesmen whose big words had to be measured against the frozen corpses of young men paving the trenches. Hemingway's youthful readers were convinced that the horrors of the twentieth century with their deadly radiations had sickened and killed humanistic beliefs. I told myself therefore that Conrad's rhetoric must be resisted: resisted, not rejected, for I never thought him mistaken. He spoke directly to me. The feeling individual appeared weak—he felt only his own weakness. But if he accepted his weakness and his separateness and descended into himself, intensifying his loneliness, he discovered his solidarity with other isolated creatures.

I feel no need now to sprinkle Conrad's sentences with skeptical salt. But there are writers for whom the Conradian novel—all novels of that sort—has become invalid. Finished. There is, for instance, M. Alain Robbe-Grillet, one of the leaders of French literature, a spokesman for "thingism"—*choseisme*. In an essay called "On Several Obsolete Notions," he writes that in great contemporary works—Sartre's *Nausea*, Camus's *The Stranger*, Kafka's *The Castle*—there are no characters; you find in such books not individuals, merely entities. "The novel of characters," he says, "belongs entirely in the past. It describes a period: that which marked the apogee of the individual." This is not necessarily an improvement; that Robbe-Grillet admits. But it is the truth. Individuals have been wiped out. "The present period is rather one of administrative numbers. The world's destiny has ceased, for us, to be identified with the rise and fall of certain men of certain families." He goes on to say that in the days of Balzac's bourgeoisie it was important to have a name and a character; character was a weapon in the struggle for survival and success. In that time, "It was something to have a face in a universe where personality represented both the means and the end of all exploration." Our world, he concludes, is more modest. It has renounced the omnipotence of the person. But it is more ambitious as well, "since it looks beyond. The exclusive cult of the 'human' has given way to a larger consciousness, one that is less anthropocentric." However, he offers in comfort a new course and the promise of new discoveries before us.

On an occasion like this I have no appetite for polemics. We all know what it is to be tired of "characters." Human types have become false and boring. D. H. Lawrence put it early in the century that we human beings, our instincts damaged by puritanism, no longer care for—worse, have become physically repulsive to—one another. "The sympathetic heart is broken," he said. "We stink in each other's nostrils." Besides, in Europe the power of the classics has for centuries been so great that every country has its "identifiable personalities" derived from Molière, Racine, Dickens, or Balzac. An awful phenomenon. Perhaps this is connected with the wonderful French saying: *"S'il y a un caractère, il est mauvais."* It makes one think that the unoriginal human race tends to borrow what it needs from sources already at hand, much as new cities have often been made from the rubble of old ones. The viewpoint is perhaps confirmed by the psychoanalytic conception of character—that it is an ugly, rigid formation, something to be resigned to, nothing to be embraced with joy. Totalitarian ideologies, too, have attacked individualism, sometimes identifying character with property. There is a hint of this in M. Robbe-Grillet's argument. Rejection of personality, bad masks, boring forms of being, have had political results.

But this is not my subject; what I am interested in here is the question of the artist's priorities. Is it necessary or even desirable that he begin with historical analyses, with ideas or systems? Proust speaks in *Time Regained* of a growing preference among young and intelligent readers for works of an elevated, analytical, moral, or sociological tendency—for writers who seem to them more profound. "But," says

Proust, "from the moment that works of art are judged by reasoning, nothing is stable or certain, one can prove anything one likes."

The message of Robbe-Grillet is not new. It tells us that we must purge ourselves of bourgeois anthropocentrism and do the classy things that our advanced culture requires. Character? "Fifty years of disease, the death notice signed many times over by the serious essayists," says Robbe-Grillet, "yet nothing has managed to knock it off the pedestal on which the nineteenth century had placed it. It is a mummy now, but one still enthroned with the same—phony—majesty, among the values revered by traditional criticism."

Like most of us, I share Robbe-Grillet's objection to the mummies of all kinds we carry about with us, but I never tire of reading the master novelists. Can anything as vivid as the characters in their books be dead? Can it be that human beings are at an end? Is individuality really so dependent on historical and cultural conditions? Is the account of those conditions we are so "authoritatively" given by writers and psychologists to be accepted? I suggest that it is not in the intrinsic interest of human beings but in these ideas and accounts that the problem lies. It is the staleness and inadequacy of the ideas that repel us. To find the source of trouble, we must look into our own heads.

The fact that the death notice of character has been signed by the serious essayists means only that another group of mummies—certain respectable leaders of the intellectual community—has laid down the law. It amuses me that these serious essayists should be empowered to sign the death notice of a literary form. Should art follow "culture"? Something has gone wrong.

A novelist should be free to drop "character" if such a strategy stimulates him. But it is nonsense to make such a decision on the theoretical ground that the period which marked the apogee of the individual, etc., is ended. We must not permit intellectuals to become our bosses. And we do them no good by letting them run the arts. Should they, when they read novels, find in them only the endorsement of their own opinions? Are we here to play such games?

Characters, Elizabeth Bowen once said, are not created by writers. They preexist, and they have to be *found*. If we do not find them, if we fail to represent them, the fault is ours. It must be admitted, however, that finding them is not easy. The condition of human beings has perhaps never been more difficult to define. Those who tell us that we are in an early stage of universal history must be right. We are being lavishly poured together and seem to be experiencing the anguish of new states of consciousness. In America, millions of people have in the last forty years received a "higher education"—often a dubious blessing. In the upheavals of the sixties we felt for the first time the effects of up-to-date teachings, concepts, sensitivities, the pervasiveness of psychological, pedagogical, political ideas.

Every year we see scores of books and articles by writers who tell Americans what a state they are in. All reflect the current crises; all tell us what we must do about them—these analysts are produced by the very disorder and confusion they prescribe for. It is as a novelist that I am considering the extreme moral sensitivity of our contemporaries, their desire for perfection, their intolerance of the defects of society, the touching, the comical boundlessness of their demands, their anxiety, their irritability, their sensitivity, their tender-mindedness, their goodness, their convulsiveness, the recklessness with which they experiment with drugs and touch therapies and bombs. The ex-Jesuit Malachi Martin in his book on the Church compares the modern American to Michelangelo's sculpture *The Captive*. He sees "an unfinished struggle to emerge whole" from a block of matter. The American "captive" is beset in his struggle by "interpretations, admonitions, forewarnings and descriptions of himself by the self-appointed prophets, priests, judges and prefabricators of his travail," says Martin.

If we take a little time to look more closely at this travail, what do we see? In private life, disorder or near panic. In families—for husbands, wives, parents, children—confusion; in civic behavior, in personal loyalties, in sexual practices (I will not recite the whole list; we are tired of hearing it)—further confusion. It is with this private disorder and public bewilderment that we try to live. We stand open to all anxieties. The decline and fall of everything is our daily dread; we are agitated in private life and tormented by public questions.

And art and literature—what of them? Well, there is a violent uproar, but we are not absolutely dominated by it. We are still able to think, to discriminate, and to feel. The purer, subtler, higher activities have not succumbed to fury or to nonsense. Not yet. Books continue to be written and read. It may be more difficult to cut through the whirling mind of a modern reader, but it is still possible to reach the quiet zone. In the quiet zone, we novelists may find that he is devoutly waiting for us. When complications increase, the desire for essentials increases too. The unending cycle of crises that began with the First World War has formed a kind of person, one who has lived through strange and terrible things and in whom there is an observable shrinkage of prejudices, a casting off of disappointing ideologies, an ability to live with many kinds of madness, and an immense desire for certain durable human goods—truth, for instance; freedom; wisdom. I don't think I am exaggerating; there is plenty of evidence for this. Disintegration? Well, yes. Much is disintegrating, but we are experiencing also an odd kind of refining process. And this has been going on for a long time. Looking into Proust's *Time Regained*, I find that he was clearly aware of it. His novel, describing French society during the Great War, tests the strength of his art. Without an art that shirks no personal or collective horrors, he insists, we do not know ourselves or anyone else. Only art penetrates what pride, passion, intelligence, and habit erect on all sides—the seeming realities of this world. There is another reality, the genuine one, which we lose sight of. This other reality is always sending us hints, which, without art, we can't receive. Proust calls these hints our "true impressions." The true impressions, our persistent intuitions, will, without art, be hidden from us, and we will be left with nothing but a "terminology for practical ends which we falsely call life."

Proust was still able to keep a balance between art and destruction, insisting that art was a necessity of life, a great independent reality, a magical power. For a long time, art has not been connected, as it was in the past, with the main human enterprise. Hegel long ago observed that art no longer engaged the central energies of man. These energies were now engaged by science—a "relentless spirit of rational inquiry." Art had moved to the margins. There it formed "a wide and splendidly varied horizon." In an age of science, people still painted and wrote poetry, but, said Hegel, however splendid the gods looked in modern works of art and whatever dignity and perfection we might find "in the images of God the Father and the Virgin Mary," it was of no use: we no longer bent our knees. It is a long time since the knees were bent in piety. Ingenuity, daring exploration, freshness of invention, replaced the art of "direct relevance." The most significant achievement of this pure art, in Hegel's view, was that, freed from its former responsibilities, it was no longer "serious." Instead it raised the soul through the "serenity of form above painful involvement in the limitations of reality." I don't know who would make such a claim today for an art that raises the soul above painful involvement with reality. Nor am I sure that at this moment, it is the spirit of rational inquiry in pure science that engages the central energies of man. The center seems (even though temporarily) to be filled with the crises I have been describing.

There were European writers in the nineteenth century who would not give up the connection of literature with the main human enterprise. The very suggestion would have shocked Tolstoy and Dostoyevsky. But in the West, a separation between great artists and the general public took place. Artists developed a marked contempt for the average reader and the bourgeois mass. The best of them saw clearly enough what sort of civilization Europe had produced, brilliant but unstable, vulnerable, fated to be overtaken by catastrophe.

Despite a show of radicalism and innovation, our contemporaries are really very conservative. They follow their nineteenth-century leaders and hold to the old standards, interpreting history and society much as they were interpreted in the last century. What would writers do today if it occurred to them that literature might once again engage those "central energies," if they were to recognize that an immense desire had arisen for a return from the periphery, for what is simple and true?

Of course, we can't come back to the center simply because we wish to, though the realization that we are wanted might electrify us. The force of the crisis is so great that it might summon us back. But prescriptions are futile. One can't tell writers what to do. The imagination must find its own path. But one can fervently wish that they—that we—would come back from the periphery. We writers do not represent mankind adequately. What account do Americans give of themselves, what accounts of them are given by psychologists, sociologists, historians, journalists, and writers? In a kind of contractual daylight, they see themselves in the ways with which we are desperately familiar. These images of contractual daylight, so boring to Robbe-Grillet and to me, originate in the contemporary worldview: We put into our books the consumer, civil servant, football fan, lover, television viewer. And in the contractual daylight version, their life is a kind of death. There is another life, coming from an insistent sense of what we are, which denies these daylight formulations and the false life—the death-in-life—they make for us. For it is false, and we know it, and our secret and incoherent resistance to it cannot stop—that resistance arises from persistent intuitions. Perhaps humankind cannot bear too much reality, but neither can it bear too much unreality, too much abuse of the truth.

We do not think well of ourselves; we do not think amply about what we are. Our collective achievements have so greatly "exceeded" us that we "justify" ourselves by pointing to them. It is the jet plane in which we commonplace human beings have crossed the Atlantic in four hours that embodies such value as we can claim. Then we hear that this is closing time in the gardens of the West, that the end of our capitalist civilization is at hand. This means that we are not yet sufficiently shrunken; we must prepare to be smaller still. I am not sure whether this should be called intellectual analysis or analysis by intellectuals. The disasters are disasters. It is worse than stupid to call them victories, as some statesmen have done. But I am drawing attention to the fact that there is in the intellectual community a sizable inventory of attitudes that have become respectable—notions about society, human nature, class, politics, sex, about mind, about the physical universe, the evolution of life. Few writers, even among the best, have taken the trouble to reexamine these attitudes or orthodoxies. Such attitudes are everywhere, and no one challenges them seriously. They only glow more powerfully in Joyce or D. H. Lawrence than in the books of lesser men. Since the twenties, how many novelists have taken a second look at Lawrence or argued a different view of sexual potency or the effects of industrial civilization on the instincts? Literature has for nearly a century used the same stock of ideas, myths, strategies. The serious essayists of the last fifty years, says Robbe-Grillet. Yes, indeed. Essay after essay, book after book, confirms the most serious thoughts—Baudelairean, Nietzschean, Marxian, Psychoanalytic, etc., etc.—of these most serious essayists. What Robbe-Grillet says about character can be said also about these ideas, maintaining all the usual things about mass society, dehumanization, and the rest. How poorly they represent us. The pictures they offer no more resemble us than we resemble the reconstructed reptiles and other monsters in a museum of paleontology. We are much more limber, versatile, better articulated, there is much more to us—we all feel it.

What is at the center now? At the moment, neither art nor science but mankind determining, in confusion and obscurity, whether it will endure or go under. The whole species—everybody—has gotten into the act. At such a time it is essential to lighten ourselves, to dump encumbrances, including the encumbrances of education and all organized platitudes, to make judgments of our own, to perform acts of our own. Conrad was right to appeal to that part of our being which is a gift. We must look for that gift under the wreckage of many systems. The collapse of those systems may bring a blessed and necessary release from formulations, from misleading conceptions of being and consciousness. With increasing frequency I dismiss as "merely respectable" opinions I have long held—or thought I held—and try to discern what I have really lived by and what others really live by. As for Hegel's art freed from "seriousness" and glowing on the margins, raising the soul above painful involvement in the limitations of reality through the serenity of form, that can exist nowhere now, during this struggle for survival. However, it is not as though the people who engaged in this struggle had only a rudimentary humanity, without culture, and knew nothing of art. Our very vices, our mutilations, show how rich we are in thought and culture. How much we know. How much we can feel. The struggles that convulse us make us want to simplify, to reconsider, to eliminate the tragic weakness that has prevented writers—and readers—from being at once simple and true.

Writers are greatly respected. The intelligent public is wonderfully patient with them, continues to read them, and endures disappointment after disappointment, waiting to hear from art what it does not hear from theology, philosophy, social theory, and what it cannot hear from pure science. Out of the struggle at the center has come an immense, painful longing for a broader, more flexible, fuller, more coherent, more comprehensive account of what we human beings are, who we are, and what this life is for. At the center, humankind struggles with collective powers for its freedom, the individual struggles with dehumanization for the possession of his soul. If writers do not come again into the center, it will not be because the center is preempted. It is not. They are free to enter. If they so wish.

The essence of our real condition, the complexity, the confusion, the pain of it, is shown to us in glimpses, in what Proust and Tolstoy thought of as "true impressions." This essence reveals and then conceals itself. When it goes away it leaves us again in doubt. But our connection remains with the depths from which these glimpses come. The sense of our real powers, powers we seem to derive from the universe itself, also comes and goes. We are reluctant to talk about this because there is nothing we can prove, because our language is inadequate, and because few people are willing to risk the embarrassment. They would have to say, "There is a spirit," and that is taboo. So almost everyone keeps quiet about it, although almost everyone is aware of it.

The value of literature lies in these intermittent "true impressions." A novel moves back and forth between the world of objects, of actions, of appearances, and that other world, from which these "true impressions" come and which moves us to believe that the good we hang on to so tenaciously—in the face of evil, so obstinately—is no illusion.

No one who has spent years in the writing of novels can be unaware of this. The novel can't be compared to the epic, or to the monuments of poetic drama. But it is the best we can do just now. It is a sort of latter-day lean-to, a hovel in which the spirit takes shelter. A novel is balanced between a few true impressions and the multitude of false ones that make up most of what we call life. It tells us that for every human being there is a diversity of existences, that the single existence is itself an illusion in part, that these many existences signify something, tend to something, fulfill something; it promises us meaning, harmony, and even justice. What Conrad said was true: Art attempts to find in the universe, in matter as well as in the facts of life, what is fundamental, enduring, essential.

WRITERS,

INTELLECTUALS, POLITICS:

MAINLY REMINISCENCE

(1993)

*W*hen the Bolsheviks took power in 1917, I was two years old. My parents had emigrated from Saint Petersburg to Montreal in 1913, so events in Russia were on their minds, and at the dinner table the czar, the war, the front, Lenin, Trotsky, were mentioned as often as parents, sisters, and brothers in the old country. Among Jews it was scarcely conceivable that the great monarchy should have fallen. Skeptical older immigrants believed that the Bolshevik upstarts would soon be driven out. Their grown children, however, were keen to join the revolution, and I can remember how my father argued in the street with Lyova, the son of our Hebrew teacher, who said he had already bought his *schiffskarte*. My father shouted that the new regime was worthless, but the young were then accustomed to respect their elders, so Lyova smiled—deferential but immovable. He went off to build a new order under Lenin and Trotsky. And he disappeared.

Much later, after we had moved to Chicago and I was old enough to read Marx and Lenin, my father would say, "Don't you forget what happened to Lyova—and I haven't heard from my sisters in years. I don't want any part of your Russia and your Lenin."

But in my eyes my parents were Russians, with agreeable Russian traits. They had brought with them a steamer trunk filled with Saint Petersburg finery—brocaded vests, a top hat, a tailcoat, linen sleeping suits with pleated fronts, black taffeta petticoats, ostrich feathers, and button boots with high heels. Of no use in the dim ultima Thule of Montreal or in proletarian Chicago, they were the playthings of the younger children. The older ones quickly and eagerly Americanized themselves in the U.S., and the rest soon followed suit. The country took us over. It *was* a country then, not a collection of "cultures." We felt that to be here was a great piece of luck. The children of immigrants in my Chicago high school, however, believed that they were also somehow Russian, and while they studied their *Macbeth* and Milton's *L'Allegro*, they read Tolstoy and Dostoyevsky as well and went on inevitably to Lenin's *State and Revolution* and the pamphlets of Trotsky. The Tuley High School debating club discussed the *Communist Manifesto*, and on the main stem of the neighborhood, Division Street, the immigrant intelligentsia lectured from soapboxes, while at "the forum," a church hall on California Avenue, debates between socialists, communists, and anarchists attracted a fair number of people. This was the beginning of my radical education. For on the recommendation of friends, I took up Marx and Engels, and I remember, in my father's bleak office near the freightyards, blasting away at *Value, Price, and Profit* while the police raided a brothel across the street—for nonpayment of protection, probably—throwing beds, bedding, and chairs through the shattered windows.

The Young Communist League tried to recruit me in the late thirties. Too late—I had already read Trotsky's pamphlet on the German question and was convinced that Stalin's errors had brought Hitler to power.

Curious how widely information of world politics was disseminated and in what odd corners around the globe positions then were taken. When the poet Mandelstam interviewed a Comintern member in 1923, he asked, " 'How has Gandhi's movement affected you in Indochina? Have you experienced any vibrations, any echoes?' 'No,' answered my companion"—identified as Nguyen Ai Quoc, known to us later as Ho Chi Minh. Mandelstam describes him to us: "At heart he is but a boy, thin and lithe, sporting a knitted wool jacket."

Few boys, I need hardly say, became Comintern members. For millions of them worldwide, however, the October Revolution was a great reverberator whose echoes of freedom and justice you could not choose but hear. That revolution was for many decades the most important, most prestigious event in history. Its partisans held that it had brought to an end the most monstrous of wars and that Russia's revolutionary proletariat had made mankind the gift of a great hope. Now the oppressed everywhere, under communist leadership, would destroy decadent capitalist imperialism. In Depression Chicago, boys at heart—and girls as well—were putting their revolutionary thoughts in order. The program was not very clear, but the prospect was immensely thrilling. Full ideological clarity would not arrive for some time.

In college (1933) I was a Trotskyist. Trotsky instilled into his young followers the orthodoxy peculiar to the defeated and ousted. We belonged to the movement, we were faithful to Leninism and could expound its historical lessons and describe Stalin's crimes. My closest friends and I were not, however, activists; we were writers. Owing to the Depression, we had no career expectations. We got through the week on five or six bucks, and if our rented rooms were small, the libraries were lofty, were beautiful. Through "revolutionary politics" we met the demand of the times for action. But what really mattered was the vital personal nourishment we took from Dostoyevsky or Herman Melville, from Dreiser and John Dos Passos and Faulkner. By filling out a slip of paper at the Crerar Library on Randolph Street, you could get all the bound volumes of *The Dial* and fill long afternoons with T. S. Eliot, Rilke, and E. E. Cummings. Toward the end of the thirties, *Partisan Review* was our own *Dial*, with politics besides. There we had access to our significant European contemporaries—Silone, Orwell, Koestler, Malraux, André Gide, and Auden. *Partisan*'s leading American contributors were Marxists—critics and philosophers like Dwight Macdonald, James Burnham, Sidney Hook, Clement Greenberg, Meyer Schapiro, and Harold Rosenberg. The *PR* intellectuals had sided with Trotsky quite naturally, during the Moscow trials. Hook had persuaded his teacher John Dewey to head a commission of inquiry in Mexico. We followed the proceedings bitterly, passionately, for we were, of course, the Outs; the Stalinists were the Ins. We alone in the U.S.A. knew what a bad lot they were. FDR and his New Dealers didn't have a clue; they understood neither Russia nor communism.

But our own movement, we began to learn, was often foolish, even conspicuously absurd. During the Spanish Civil War, the issue of material aid for the Spanish Republic was furiously debated by comrades who didn't have a dime to contribute. A more serious challenge to our loyalty was the invasion of Finland by the Red Army. Trotsky argued that a workers' state could not by definition wage an imperialist war. The invasion was progressive, since it would nationalize property, an irrevocable step toward socialism. Faithful to the October Revolution, Trotsky fought the dissenters, of whom there were now many. The split this led to did not come to the attention of the American public, which in any case would have preferred Disney's *Fantasia* to our kind.

Although I now drifted away from Marxist politics, I still admired Lenin and Trotsky. After all, I had first heard of them in the high chair while eating my mashed potatoes. How could I forget that Trotsky had created the Red Army, that he had read French novels at the front while defeating Denikin. That great crowds had been swayed by his coruscating speeches. The glamour of the Revolution still cast its spell. Besides, the most respected literary and intellectual figures had themselves yielded to it. Returning from a visit to Russia, Edmund Wilson had spoken about "the moral light at the top of the world," and it was Wilson who had introduced us to Joyce and Proust. His history of Revolutionary thought, *To the Finland Station*, was published in 1940. By that time, Poland had been invaded and France had fallen to the Nazis.

Nineteen forty was also the year of Trotsky's assassination. I was in Mexico at the time, and an acquaintance of the Old Man, a European lady whom I had met in Taxco, had arranged a meeting. Trotsky agreed to receive my friend Herbert Passin and me in Coyoacan. It was on the morning of our appointment that he was struck down. Arriving in Mexico City, we were met by the headlines. When we went to his villa we must have been taken for foreign journalists, and we were directed to the hospital. The emergency room was in disorder. We had only to ask for Trotsky. A door into a small side room was opened for us, and there we saw him. He had just died. A cone of bloody bandages was on his head. His cheeks, his nose, his beard, his throat, were streaked with blood and with dried iridescent trickles of iodine.

He is reported to have said once that Stalin could kill him whenever he liked, and now we understood what a far-reaching power could do with us; how easy it was for a despot to order a death; how little it took to kill us, how slight a hold we, with our historical philosophies, our ideas, programs, purposes, wills, had on the matter we were made of.

The Great Depression was a time of personal humiliation for those who had worked and lived in respectable prosperity. Capitalism seemed to have lost its control over the country. To many, the overthrow of the government looked like a distinct possibility. In the early Depression years, the policies dictated by the communist leadership during its rigid and grim third period had had little success in the U.S.A. A new Popular Front policy was announced when Hitler began to demolish the parties of the left. For American communists, the Popular Front, temperate and apparently conciliatory, was a bonanza. The Party was freed from its foreign-sounding jargon and began instead to speak the language of Wobblies and working stiffs. Embracing native populism, it sang folk songs and played guitars. Not Lenin and Stalin but Jefferson and Lincoln sat at the center of the new pantheon. The New Deal philosophy of FDR as we heard it in fireside chats generated warmth and confidence. Henry Wallace announced that this was the century of the common man. The Popular Front identified itself with this new populism, and the CP learned for the first time how heady it was to be in the mainstream of national life. The country appeared to be having a great cultural revival. Writers and actors were attracted by well-endowed front organizations and fellow-traveling groups. The left had struck it rich.

I was myself a not ungrateful beneficiary of the New Deal. Toward the end of the thirties, I was employed by the WPA Writers' Project. Our stars in the Chicago office were Jack Conroy and Nelson Algren—neither of them out of favor with the Communist Party. Algren was indeed an original, unfortunately susceptible to ideological infection, a radical bohemian in a quickly dated Chicago style. Few of the younger generation of gifted writers were untouched by the Popular Front influence. I refer not only to those who were later victimized in the hysteria generated by McCarthy but also to certain of the more prestigious contributors to *The Nation* and the *New Republic* who had gone along with the CP during the civil war in Spain (e.g., Malcolm

Cowley). The Popular Front style was distinctive, and its "culture" was easily recognizable in writers like Clifford Odets, Lillian Hellman, or Dalton Trumbo, or in critics or radio writers who may as well remain nameless. It survives even now, and you need do no more than mention Whittaker Chambers or Alger Hiss or J. Robert Oppenheimer or the Rosenbergs at a dinner table to learn how durable the issues and dogmas of the thirties and the early postwar years have remained.

It is perfectly true, as Charles Fairbanks has suggested, that totalitarianism in our century has shaped the very definition of what an intellectual is. The "vanguard fighters" who acted under Lenin's direction in October were intellectuals, and perhaps the glamour of this event had its greatest effect on intellectuals in the West. Among political activists this was sufficiently evident, but the Bolshevik model was immensely influential everywhere. Trotsky and T. E. Lawrence were perhaps the most outstanding of the intellectual activists to emerge from World War I—the former as Lenin's principal executive, Lawrence as the delicate scholar and recluse, a Shakespearean Fortinbras materializing in the Arabian desert. Malraux was inspired by both men, obviously, an aesthete and a theorist, eager in his first phase for revolutionary action and manifesting a curious relish for violence in a great cause. It was he who set an example for French writers of the forties. Sartre was certainly one of his descendants, and many in France and elsewhere modeled themselves upon him, up to the time when he abjured revolution. There was a trace of this also in Arthur Koestler, who so often exposed himself to personal danger, but it was in France, between the thirties and the time of Régis Debray, that leftist intellectuals presented themselves in the West as soldiers of the revolution.

The Leninist style was adopted by Berlin intellectuals in the twenties. Bertolt Brecht's *The Measures Taken* represents the central precept of Leninism, namely the primacy of the Party, and it dramatizes with great power the tragedy of disobedience—the failure of a Party worker to achieve the utter self-effacement demanded by "History." Martin Esslin tells us most vividly about Brecht himself—the public persona of the literary *enfant terrible*, the truckdriver's jacket and dirty visored cap he wore. In proletarian costume, he "drove around Berlin at great speed" but wore the steel-rimmed glasses of a "minor civil servant or village schoolmaster." Lenin himself has been characterized as a gymnasium teacher from Simbirsk: the Great Headmaster is what Wilson calls him. A powerhouse disguised as a pedant. The Lenin style was also favored by bohemian intellectuals in Greenwich Village. A valuable comment on this has been made by the art critic Clement Greenberg, who was himself preoccupied with the Great Headmaster's personality. He says of Brecht: "Lenin's precepts became for him an eternal standard of conduct, and Bolshevism a way of life and a habit of virtue." And in another place: "the followers of Lenin and Trotsky—like little men aping the externals of those they follow—have cultivated in themselves that narrowness which passes for self-oblivious devotion, that harshness in personal relations and above all that devastating incapacity for experience which have become hallmarks and standard traits of the Communist 'professional revolutionary' . . . it is the cultivated and trained narrowness . . . which frightens away imagination and spontaneity." These animadversions, when I read them years ago, increased my respect for Greenberg; I found in them an unusual gift for self-insight. He had carried himself like a Lenin of the arts. Many of the gifted intellectuals of that time took on a Leninist coloration. They were "hard." To them "lives" and "personalities" were unreal bourgeois conceits, extensions of the idea of property. You eliminated, you cut down to size, you put down frailties and fashions, you welcomed the avant-garde and destroyed kitsch with revolutionary mental rays.

The Russian Revolution was made by a small band of intellectuals under the direction of Lenin, their chief theoretician. Small wonder that intellectuals in the West should have been intoxicated by such an example.

Some of these people were authentic originals and impressively intelligent (Harold Rosenberg, for example). The more clearheaded of the Village intellectuals toward the end of the thirties were beginning to understand that the Revolution was a disaster. Few of them, however, turned away from Marxism. One way or another, they clung to the texts that had made intellectuals of them. The Marxist fundamentals had organized their minds and gave them an enduring advantage over unfocused rivals educated helter-skelter in American universities. What you invest your energy and enthusiasm in when you are young you can never bring yourself to give up altogether. I came to New York toward the end of the thirties, muddled in the head but keen to educate myself, and toward the end of the forties I had become a contributor to *Partisan Review* and a Villager. All around us was commercial America. The Village was halfway between Madison Avenue and Wall Street. Its center lay in Washington Square. From her apartment facing the benches and the elms, Eleanor Roosevelt might have seen, had they been pointed out to her, some of the most eminent intellectuals in the country discussing French politics, American painting, Freud and Marx, André Gide and Jean Cocteau. Everyone was avid for high-minded, often wildly speculative talk.

For Darwin it was the struggle for existence that mattered; for me, in those years, it was the struggle for conversation. There was no existence without it. There were notable talkers in this group of anti-communist leftists: Dwight Macdonald, tall, loosely held together, bearded, goggled, a rapid stammerer; Philip Rahv with his deep, breathy Russian rumble; Harold Rosenberg, extraordinarily fluent, persuasive, domineering, subtle, and sharp; Paul Goodman, both canny and visionary, looking beyond you as he laid down the law on psychiatry, poetry, anarchism, and sex.

Among these thinkers, small distinction was made between an intellectual and a writer. The culture heroes who mattered were those who had ideas. Sidney Hook, in many respects a sensible man, once said to me that Faulkner was an excellent writer whose books would be greatly improved by dynamic ideas. "I'd be glad to give him some," he said. "It would make a tremendous difference. Do you know him?"

There was indeed much for us to understand: history, philosophy, science, the cold war, mass society, pop art, high art, psychoanalysis, existentialism, the Russian question, the Jewish question. Yet I quickly saw—or rather (since I don't see quickly) I intuited—that writers seldom were intellectuals. "A bit of ideology and being up to date is most *apropos*," Chekhov said—tongue in cheek, I suspect. In a more serious vein, he wrote that writers "should engage in politics only enough to protect themselves from politics." "Absence of lengthy verbiage of a political-social-economic nature" was one of his rules, and he recommended also objectivity, brevity, audacity, the avoidance of stereotypes, and compassion. (Ah, for the days before such words had fallen into disrepute.)

I don't intend just now to go farther into the differences between cognition and imagination; I simply note that I avoided anything resembling a choice by following my bent. I can't remember that I ever tried to discuss art versus politics with other writers. At a visiting firemen's dinner, years later, I once asked Günter Grass why he was campaigning so hard for Willy Brandt. Should writers go into politics? He turned a silent glare upon me, as if it outraged him (on this evening, he was the fireman) to be seated beside a village idiot.

Only in America! he may have thought.

For in Europe, writers accepted politics as their absolute. This, as I learned during my Paris years (1948–50), was the thing to do. The year 1948 was a peculiarly bleak and bitter one. Coal, gasoline, even bread, were still being rationed. That Paris was the capital of world civilization could no longer be taken for granted. French thinkers and writers struggled to maintain its preeminence. Americans, recently cheered as liberators, were not warmly received, the right being nearly as hard on them as the left. Mauriac in his columns expressed a decided preference for the Russians—for Russian rather than American literature. (Up to a point, I could agree with him.) On the left, only Americans who had been ideologically vetted were accepted. The rest were thought to be spies. And French-speakers were especially tricky—very likely double agents. Lifelong Francophiles like my friend H. J. Kaplan were suspect, whereas Richard Wright was immediately welcomed, and the existentialists who met in the bar of the Pont-Royal soon had him reading Husserl, whom I ignorantly held in great respect. I *might* have become an intellectual, but this makes me think of the prostitute in the French cartoon who said, "*J'aurais pu faire la religieuse.*" Seeing Wright in Saint-Germain-des-Prés, deep in a thick, difficult book, I asked him why this was necessary, and he told me that it was indispensable reading for all writers and that I had better get a copy of my own. I wasn't quite ready for Husserl. As often as possible I went to music halls and the Cirque d'Hiver. Still, I did keep up with French ideas, read Sartre in *Les Temps Modernes* and Camus in *Combat*. I also took in an occasional lecture at the Collège de Philosophie.

The bitterness of defeat, occupation, and liberation pervaded postwar Paris. An atmosphere of disgrace and resentment darkened the famous facades and made the Seine (at least to me) look and smell medicinal. This oppressiveness, I was later persuaded, was an early symptom of the cold war. For the time being, the French lay helpless between the U.S.S.R. and the U.S.A. The communist alternative, so far as I could judge, held an edge in public opinion, so that you couldn't have your hair cut without enduring torrents of Marxism from the barber. I had come to Paris as Americans generally did, to be educated, and the general ignorance of the history of the Soviet Union in all quarters came as a great surprise. Reading Sartre, I said to myself, Chicago style, "This has got to be a con." A con on my turf was a shade more venial than a lie. I preferred to believe that Sartre's curious behavior was deliberate, Machiavellian. His hatred of the bourgeoisie was so excessive that he was inclined to go easy on the crimes of Stalin. On the intellectual Dow-Jones—if there had been such a thing—his credentials, before I began to read him, would have been comparable to preferred stock. But the facts were readily available, and that he should know so little about them was a great disappointment. He spoke in Marxist style of an oppressive bourgeois ideology, and while he admitted his bourgeois origins, his aim was to create a revolutionary public. Himself an heir of the eighteenth-century *philosophes*, he would speak to the proletariat as his literary ancestors had spoken to the bourgeoisie, bringing political self-awareness to those who were to be the revolutionaries of today. He asserted that the workingman seeking liberation would liberate all of us as well, and for all time. The French CP was an obstacle standing between Sartre and the working class. As for existentialism, he readily conceded that it was a phenomenon produced by the decomposition of the bourgeois carcass. The only public at present available to him came, disgustingly, from the intelligent sector of the rotting bourgeoisie (victims, no doubt, but tyrants also).

"Were the author an Englishman we should here know that our leg was being pulled," wrote Wyndham Lewis in *The Writer and the Absolute*. "But Sartre does not smile . . . he is at his wits' end what to do." Lewis seems wryly sympathetic. And he does here and there agree with Sartre and quotes him approvingly when he declares that we are living in the age of the hoax. "National Socialism, Gaullism, Catholicism, French communism are hoaxes—consciousness is deluded and we can only safeguard literature by disillusioning or enlightening our public. . . . Sartre believes all that the communists believe," Lewis concludes. "But he did not wish to convert this *collage* into a marriage." He says that Sartre was a fellow traveler in the *front populaire*. "He engaged in a path in those days which leads either to communism or to nothing. It was the *néant* that he chose."

My own guess in 1949—when I was immature: not young, only, as I now see, underdeveloped—was that French intellectuals were preparing themselves, perhaps positioning themselves for a Russian victory. Their Marxism also reflected the repugnance they felt for the other superpower. There were comparable anti-American sentiments in England. Graham Greene, like many writers (and civil servants) of his generation, abominated the U.S.A. and its politics. Successive English governments agreed on the whole with the American line, but Greene found ways to transfer at least part of the odium from London to Washington. On our side of the Atlantic he had a big following. Educated Americans, establishment haters, dearly love to see our society and its official policies loused up. "The main enemy is at home" was Lenin's wartime slogan. Of all his ideas, it may well be the most durable.

When I revert to those times, I can take no pleasure in having spotted the errors of Sartre et al. I am disheartened rather by the failure of all these aspirations for justice and progress. I can understand that as crisis succeeded crisis, no one wanted to surrender to passivity. It is sad to watch so much ingenuity invested in leaky theories. Behind the iron curtain, experiencing totalitarianism directly, people had a clearer orientation.

In the West, there was a certain opinion consumerism. One asked oneself, What shall I think, this or that? Sidney Hook in his autobiography scorns the *Partisan Review* intellectuals, the respectable left. His description of them makes them look like small-business types, importers of foreign specialties in a highbrow artistic mall. Mere talkers, Hook thought, some of them had no taste for real politics. Moreover, they believed that World War II was an imperialist war, exactly like the first. Since they were not the kind of Leninists who aimed to lead a putsch in Washington, their analyses of England and Germany did bring to mind the theologians of Lilliput. The account given by Hook, the stalwart cold warrior, of their confused Marxism was, four decades later, still edged with bitterness. But the fact that we can do nothing does not preclude wanting to be right, and everyone was then intent on the one true position. "I had to turn my heavy guns on Dwight Macdonald and the others," Hook would tell me in his last years. But no one has ever examined the connection between helplessness and holding the right views. Following contemporary events is in a way like reading history. To read history is essential, but what in actuality can we do about it? The novelist Stanley Elkin, in an essay called "The First Amendment as an Art Form," asks: "Who in old times ever held anything so uncalled for as an opinion? . . . History, history *really* was, still is, the agenda of activists. The rest of us, you, me, the rest of us are mere fans of a world view and use the news like theater—episodes, chapters in some Sabbath soul serial." He goes on to say that if we don't have the gift for effecting change, we have "the solace of criticism."

Granted, activists like Hook made a difference. Their contribution to victory in the cold war can't be measured but must be acknowledged. It was Hook—taking Hook as representative of any number of thinkers and activists—Hook, not Sartre, whose views prevailed, and should have prevailed. And what Mr. Elkin does is to report accurately on the state of opinion in a democracy like ours. What we need to consider is the combining of theorizing with effectiveness. I give Hook full marks for the wars he fought and admire him despite his evident lack of sympathy with my way of looking at things. He was the active, not the contemplative, sort, not so much a philosopher as an ex-philosopher. On one of the last evenings I spent with him, he told me that philosophy was no more. I asked what the Ph.D.'s he had educated were doing with themselves. They were working in hospitals as ethicists, he said. That didn't make him unhappy either. I don't think that the end of the cold war signifies that theorizing is bankrupt. To obtain a clear picture of the modern project, to give the best possible account of the crisis of the West is still a necessity.

Politics as a vocation I take seriously. But it's not my vocation. And on the whole, writers are not much good at it. The positions they take are generally set for them by intellectuals. Or by themselves, insofar as they are intellectuals (e.g., the case of Sartre). Those anticommunist intellectuals and publicists with whom I have agreed on issues of the cold war, though they tend to be high-toned and swollen with cultural pride and *suffisance*, are often philistine in their tastes. Their opposite numbers on the left are, in this respect, a mess entirely.

My policy has therefore been to avoid occasions that bring writers together. When President Johnson invited some twenty or thirty "leaders of the arts" to the White House, I foolishly accepted. I thought I would announce my opposition to Vietnam in a letter to the *Times*, and I could then attend the jamboree—in order to show my respect for the presidency. These principles! I have a weakness for stupid loftiness. Robert Lowell, who boycotted the event, had telephoned me more than once to concert a strategy for the afternoon. I gathered that he and his group were giving me a clearance to participate—somebody like me *should* be inside. The White House that day was filled with the cries of Lowell supporters, whom I will call the pros; the cons were in the minority. The journalists covering the event were as noisy and furious as the writers. The climax for me was the appearance of the uninvited Dwight Macdonald, tall, satyr-bearded, walking into the Rose Garden in sneakers, the great bohemian himself going around with a resolution endorsing Lowell's boycott. Many signed. LBJ afterward said the whole thing was nothing but an insult. "They insult me by comin', they insult me by stayin' away."

Philip Rahv set me straight about this. "You got put on the spot by Cal Lowell. He's a crafty schemer. When he gets into maneuvering that way, nobody has a chance with that dreamy poet."

The last literary meeting I can remember to have attended was the International PEN Congress in New York. There I was assigned to a panel on "The State and the Alienation of the Writer"—a superfluous and foolish topic. In a short talk (the shorter the better on this occasion), I said that our government hardly bothered with writers at all. The Founders had put together an enlightened plan for equality, stability, justice, relief from poverty, and so forth. Art, philosophy, and the higher concerns of mankind are not the business of the state. The emphasis here is on well-being and on a practical sort of humanitarianism. With the help of science, we would conquer nature and force her to provide for us. Scarcity was to be abolished. On the whole, I believed this program had met with success. In a commercial society, nothing prevents one from writing novels or painting watercolors, but culture does not get the same attention as crops or manufacture or banking. I concluded by saying that many of the material objectives of the Founders had been successfully realized.

Before I could step down, Günter Grass had risen to attack me from the floor. He said that he had just visited the South Bronx and that the poor blacks who lived in those monstrous streets could not agree that they were free and equal. The horrors they endured were not at all like the picture of American success that I had described. The hall was crowded with writers and intellectuals. Grass had just lighted the ideological fuse and out came a tremendous boom, a blast of anger from delegates and visitors. Replying as well as I could in the uproar, I said that of course American cities were going to hell in a hurry; they had become monstrous. I tried also to indicate that corrective actions, if there were any, could be taken only by a rich society, and this seemed to prove that the material objectives of the Founders had indeed been met. I added, since this was a PEN conference, that writers in politics hadn't done at all well. In this connection I mentioned Brecht and Feuchtwanger in Germany. Grass protested that he was always being put down in America as a communist.

You have to hand it to the social visionaries and liberators: they know how to get the high ground and keep it. They are masters also of the equivalence game: you have spoken well of the American system because you are an apologist for it and a stooge; you are not concerned about the poor, and you are a racist to boot.

He had pressed the agitprop button; up went a familiar semaphore. To this semaphore the agitated crowd responded with a conditioned reflex.

"I am afraid that great German writers do not have to know in order to pronounce," Melvin Lasky has written apropos of Grass.

Grass seems to have believed I was justifying the establishment —that moth-eaten shroud. No, I was simply describing what there is to see.

A brief quotation from an exceptionally clear-minded political theorist, Allan Bloom, will show better than I can the direction I meant to take in my speech before the PEN vipers: "Civil societies dedicated to the end of self-preservation cannot be expected to provide fertile soil for the heroic or the inspired. They do not require or encourage the noble. . . . One who holds the 'economic' view of man cannot consistently believe in the dignity of man or in the special status of art and science."

These are the basics, the first principles of modernity, of the Enlightenment conviction that this is what would be best for most of us. The objectives of Lenin's revolution never materialized in Russia, but they are all about us here in bourgeois America, says the philosopher Kojève. But in the process, everything worth living for has melted away.

Eastern Europe was "spared" our revolution. Instead Russia had seven decades and more of Stalin, an Oriental despot; and Poland, Hungary, and the rest came in for nearly half a century of Soviet rule. The writers who stood their ground against totalitarianism and went to the Lubyanka and the gulag move us deeply as moralists and artists. I particularly admire Shalamov, the author of *Kolyma Tales*, and Aleksander Wat, who wrote *My Century*, together with many others, Russians, Poles, and Jews, who endured Stalin's prisons and Hitler's death camps.

In the West, people excused from such torments are, I think it fair to say, inclined to mix self-reproach with their admiration. They wonder how they would have fared under pressure. Terror is the test of tests, and I suspect that the Hobbesian or the Darwinian states of nature challenge many of us imaginatively. Intellectuals are particularly susceptible to such challenges and possibly speculate whether living through such ordeals might not have healed their divided souls.

It comes back to me now that Lenin loved Jack London's stories of the Yukon. His favorite, "To Build a Fire," is about a man stopping for the night in vast snowfields and finding that he has only a single match left. He will freeze to death if it fails to light. I can remember when I was a boy holding my breath as I read the story. Jack London, I later discovered, had a great following in Eastern Europe. This turning back to what precedes civilization is common also among refined people, as is an admiration for elemental men, men capable of exceptional violence. Dostoyevsky, for instance, was greatly impressed by the criminals he came to know in Siberia. One murderer said to him, "'You are very innocent, so innocent that it's pitiful.' . . . Whether it was that he looked on me as somebody immature, not fully grown up, or whether he felt for me that sympathy which every strong creature feels for a weaker, I do not know . . . even in the act of stealing from me he was sorry for me."

Do I seem here to be making a case against the intellectuals, criticizing even the way they read Solzhenitsyn or Shalamov? Well, yes—insofar as they allow tyranny to define the ground rules of existence. The tyrant tells us what true being is and how it should be judged. A scale of suffering is set up for us, with the camps at the top and Western societies at the bottom. Those who undergo the most dreadful torments are "serious," the rest of us are not worth bothering about.

My case against the intellectuals can be easily summarized: Science has postulated a nature with no soul in it; commerce does not deal in souls and higher aspirations—matters like love and beauty are none of its business; for his part, Marx, too, assigned art, etc., to the "superstructure." So artists are "stuck" with what is left of the soul and its mysteries. Romantic enthusiasm (resistance to bourgeois existence) was largely discredited by the end of the nineteenth century. The twentieth inverted Romanticism by substituting hate for love and nihilism for self-realization. Intellectuals seem to me to have turned away from those elements in life unaccounted for in modern science and that in modern experience have come to seem devoid of substance. The powers of soul, which were Shakespeare's subject (to be simple about it) and are heard incessantly in Handel or Mozart, have no footing at present in modern life and are held to be subjective. Writers here and there still stake their lives on the existence of these forces. About this, intellectuals have little or nothing to say.

We yield to these forces when we read a Shalamov or an Aleksander Wat. We recognize them as coming directly from human nature when that nature rejects the imposition of slavery and totalitarian injustice. But among ourselves, in the West, the forces are not acknowledged, they cannot even be recognized.

Here I have no choice but to go overboard. Russia's Oriental despotism comes from the past, and the sympathies generated by those who fought for their lives against it have little to do, I suspect, with this present world of ours. Our American world is a prodigy. Here, on the material level, the perennial dreams of mankind have been realized. We have shown that the final conquest of scarcity may be at hand. Provision is made for human needs of every sort. In the United States—in the West—we live in a society that produces a fairytale superabundance of material things. Ancient fantasies have been made real. We can instantaneously see and hear what is far away. Our rockets are able to leave the earth. The flights we make are thoughts as well as real journeys. This is something new, and it is of a magnitude too vast to be grasped. To contemplate this can make us tremble for the humanity we miss in everything we see in the incredible upwelling of inventions and commodities that carries us with it. We can't say whether this humanity has been temporarily diminished or has gone for good. Nor can we tell whether we are pioneers or experimental subjects. Russia is perhaps done with tyranny and privation. If it develops a free market and becomes a union of commercial republics, it will have to do as we have been doing all along. Kojève hints that we are irreversibly trivialized by our unexampled and bizarre achievements, so that neither life nor death can now be grasped. He seems to accept Nietzsche's appalling vision of the degenerate "Last Man."

I myself believe that everything that can be imagined is bound to be realized at least once—everything that mankind is capable of conceiving it seems compelled to do. These, for better or for worse, are the thoughts the end of the cold war suggests to me.

PART THREE

The Distracted Public

THE JEFFERSON LECTURES

(1977)

I

*C*hicago is a prairie city with a waterfront. In the twenties, it was a mark of privilege to live within sight of the lake. The ultrarich had built their fine houses near it. Landlocked slum dwellers coming eastward on streetcars in the heat of July with their picnic beach blankets and baskets headed for the shore. They straggled through the streets of the Gold Coast, for the car lines ended several blocks to the west of its mansions, hotels, and apartment buildings. This was how the children of immigrant laborers first came to know the smell of money and the look of luxury. And although the Potter Palmers had gone off years earlier, as the buffalo had gone before them, you still made progress in Chicago by moving toward the water.

Since those times, middle-class residential buildings have risen along the shore on the north side of the city. If you live in one of these and your windows face eastward, Chicago is at your back; its brick six-flats, its schools, hospitals, factories, cemeteries, and used-car lots can still be seen if you look westward from the balcony. But you can't stand on the balcony now. On this January day, the thermometer is well below zero, and Lake Michigan resembles Hudson Bay, scaly white and gray, with slabs of ice piled offshore by high winds. Oceangoing ships, late in leaving Calumet Harbor, seem to be stuck on the horizon, and their coast guard rescuers also appear to be immobilized. In this weather, Chicago, which has changed so much in the last forty years,

I. Washington, D.C., 30 March 1977.
II. Chicago, 1 April 1977.
(National Endowment for the Humanities.)

looks its old self again in its ice armor of frozen grime, fenders and car doors whitened with salt, smoke moving slowly from the stacks, the fury of the cold shrinking the face and the heart as it did in the good old days. Then other resemblances come back: pyramids of oranges behind frost-engraved plate glass, the smell of blood at the butcher's, the black and white of newsprint matching the black and white of the streets. I try to remember who it was that said opening the newspaper was like tearing the bandage from a wound. This winter makes me feel *that* time, when I was starting out, when there was a Great Depression, when gangs of unemployed men in public works projects reported at daybreak and stood in the dim frost that drifted like a powder toward the dim sun. At their make-work jobs, the unemployed picked up the paving blocks, chipped them clean, and laid them down again.

Lately, I have been rereading some of the books I was reading in the thirties, the novels of John Dos Passos and Scott Fitzgerald, Lewis's *Babbitt*, Dreiser's *The Titan*, Sherwood Anderson's *Mid-American Chants*. What a good idea it seemed during the Depression to write about American life, and to do with Chicago (or Manhattan or Minneapolis) what Arnold Bennett had done with the Five Towns or H. G. Wells with London. By writing novels and stories, Dreiser and Anderson had added our American life, massive and hardly conscious of itself, to the world and its history. People who in the past would have remained inert and silent, sons and daughters of farmers, laborers, servants, and small tradesmen, had become capable of observation and comment. European literature had taught the children of workers and farmers that novels might be made about American small towns and back streets, about actresses from Wisconsin and speculators from Philadelphia. Highly finished works of art were not produced by American and British writers like Dreiser in the Midwest, or Arnold Bennett and H. G. Wells in provincial England, but it was wonderful what they could do, how intensely interesting they could be, how much they extracted from the experiences of obscure young women like Jennie Gerhardt or Sophia Baines. Such books didn't satisfy every taste, of course. Ezra Pound complained, "The post-Zolas or post-realists deal with subject matter, human types, etc., so simple that one is more entertained by Fabre's insects or Hudson's birds and wild animals." But in the same essay he made the following handsome concession: he said, "Art very possibly *ought* to be the supreme achievement, the 'accomplished,' but there is the other satisfactory effect, that of a man hurling himself at an indomitable chaos and yanking and hauling as much of it as possible into some sort of order (or beauty), aware of it both as chaos and as potential." There are books, Pound added, "which despite their ineptitudes and lack of 'accomplishment' or 'form' and finish contain something for the best minds of the time, a time, any time." I see this as a fair statement of the case. As an adolescent in Chicago I already felt the truth of it. I could not be expected to grasp it fully, but stimulated by the Russian, French, English, and German books I read, I felt it strongly. On winter afternoons when the soil was frozen to a depth of five feet and the Chicago cold seemed to have the headhunter's power of shrinking your face, you felt in the salt-whitened streets and amid the spattered car bodies the characteristic mixture of tedium and excitement, of narrowness of life together with a strong intimation of scope, a simultaneous expansion and constriction in the soul, a clumsy sense of inadequacy, poverty of means, desperate limitation, and, at the same time, a craving for more, which demanded that "impractical" measures be taken. There was literally nothing to be done about this. Expansion toward what? What form would a higher development take? All you could say was that you accepted this condition as a gambler would accept absurd odds, as a patient accepted his rare disease. In a city of four million people, no more than a dozen had caught it. The only remedy for it was to read and write stories and novels.

I used to do my writing forty years ago on yellow second sheets from the five-and-dime, and I became attached to this coarse yellow paper, which caught the tip of the pen and absorbed too much ink. It was used by those young men and women in Chicago who carried rolls of manuscript in their pockets and read aloud to one another in hall bedrooms or at Thompson's or Pixley's—cafeterias known as "one-arm joints." No one had money, but you needed very little to be independent. You could rent a small bedroom for three dollars. A fifteen-cent breakfast was served at all soda fountains. The blue-plate dinner at thirty-five cents was perfectly satisfactory. We smoked, but we hadn't yet learned to drink. And my late friend Isaac Rosenfeld said that it cost less than a thousand dollars a year to be poor—you could make it on seven or eight hundred. But to be poor in this way meant also to be free. We were in our early twenties. Some of us were re-leased from our families by the death of parents; some of us were *sup-posed* to be university students. Stenographer sisters who should have been laying up a trousseau were sacrificing their savings for student brothers, but no one was studying much. To feel these sisterly sacri-fices too keenly was to lose some of your delicious freedom. Instead you could have wonderful discussions about remorse, drawing on Freud or on the class morality denounced by Marx and Engels. You could talk of Balzac's ungrateful children on the make in Paris, of Dos-toyevsky's Raskolnikov, the student with the ax, or of the queer bad boys of André Gide. The children of Chicago bakers, tailors, peddlers, insurance agents, pressers, cutters, grocers, the sons of families on re-lief, were reading buckram-bound books from the public library and were in a state of enthusiasm, having found themselves on the shore of a novelistic land to which they really belonged, discovering their birthright, hearing incredible news from the great world of culture, talking to one another about the mind, society, art, religion, episte-mology, and doing all this in Chicago, of all places. What did—what could—Chicago have to do with the mind and with art? Chicago was a complex of industrial neighborhoods, a string of immigrant communi-ties, Germans, Irish, Italians, Lithuanians, Swedes, German Jews on the South Side, Russian Jews on the West, blacks from Mississippi and Alabama in gloomy vast slums; even more vast were the respectable endless bungalow-filled middle-class neighborhoods. What else was there? There was the central business district where adventurous ar-chitects had pioneered the skyscraper. And we were known to the world for our towers, stockyards, railroads, steel mills, our gangsters and boosters. Oscar Wilde had come here and tried to be nice, Rud-yard Kipling had looked us over and written a nasty report. Mr. Yerkes had made millions out of car lines and el trains and Mr. Insull out of the utilities. Jane Addams had worked in the slums, and Harriet Mon-roe had worked in poetry. But the slums got bigger, while the poets left for New York, London, and Rapallo. If you looked here for the sort of natural beauty described by Shakespeare, Milton, Wordsworth, Yeats, you would never find it. Nature on the prairies was different, coarser. The soil, the air, the plants, the blasting heat, the blasting cold, the winds, the storms, the horizons—all different. Modern Europeans might complain of their excessively humanized environment—too much history and tradition, too many ghosts, the soil sifted by the hands of too many generations, the landscapes too smooth and the flowers too tame—but they didn't know what it was like here, you thought. Were the spirits of this place going to be friendly to art and culture? Most of the time you felt that those spirits would have no truck with your effeminate European cultural frills.

So you sat in your three-dollar room, which you had anxiously civilized with books (your principal support in life) and with a few prints from the Art Institute: a Velázquez Job who said *Noli Me Condemnare*, a Daumier Don Quixote riding featureless over the Castilian wasteland; and in this dusty cubicle you recognized that you were out of line, you were a strange deviant. With the steelmaking dinosaurs just to the south, and the stockyards, the slaughter rooms blazing with aereated blood where Croat or Negro workers sloshed in rubber boots, right at your back, and the great farm-machinery works and the automobile assembly lines and mail order houses, and the endless railyards and the gloomy Roman pillars of the downtown banks, this was a powerful place, but the power was something felt, not shared. And what had these labors or these transactions to do with you and your books? The meaning of this prodigious power lay in things and the methods by which things were produced. What Chicago gave to the world was goods—a standard of living sufficient for millions. Bread, bacon, overalls, gas ranges, radio sets, telephone directories, false teeth, light bulbs, tractors, steel rails, gasoline. I asked a German-Jewish refugee, just arrived, to tell me quickly, without thinking, his opinion of the city. What had impressed him most in Chicago? He said at once, "Stop and Shop"—the great food store on Washington Street, with its mountains of cheese, its vats of coffee, its ramparts of canned goods, curtains of sausage, stacks of steaks. Goods unlimited and cheap, the highest standard of living in the world, "and for the broad masses, not for an elite." The "struggle for existence" went on under your eyes, but the very fact that we could even think about such a struggle meant that millions of well-fed people could afford to sit theorizing about the human condition. What we were thinking as adolescents is succinctly summarized in a recent book by Norman Macrae of the *Economist*—*The Neurotic Trillionaire: A Survey of Mr. Nixon's Amer-*

ica. He says of the United States: "For this, after all, is the society in which the last important stage of man's long economic revolution is succeeding."

What is the place of poets and novelists in such a revolution? Can a nation preoccupied with such objectives be asked not only to complete mankind's economic and political destiny but also to pursue the pure sciences, philosophy, and art?

But I am going too fast. Let me turn back four decades to my three-dollar room in the middle of an America where people saw themselves in a collective image as inhabiting down-to-earth, bread-and-butter, meat-and-potatoes, dollar-and-cents, cash-and-carry Chicago. Wealth and ostentation, upper-class society with its Oriental and European connections, its picture galleries and opera houses, might pretend that there was another Chicago. But that was phony, for the money came from lard, steel, coke, and petroleum, and the material standard was the only genuine one. Even a gifted writer like Ring Lardner saw it that way. Here are a few sentences from the account of a performance of *Carmen*, given by one of his lowbrow narrators, dragged unwillingly, Maggie-and-Jiggs style, to Chicago's Auditorium Theater. "*Carmen*," he says, "ain't no regular musical show where a couple o' Yids comes out and pulls a few lines o' dialogue and then a girl and a he-flirt sings a song that ain't got nothin' to do with it. *Carmen*'s a regular play, only instead o' them sayin' the lines, they sing them, and in a for'n language so's the actors can pick up some loose change offen the sale of the librettos." Lardner's American animal is snarling here against the show-off women in formal dress who drag their husbands in soup-and-fish to an evening of fancy foreign culture. It was possible for H. L. Mencken of Baltimore, a he-man himself, to declare openly his admiration for Wagner, but in Chicago the normal male despised this female sickliness, the phony singing dagos wearing rompers and carrying knives. Lardner on the whole sided with Boobus Americanus, the Chicago wise guy who drank whiskey, played rummy for small stakes, slept in a Kelly bed—a shrewd, proud lout. I know those attitudes well. As a student usher at the same Auditorium Theater during the annual visits of the San Carlo Opera Company, I struggled with my own vulgarity, and when I read the *Autobiography of Lincoln Steffens*, I marked the passages where Steffens confesses that as an undergraduate in Germany he had had to turn his back to the stage, eliminating the obese costumed singers, who interfered ridiculously with the music. When Leonid Massine's Ballet Russe came to town, I offered to get one of my pals an usher's job, but he said he preferred jazz joints and prizefights. This was an American statement, and in my heart I sympathized with it. In adopting such a Know-Nothing attitude, strictly American, no one was more self-congratulatory than the sons of Russian-Jewish immigrants. By God! We belonged to the heart of the country. We were at home in the streets, in the bleachers. I remember portly, sonorous Mr. Sugarman, the *schochet* on Division Street, singing out the names of the states during the Democratic roll call, broadcast on the radio, that nominated FDR. He did this in cantorial Jewish style, as though he were standing at the prayer desk, proud of knowing the correct order from A to W, an American patriot who wore a black rabbinical beard.

I summon up the furnished rooms in which I lived in the late thirties. At Sixty-first and Ellis there is now a gas station; on the site of the Beatrice, where you had to pull a primitive hawser to get the elevator started, there is now a community vegetable garden; the building on Ingleside where I awoke covered with bedbugs has been torn down; the small brick house at Fifty-seventh and Kenwood where Mr. Hrapek burned rags and garbage in the hot-air furnace, poisoning the air, has made way for a playground. The best-known student rooming houses—Kootich Castle, Petofsky's on Woodlawn Avenue, Kenwood Gardens, with the skylighted court and wandering corridors and galleries—have vanished. I was dealing with the void before the existentialists put a name to it. Life in these houses was entertaining, but when you had your degree and your friends had gone to take up their professions in New York, in California, or in North Africa, it became hard to explain why you were still here. In 1939, when I was writing a book, I met on the street a professor who put a difficult question to me. He, Dr. L., was a European scholar, immensely learned. Growing bald, he had shaved his head; he knew the great world; he was severe, smiling primarily because he had occasion to smile, not because anything amused him. He read books while walking rapidly through traffic, taking notes in Latin shorthand, using a system of his own devising. In his round, gold-rimmed specs, with rising wrinkles of polite inquiry, he asked, "Ah? And how is the *romancier*?" The *romancier* was not so hot. The *romancier*'s ill-educated senses made love to the world, but he was as powerfully attached to silliness and squalor as to grandeur. His unwelcome singularity made his heart ache. He was, so far as he knew, the only full-time *romancier* in Chicago (apart from Nelson Algren), and he felt the queerness (sometimes he thought it the *amputation*) of his condition. He was angry, obstinate. With his ideas of beauty, harmony, love, goodness, friendship, freedom, etc., he was altogether out of it. He hated Professor L. for his sarcasm and for being right. The *romancier* was *dans la lune*. And Professor L.? The professor held an excellent degree from a European university. He had a position, an office, students; he had an apartment—he had status. In his office was a folding cot, on which he lay annotating his many volumes of Toynbee and Freud, and cutting articles from the world press. In five or six languages, he studied history, psychology, and politics. What was even more enviable was his grasp of the real world, his total comprehension of Hegel, Marx, Lenin, his detailed knowledge of society and of the history of civilization. My own relation to society was misty, dubious. I, too, was supposed to understand, but on my own peculiar conditions. Solitary, I was mystically connected to all this on unilateral terms. Through it all I appeared to be walking the streets minding my own business. I was on a mission of an esoteric sort. On detached service, as they used to say in the military, but drawn by powerful and vivid longings and sympathies, hungry for union and for largeness, convinced by the bowels, the heart, the sexual organs, and, on certain occasions, by clear thought that I had something of importance to declare, express, transmit.

I had one of my three-dollar rooms that seemed, to a young man of depressive tendencies, abandoned by life and purpose—musty, sour. I slept in see-through sheets, the wallpaper was buckling, the dry paste sifted down behind it. Shades of the city dump and the auras of bonfires hung over the table and the dresser; you knew how the varnish would smell when it burned; the carpet was trodden down to the fiber. Wood-boring insects had for decades been eating their way through chair legs. Their wood chewing and my yellow second-sheet manuscripts—there were days when such comparisons forced their way forward. Your acquaintances had real tasks and belonged to teams, institutions—even the termites were bound by instinct to an organized will and collective purpose and had their reasons for gnawing. Happy were those, said Baudelaire (I always had all the texts I needed), who could say at nightfall, *"Aujourd'hui nous avons travaillé."* Often I couldn't say that to save my soul. I looked into the letters of D. H. Lawrence and found his bitter protest against that "savage pilgrimage" his wandering life, and "the privation of the social instinct" from which he had suffered. But of course the prevailing assumption—and the Romantic assumption still prevailed—was that man could find the true meaning of life and of his own unique being by separating himself from society and its activities and collective illusions. If walking in the mountains as a solitary Rousseau didn't turn the trick, you could go and derange your senses artificially, as Rimbaud recommended.

It looked, then, as if my wide-awake and energetic peers were going to take all the active roles in "serious" life—in the professions, in business or research. They were qualified by health, strength, race, social class, birth. I didn't belong to a class that could bring me into a significant life. Therefore I had to seek a significant life in my own way. My way was to write. Nothing seemed more wonderful, but I wasn't absolutely sure of my qualifications. What was there for me to write? Did I know English well enough to write it? I had thoughts. I had a heart full of something. I studied my favorite authors. I rode the bobbling el cars reading Shakespeare or the Russians or Conrad or Freud or Marx or Nietzsche, unsystematic, longing to be passionately stirred. I thought I might confirm my own truths from hints provided by my chosen thinkers. So I moved completely equipped, like a Roman legion, as ready for Parthia as for wild Britain, setting up camp with my books, hanging up my Velázquez and my Daumier prints, spreading a hand towel over the grease stains of the armchairs. Fastidiousness was a handicap here, and it could not last long. You had to forget those who had smoked, slept, eaten, lolled, dreamed, sickened, and grieved before you. I disapproved strongly of my orphan's emotions, my castaway's sinking heart, and did my best to develop bohemian attitudes toward cockroaches and mice. As a bohemian, driving your cart and your plow over the bones of the dead, living cheerfully, you stood for something, you fought for your freedom, you were cured of bourgeois squeamishness about dirt, debt, property, or sex, and you were not afraid of idleness. But you couldn't fully train yourself into bohemianism, and as you faced the horror of the room you had just rented, your bohemian attitudes sometimes crumbled away. You inspected the mattress, smelled the decay, turned over the desk blotter to see if it had a clean side, and you longed boundlessly, frantically, for contact, interest, warmth, order, continuity, meaning, real reality. Community, kinship, roots? It was the essence of your situation that you had no such connections. You were, if you could bear it, ideally free.

That, certainly, was how Walt Whitman saw the American condition. What an opportunity! he exclaims in "Song of the Open Road." The earth, that is sufficient. The new man needs no good fortune; he himself is good fortune. Henceforth he whimpers no more, postpones no more. "Done with indoor complaints, libraries, querulous criticisms, / Strong and content I travel the open road." The universe itself, conceived as such a road, draws you into happiness; happiness, an efflux of the soul, pervades the open air. Nor is this a solitary, self-absorbed freedom and happiness; it is the happiness of friends, lovers, and camerados. The poet does not reject the "old delicious burdens" but carries them, together with the men and women whom they afflict, wherever he goes. Receptive to all, he neither prefers nor denies, welcomes the black, the felon, the sick, the beggar, the drunkard, the mechanic, the rich person, the sleeping couple, the market man, the furniture mover, the hearse.

I would have been glad to embrace this blissful freedom (something like Rousseau's *"sentiment de l'existence"*), but it wasn't as easy as it sounded. It required thought and discipline. Impulse wasn't enough. Besides, I couldn't find Whitman's America in Depression Chicago. There were many thousands of sleepers near me nightly in apartment buildings and rented rooms, but in the morning those who were fortunate enough to be employed went to their factories, offices, warehouses. By the time I got to my window, the streets were already vacant, the children at school, the housewives washing up. Dogs and cats were irresponsibly free. The unemployed (in those days) were most responsibly sad. There were no carefree mechanics having a lark on the street corner. If I wanted to mingle with friends, lovers, and camerados, I had to take the train downtown.

I had no intention of succumbing to complaints and to libraries. I agreed in principle with Whitman about the evils of solitary self-absorption. Nevertheless I am bound to point out that the market man, the furniture mover, the steamfitter, the tool-and-diemaker, had easier lives. They were spared the labor of explaining themselves.

What was the meaning of my unpractical life? Ordinary gainful employment was better, wasn't it? The tool-and-diemaker understood penniless idleness, but what was he to make of toilsome pennilessness? What was the sense of this self-imposed discipline? It was worthwhile in principle, no doubt, it was courageous to assert that a world without art was unacceptable. But it was no more than the simple truth that the hero of art was himself unstable, stubborn, nervous, ignorant, that he could not bear routine or accept an existence he had not made for himself. This militant life, in which the purpose of militancy was not perfectly clear, developed strength of will certainly, and the answer to Professor L.'s question might have been: The *romancier* certainly is making something of himself. Something perhaps free, perhaps generous, firm of purpose, whatever else. But what is the purpose? The *romancier* has an idea, but he doesn't yet know quite what it is.

I think I can see now what I was getting at. Pioneering America, immigrant America, political America, the industrial America of the Carnegies, Du Ponts, and Henry Fords, did not entirely engross the human spirit in the New World. Something that humankind was doing in this American setting was beyond all these activities and innovations, which so impressed or frightened or antagonized the whole world. That something had not found full expression, and this was the intuition that made solitary young men and women so obstinate in their pursuit of art.

On the open road, separateness was ideal because it ended in joining, but no such choice was ever offered in our century. At least we believed that 1914 and 1917 and, later, Hitler, Holocaust, and Hiroshima had made a special case of us and that the camerado to whom Whitman held out his loving hand had become far too kinky a bird for the wholehearted simplicity of such a gesture. Take, for contrast, Hemingway's view of the separate self. With him isolation is a permanent kind of despair. "Moral vacancy" is what John Berryman called it in a short essay on Hemingway's "A Clean, Well-Lighted Place." This modern condition of emptiness suited me no more than the open road. I recognized the truth of it for Hemingway—as *his* truth, it was impressive. Borrowed, the same truth was shabby. The mind in its incessant activity makes all possible suggestions, conceives everything. Hemingway's dignity in the face of nothingness is not a negligible conception; its attraction is understandable. But one need not go down with the decay of religious beliefs that have lost their power to bind us to life. "Moral vacancy" is nihilism, and nihilism acknowledges the victory of the bourgeois outlook. The bourgeois outlook is that if you can't beat 'em you had better join 'em. But other responses may be possible.

Rootlessness, so frightening to some, exhilarates others. Wyndham Lewis, who has given this question more thought than anyone else in our time, wrote that no American worth his salt should long for *Gemeinschaft* or go about looking for roots. The American's most conspicuous advantage is that he is pleasantly detached or disembodied; the sensation he has is that of being in the world, not necessarily in a nation. He is liberated from castes, czars, masters, corvées, and he is attached to the *absence* of burdens and limitations and has learned to be at home in a "slightly happy-go-lucky vacuum in which the ego feels itself free. It is, it seems to me, something like the refreshing anonymity of a great city, compared with the oppressive opposite of that, invariably to be found in the village," said Lewis in *America and Cosmic Man*. "Everything that is obnoxious in the Family is encountered in the latter; all that man gains by escape from the Family is offered by the former." A "rootless Elysium," as he calls it, is enjoyed "by the great polyglot herds in American cities." In old Europe, this Elysium was enjoyed by kings, who had connections in all countries. In modern Europe, it is behind the iron curtain that people stay put and that the "rootless cosmopolitanism" of the West is denounced. If you reply that the cruel dullness of police states does not justify the whirling of random human particles in the West, I will agree. Wyndham Lewis saw the promise of Elysium in this happy-go-lucky vacuum. He had a strong head and was ready for a universal future in which writers, painters, and thinkers would become strong enough to lead a free life. But most of us are aware that many of the human attachments cut in the process of liberation will have to be restored and renewed. Such renewal can occur only because we will it and think it. We will it and think it not because we are nostalgic but because there is no human life without the attachments that we express in words like "good," "moral," "just," "beautiful." The restoration of these connections is to be undertaken only out of the soul's recognition of their necessity. It will not happen because we join political parties or take up causes. It will begin when the intellect confirms what the soul desires.

It will be objected that if thinking be the first step in our recovery, we are done for. In saying this, I am not being dreamy or hypothetical. Rather, I am taking into account what is visible to everyone: namely, the increase of concepts and abstractions in ordinary life and the grip that "science" has on it. The weakening of traditional culture, the thinness of aesthetic and religious influences, drive Americans, as they do modern men everywhere, to look for guiding ideas. Their thinking is invariably poor, their ideas are unfortunately wretched, but since we are deprived of the old ways of life, of dependable customs and of saving inertias, we have no alternative but to think. Our way of going about thinking is not something on which we can congratulate ourselves. The ideas around us are apt to produce more confusion than order. One sits down, for instance, to watch a private-eye movie set in southern California and then finds oneself called up to review a variety of literary, psychological, and philosophical notions from André Gide and his more important predecessors—views of family life that date from the days of Ibsen and Strindberg, plainly adapted from Sorel and ultimately from Nietzsche. In every scene of the picture you can see a sort of dandruff of existentialism on the shoulders of the actors.

So it comes down to this: the living man is preoccupied with such questions as who he is, what he lives for, what he is so keenly and interminably yearning for, what his human essence is, and instead of the bread of thought he is offered conceptual stones and fashionable non-ideas. And so, immensely needy, people are engaged in thought or with the products of thought, taking attitudes that presuppose thought—attitudes toward public responsibility, or personal adjustment, or crime, morality, punishment, abortion, child care, education, love, race relations. This is what people, aided or misled by advisers, teachers, experts, therapists, social scientists, newspaper columnists, television writers, actors, and political leaders, are attempting to work out.

A recent television program introduces to the public a psychiatric social worker who deals at a "halfway house" with juvenile delinquents. In his conversation with a young parolee, the social worker elevates the dialogue to the conceptual plane. "Suppose you were to kill one of your holdup victims, what would you feel? *Have* you killed anyone?" The boy smiles, neither affirming nor denying, but leaving the impression that he has committed a murder (it would be strange, with such a record, if he hasn't). He answers, "I wouldn't feel much of anything. I keep on going the only way I know how to go along." The social worker speaks of asocial behavior. The term is familiar to the young criminal. The social worker is able to explain the causes of this asocial behavior. But the delinquent could do it too, and in the very same terms. So they bandy abstractions with equal ease and familiarity. "I don't owe anybody no different, because of the way I grew up and what they done to me." The social worker indicates that he understands this. The delinquent accepts his understanding, shares it, but does not appear to be touched in any deeper place by it. Indeed, no deep place is mentioned. It is absent from the "concepts" used by both parties. The young criminal evidently sees himself as the significant person who is the object of the concepts. He is formulated by them, he formulates in his turn, and these formulations constitute his mental life, which is perhaps not less exiguous than that of the intellectuals who study criminology, teach courses, and give degrees. A mental life, I say, and not a moral life.

It is not too much to say that the young writer in his Chicago rooming house had already begun to understand this condition when he read Dostoyevsky, for Dostoyevsky's subject was, after all, the condition of mankind at the beginning of this new age of consciousness. Dostoyevsky would have felt about the post-realists very much as Pound was to feel: namely, that they dealt with subject matter, with human types, so simple that one was more entertained by the insects of Fabre or the birds of W. H. Hudson. But then Pound added, as we have just seen, that while art *ought* to be the supreme achievement, the artist looks like a man hurling himself at a chaos and hauling as much of it as possible into some kind of order. There are modern books, he insisted, that, despite their lack of accomplishment, "contain something for the best minds of the time, . . . any time." With this I agreed and still agree. But how useful are even the best instruments developed by modern literature for this purpose? What good is what we have come to know best, we writers—the lessons of Symbolism with its Romantic legacy, of modernism and the various kinds of vanguardism? In asking what good Proust, Joyce, Mann, Lawrence, Kafka, Hemingway, can do us, I intend no disrespect. These writers have formed my mind. But it is for that very reason that I can see why they should perhaps be put aside by the contemporary American novelist. Educated America would be pleased to see its writers continue to Joyce-ify or Lawrenceize. People have become accustomed to take their cultural pleasures in these familiar ways, writers have learned to gratify these tastes, but the game can't interest writers whose art binds them to the modern reality of disorder, to American society as it is now and the mixture of mind and crudity it offers.

A recent correspondent writes to me about the culture of Chicago and speaks of it as a "white-knuckle" city. A native Chicagoan, he writes: "I clearly remember long afternoons in the alley digging up rusty nails and bottle caps from the blacktop. That stuff is really Chicago's culture—an oily, foul-smelling matrix that binds together people and their jobs, brick and building." I cite this not as a judgment that I share but as a common attitude for which there is something to be said. This Chicago does not inevitably possess us, but it most palpably surrounds us. The columnist Mike Royko, in his obituary on Mayor Daley, said that it was the powerful, semiliterate Daleys who spoke for Chicago, not the S. Bellows. Up to a point, he was right. No novelist can be Chicago's representative man. But the novelist can see, perhaps, what is coming. What he did he did not do for the sake of being different or out of arbitrariness. He did it because of his intuition that something humanity was up to in its American setting was not yet visible and clear and that he must not take what was manifest as final. The manifest Mayor Daley was incoherent and sometimes vulgar. There was another Mayor Daley, who was infinitely knowledgeable and subtle. Both of these Daleys were real. The relations between the two of them must have been fascinating. For things are not what they seem. Even Longfellow knew that. Chicago's crudities do not lack a certain theoretical background, an idea not too far below the threshold of consciousness. I was aware, in a word, that if the post-realists of my youth, in describing white-knuckle Chicago, thought they were representing human types as simple as Fabre's insects or Hudson's birds, they were badly mistaken.

It was, then, in blacktop Chicago, among the white knuckles, that an apprentice novelist was reading refined and exquisite poets and grave philosophers, while he sat on park benches or in the public libraries. He read not only his American contemporaries but journals like *transition*, *The Dial*, and *The Little Review*, which published the French, German, and Irish geniuses of the early twenties. In Chicago, we were well aware that Paris was the center of an international culture. To this center belonged decadents, nihilists, surrealist cubists. Mondrian, Picasso, Diaghilev, were there. A cultural Klondike, Harold Rosenberg has accurately called it (in "The Fall of Paris"), in which the century found its fullest expression. This international culture was peculiarly appreciated in Chicago, a city of Italians, Hungarians, Poles, blacks just up from the South, Irish stockyard workers and politicians, German mechanics, Swedish cabinetmakers, Jewish garment workers, Greek cooks, Iowa dirt farmers, and Hoosier small-town storekeepers, a city of foreigners, roughnecks, and working stiffs. Anyone might become a prospector and strike it rich, find the gold of art under the el tracks. Such was the hope emanating from Paris in those great years.

This is what Rosenberg has to say in his memorable essay:

> In all his acts contemporary man seems narrow and poor, yet there are moments when he seems to leap towards the marvelous in ways more varied and whole-hearted than any of the generations of the past. . . . Released in this aged and bottomless metropolis [Paris] from national folklore, national politics, national careers; detached from the family and the corporate taste, the lone individual, stripped, yet supported on every side by the vitality of other outcasts, with whom it was necessary to form no permanent ties, could experiment with everything that man today has within him of health or monstrousness. . . . Because the Modern was often inhuman, modern humanity could interpret itself in its terms.

Elsewhere he speaks of "a dream living-in-the-present and a dream world citizenship—resting not upon real triumphs but upon a willingness to go as far as was necessary into nothingness in order to shake off what was dead in the real." Germany was ready by the end of the thirties to transfer these modern formulas from art to politics. "In that country," he writes, "politics became a 'pure' (i.e. inhuman) art, independent of everything but the laws of its medium. The subject matter of this *avant-garde* politics was, like that of the earlier art movements of Paris, the weakness, meanness, incoherence and intoxication of modern man."

Rosenberg's propositions are highly suggestive; I don't know how many of them I would call true. Can we all agree upon what it was in the "real" that was dead? We can only agree that many people were profoundly convinced that they were being asked to submit to enslavement, to surrender their lives to the service of dead realities. Another question: Was it necessary to plunge into nihilism in order to be purified, to shake off what was dead? Or was this revolutionary attitude not, in many cases, a screen for perversity, an excuse for the craving to make war, to destroy men, women, children, cities, peoples? Was Hitler the "pure" inhuman artist whose medium was politics? But it is not necessary to agree in detail with Rosenberg. He has located a phenomenon and brings us in a few sentences before one of these giant manifestations that, prompted by a desire for "normalcy" or "sanity," we would rather not see. It is useless to talk about literature if we are not prepared to think about the facts of life in this present staggering century.

Observe that Rosenberg speaks of the lone modernist sustained "by the vitality of other outcasts," with whom he did not need to form ties. But the Picassos, Apollinaires, Diaghilevs, Joyces, Kandinskys, and Wyndham Lewises were a relatively sociable and jolly crew. I am reminded, as I read these words about the mutual aid of these modernist outcasts, of the far more drastic isolation of artists in modern Russia, of poets who had only their own resources to sustain them and were not at all inclined to experiment with "everything that man today has within him of health or monstrousness." People utterly cut off from all institutions, all social support, poets like Osip Mandelstam or Akhmatova, formed attachments to Pushkin or Dante. Dante was Mandelstam's inseparable companion. He carried a pocket edition of *The Divine Comedy*, says his widow, "just in case he was arrested not at home but in the street." The volume he took to Siberia with him was a bulky one. Nadezhda doubts that it was still in his possession when he died, for "in the camps under Yezhov and Stalin nobody could give any thought to books."

The subject matter of poets who continued in Soviet Russia to be poets was not "the weakness, meanness, incoherence and intoxication of modern man." Writers were more apt to concern themselves with the life they were denied, with the deeper meaning of the art they were forbidden to practice, with the rights and powers of the individual apparently so defenseless, with the artist as artist, who was, in the gangster state, so insignificant.

This is not to deny that "the weakness, meanness, incoherence and intoxication of modern man" are real themes. But they are not the only genuinely modern themes. And it was not because the Russian poets I have mentioned were eager to go the way of their modernist colleagues in the West that they resisted Stalin. You do not defy terror or risk exile because you have accepted as an artist the task of chronicling weakness. Terror has won you the right to wider scope.

Nearly forty years ago, in the year 1940, I sat on a park bench in Chicago and read Rosenberg's essay. "In all his acts," he said, "contemporary man seems narrow and poor. Yet there are moments when he seems to leap towards the marvelous in ways more varied and whole-hearted than any of the generations of the past." What I felt, in isolation, was my privilege, my painful freedom, to think and feel. Workers in factories, doctors in hospitals, clerks in the shops, even criminals in prison, belonged to a community of some sort, but a young man who had left his rooming house with a copy of *Partisan Review* in his pocket to sit in Jackson Park, detached indeed from family and corporate taste, considered the oddity of his calling, so remote from workers, clerks, doctors, even criminals, and yet so intimately connected with the vital needs of them all. The consciousness of this intimacy was mine only. For how were others to guess what I had privately determined to attempt. If they knew, they would think it very curious indeed. And to tell the truth, they were curious to me too, living without the higher motives of which I was so wildly, perhaps ridiculously, proud. But I would, for the sake of us all (I was very young then), narrow and poor as I was, try myself to leap towards the marvelous. Here we were only beginning to understand what a decade of horrors we had entered. The Depression was ending, and the factories were stoking up again, people were returning to work. But Warsaw had been destroyed, and Rotterdam, and hundreds of thousands of people, just massacred, were still in the first stages of decay, under the rubble or in mass graves. And Paris, which for a few years had been the seat of an international modern culture, was now a conquered city.

I shall not go on talking about the disasters of the century. We don't need any more of that. But it is, I think, necessary to consider what sort of person these experiences, these strange turns, have produced. This person is our brother, our *semblable*, our very self. He is certainly in many respects narrow and poor, blind in heart, weak, mean, intoxicated, confused in spirit—stupid. We see how damaged he is, how badly mutilated. But the leap towards the marvelous is a possibility he still considers nevertheless. In fact, he is well qualified by his peculiar experiences to try jumping. He dreams of beating the rap, outwitting the doom prepared for him by history. Often he seems prepared to assert that he is a new kind of human being, whose condition calls for original expression, and he is ready to take a flier, go for the higher truth. He has been put down, has put himself down too, but he has also dreamed of strategies that will bring him past all this detraction, his own included. For he knows something. Anyone who has lived attentively through five decades of this epoch has had centuries of history thrust upon him, ages of mental experience. He is (or can be) skeptical, cant-free, heedful of his own intuitions. He has seen orthodoxies come and go, and he has learned that he must trust the communications coming from his own soul—stipulating that his soul should know the dry taste of objectivity. The principal characteristic of this survivor is that he has made himself lighter by putting off, by setting aside, the ideas and doctrines that have dominated this century, its leading psychologies and philosophies, its wilder political beliefs, the endless horrible comedy of public lying. What is observable in our best contemporaries is a lightening, a divestiture. They lighten themselves not because they care less but because they care more, not because they are attracted by the silliness of a cynical style but because they are repelled by that form of theatrical vanity precisely and have come to detest the worldly-wise man. Perhaps they have come to see that the theories they accepted for decades had nothing to do with their most significant intentions and actions. We "square" ourselves with our ideas, but in time we recognize that the unacknowledged soul has somehow saved us from the worst effects of those ideas.

I occasionally encounter persons who have been "lightened." They are by no means fault-free, redeemed from error, heroes and heroines of love, or saintly characters. They have moved away from the prevailing prejudices of the century. There are more of these "lightened" persons in real life than in books, but now and then a poem or a story may emit the welcome signal. I saw it recently in a short book by Christina Stead, *The Little Hotel.* There are signs of it also in one of her earlier novels, *Places of the Heart.* One of her characters says, "I often wonder at my strange fate to be born into the first generation that understands humanity's birthright, the perfect consummation." The lady who is speaking is an oddball, somewhat crazy in her generosity, a deserted woman who can know very little about the "birthright" of erotic consummation. That sort of bliss is not for her. And perhaps there is no such bliss as the deprived imagine. I put the emphasis in another place. She is one of those who feel that they can understand the "birthright" of humanity. It may be an illusion merely, but it can be strongly argued that it is based on a genuine intuition.

In the journal of the poet George Seferis, I meet other "lightened" people, himself the most distinctly "lightened" of them. The signs are all there: a mind of great clarity and evident power, experienced in despair, a witness to murder, war, ruin. He is by the sea, the Aegean, and he writes: "It was impossible to separate the light from the silence, the silence and light from the calm. . . . There was a sense that another side of life exists." Again, he writes, after rowing, walking, and swimming: "*Myself* has come *out.*" And he continues: "The day holds its breath. Such calmness that every motion—a leaf, a sound, a boat in the canal—stays for a long time suspended in the light as if there were no end. . . ." Then he speaks of desires and plans, and he says: "It's strange (for me) to have any feeling for this sack full of 'personal sentiments' that is now loosened and drives me mad (literally) with these unsettled winds. I had kept them all tightly shut up during the war years, for six years at least." He mentions dreams and says: "It's natural that the language of dreams pertains even to trifles; messengers condescending even to humble errands. The intellectuals have made them speak only with the trumpet of Jericho or with bagpipes." The man who has been lightened reserves for himself the right to consider what a dream is, not to submit it to intellectual professionals who will tell him what to make of these most intimate mysteries. And here are sentences from a letter Seferis received from his friend Angelos, who went to America and died there. "The feeling of New York. 'This country is starving spiritually amid her gold, like Midas. All this is relative of course . . . ,' " writes Angelos. " 'There is no place where you see man's naked soul more than over here; blacks with bloody faces, women crying in the subway.' " By the light of one's own judgment, and in one's own style, and with one's own powers, one sees the naked soul. When *oneself* has come *out*, many things become visible.

We have long been locked in by respectable opinion, by the prestigious sciences, by ideologies, locked in even by those modern masterpieces that have for a few decades now become a part of us. And I am speaking of that freedom to approach the marvelous which cannot be taken from us, the right, with grace, to make the most of what we have, to make as much as human beings ever have made of their condition. To do this by means of an art that, admitting defects and impurities and making the most realistic concessions, fully aware also of the sackful of "personal sentiments" that have the power to drive us mad, taking into account, finally, the cruelty, abasement, monstrosity, and evil that we know, is nevertheless true and powerful. Perhaps even, in spectacular defiance of this chaos that surrounds us, a divinely beautiful art.

II

A kind friend, worried about my soul, has sent me a handsomely printed little book called *The Bitch Goddess Success*. It was William James who first called success a bitch and identified her as the source of our most serious disease—the squalid cash interpretation of realized ambition. She was to blame, he thought, for the moral flabbiness of so many Americans.

I was glad to receive this anthology, for like a great many of us, I am aware of shameful shortcomings and I am eager for accurate diagnosis and grateful for correction and cure. The easiest way to get my attention is to approach me from the side of reform. So I sometimes sit down with this handy book and read a few frightening but improving sentences from Thoreau or Walt Whitman. But it occurred to me the other day that these great and lucky men were having it both ways: they were doubly successful. Whitman not only succeeded in writing poems of great beauty but saw through success as well and transcended it. He stands in the American heavens as a twin star—poetic and monitory.

We have always been as fascinated by admonition as by success.

America, please remember, is (or used to be) the land of the sampler and of Poor Richard. Grandmothers no longer embroider bracing sayings about sleeping sluggards, but the critical spirit, although changed, is very strong and omnipresent in its new forms. There was a Goddess of Rebukes, who worked in the shadows behind the Goddess of Success. Less prominent, she was perhaps more powerful and enduring. She makes herself felt today in the pervasive uneasiness experienced by all Americans. When the first Rockefeller declared that he was the trustee of common property, committed to his care by God's providence, he was defending himself sturdily against the second goddess. Is there a banker on Wall Street who would say any such thing today? God is no longer invoked by capitalists. When a member of President Eisenhower's cabinet said a few years ago that what was good for General Motors was good for the country, he caused a scandal. The wisdom of tycoons is no longer respected. Skepticism of success has increased. Make no mistake about it, the Rebuke Goddess is stronger than the Bitch Goddess. Tame executives who have learned of Max Weber at seminars in Aspen mention the Protestant Ethic but only as a phantom, one of the vanished forces of religion. What has carried over from the days of sin and preaching is a diffuse awareness of moral defectiveness, a sense of undeserved advantages, of ingratitude for good fortune; a feeling that this miraculously successful country has done evil, spoiled and contaminated nature, waged cruel wars, failed in its obligations to its weaker citizens, the blacks, the children, the women, the aged, the poor of the entire world.

Are we wrong thus to reproach ourselves? I haven't said that.

At the moment I am considering only our extraordinary sensitivity and our appetite for rebuke. Many of our intellectuals serve as priests of the Goddess of Rebuke, nagging, scolding, and infecting a vulnerable people with gnawing anxiety and remorse. In so doing *they* have become successful. They can claim that they do not serve the Bitch Goddess. Personally immune to her, they merely refer to her for purposes of rebuke. This was why my considerate friend sent me the handsomely printed little anthology.

Really, the Bitch Goddess is as dated as Thomas Edison's gramophone.

Anthologists have made Walt Whitman sound like a scold. Whitman is too grand for that. His denunciations of America's literary and moral failures—corruption, hollowness of heart, depravity, the hell under the breastbones—are as fresh and true as when I first read them in his *Democratic Vistas* half a century ago. Some of the other contributors to the Bitch Goddess volume are less impressive moralists, but I welcome their attacks too, because I believe with H. L. Mencken that being attacked does more good than harm. In a letter written to Theodore Dreiser in 1920, he said: "There is always a certain amount of truth in every attack, however dishonest. . . . I have learned more from attacks than from praise. In even the most vicious of them there is a touch of plausibility. There is always something embarrassing about unqualified praise. A man knows, down in his own heart, that he doesn't deserve it." Thus even the iconoclastic Mr. Mencken proves to be a genuine American who feels that we sinners need all the help we can get, that it is more useful and bracing to be damned than blessed, that if the soul is to build more stately mansions, it cannot do without the shaping suggestions only your enemies can make. Americans must be the most sententious people in history. Far too busy to be religious, they have always felt that they sorely needed guidance. I have a friend who tells me he thinks that the most powerful moral document in America was, for a time at any rate, the Boy Scout's Handbook. He believes the moral sentiments of this book caused untold harm to several generations of young men pure in heart by preparing them for high-principled victimization. Girls, he argues, were not hampered by such teachings. Their mothers brought them up in the real world. They saw their advantages clearly and took them up nimbly. Out of this comes what he calls the "Big Galahad Disaster." He goes on to draw a picture of sexual misery, mother hatred, alcoholism, and blasted illusions such as . . . well, such as you may find in five hundred American novels written since *The Great Gatsby*.

But I must hold to my subject. I was saying that I had taken to reading daily in *The Bitch Goddess Success* because I found it full of helpful suggestions, mantras for meditation. Mr. Charles Ives, for instance, in criticizing prize competitions in the arts, says that "a close union between spiritual life and the ordinary business of life is necessary" and that we must keep the balance between ordinary life and spiritual life. Well, this is of course the name of the game. But the maddening fact is that after you have said these obviously true things, you are up against it still. For when Mr. Ives, casting about for an example of the ordinary, says that "a month in the Kansas wheatfields may do more for a young composer than three years in Rome," you ask yourself when he himself last looked at ordinary life in Kansas. Again, he says: "If, for every thousand dollar prize, a potato field be substituted, so that these candidates of Clio can dig a little in real life . . . art's air might be a little clearer." Then he checks himself slightly by quoting a French moralist: *"On ne donne rien si liberalement que ses conseils."* But he has not checked himself in time. Digging potatoes? Kansas wheatfields? The last American artist to try those wheatfields was Vachel Lindsay when he went forth to preach his Gospel of Beauty in the days before the First World War. The ordinary business of life in the United States and its great cities is what it is because out in Kansas they aren't bringing in the sheaves as they did in 1910.

For further enlightenment I turn, in the same little book, to the contribution of the famous architect Louis H. Sullivan, who worked for so many years in Chicago. What he tells us is this: "As you are, so are your buildings; and, as are your buildings, so are you. You and your architecture are the same. Each is the faithful portrait of the other. To read the one is to read the other. To interpret the one is to interpret the other." If this is true, Mr. Sullivan has accounted in full for the proposition of Mr. Ives. The balance between ordinary life and spiritual life is manifest in what you see before your eyes. Now, I have spent most of my life in Chicago and have undoubtedly been influenced by its streets, houses, factories, office buildings, six-flats, sky-scrapers, but I can't agree that Chicago and I are completely reflected in each other. Mr. Sullivan is here driven into polemical exaggeration. You expect this from prophets. They must exaggerate. "Take heed!" Sullivan cries, when he has reached his prophetic altitude.

Did you think Architecture a thing of books—of the past? No! Never! It was, always, of its present and its people! It, now, is of the present, and of you! This Architecture is ashamed to be natural, but it is not ashamed to lie; so, you, as a people, are ashamed to be natural but not ashamed to lie. . . . This Architecture is filled with hypocrisy and cant. So, likewise, are you, but you say you are not. This Architecture is neurasthenic, so have you burned the candle at both ends. Is then this Democracy? . . . This Architecture has no serenity—sure sign of a people out of balance. . . . You know not what fullness of life signifies—you are unhappy, fevered, perturbed. In these buildings the Dollar is vulgarly exalted—and the Dollar you place above Man. You adore it twenty four hours each day: it is your God! These buildings show lack of great thinkers, real men—though you now, in your extremity, are in dire need of great thinkers, real men—Yet, here and there, a building bespeaks integrity—so have you that much of integrity. All is not false. What leaven is found in your buildings—such leaven is found in you. Weight for weight, measure for measure, sign for sign—as your buildings are, so are you!

So people are scolded and, in a Sunday mood, find it refreshing and beneficial. Well, of course there's a lot in this. Ruskin's message was similar. And there was William Morris too, and even, if you like, Blake with his Satanic Mills and London's chartered streets—though Blake would never have said that as our chartered streets were, so were we. You would have to be an architect to make precise counterparts of souls and houses. Still, one can easily understand what Chicago at the turn of the century must have done to a man like Sullivan as he inspected its hovels, slums, bungalows, workrooms, depots, plush hotels, flophouses, its railyards and warehouses and the mansions and tombs of the rich. Sullivan is easily identified as a man of the single-minded type. Democracy might be saved if we built not for the buck but for the occupant. Each of the Romantic friends of mankind knew exactly where the remedy was to be found. Assigned in high school to study Carlyle's famous essay on Robert Burns, I read: "Let me write the songs of a people, and you may write its laws." I was not surprised by this. Having grown up in Chicago, I had heard dozens of similar claims. Vegetarians argued that wars would stop if only we ceased to butcher animals. Bread cranks demanded that we check the decay of society by banning white flour. The temperance lecturers, the enemies of tobacco, saw in booze and in smoking dangers of the same dimensions that made Sullivan cry, "Take heed!" Moving into a more respectable intellectual sphere when I left high school, I learned from more refined theorists of the class struggle and the proletarian revolution; or about character neuroses of sexual origin that were destroying civilization; about the semantic chaos that made opposing interests incomprehensible to each other. One cause of misery, one remedy.

I was pleased to read some months ago what the Austrian writer Karl Kraus had said on his deathbed when he heard the news that the Japanese had gone into Manchuria: "None of this would have happened if people had only been more strict about the use of the comma." For the poet, it is the corruption of language and good usage that starts all the trouble. But Kraus spoke like a wit, and not like a monomaniac convinced that he knew the one remedy that would bring peace and happiness to everyone. The dying Kraus seems to have remained faithful to his vocation while conceding under the full weight of death that no conviction can be wholly free from absurdities. Bad punctuation no more nails down the case than class struggle, sexual neurosis, mass-produced bread, or ugly buildings—that is how I translate Kraus's comment.

The artist cannot avoid the disorder of contemporary reality, calling on bankers, builders, and the public to redeem democracy by building with honor or by adopting psychological, sexual, or political doctrines. He is bound, bitterly at the best of times, to the *amor fati*, as Nietzsche calls it, the imperative to embrace what is. Such an embrace is not a surrender; it is the necessary acceptance of a mass of complexities. To limit himself to any one of these single views would result in his segregation, would cut him off from seeing and from understanding what he sees. This mountain of complexities is the supreme datum. It is our great given. And it is *ours*.

Reading the journal of the Greek poet Seferis, I come upon a valuable entry. Seferis is speaking to his friend Sikelianos, who is ill. "I asked about his health. 'Yes, I do have high blood pressure,' he answered, 'but it is Sikelianos' high blood pressure!' "

Similar terms may be applied to the American writer's relations to his country—this antipoetic country: for it has been called antipoetic even by those who, like Tocqueville, found so much of it admirable. The poet Karl Shapiro writes (in a book of essays called *To Abolish Children*):

> It takes a good deal of courage (either that or a powerful inertia) to live in America. . . . Living in an antipoetic climate, in fact, is our chief form of poetic stimulation. An anthology of twentieth-century United States poetry will bear this out. Thematically, the poems are almost all of a piece: life in the land of

the airconditioned nightmare. That twentieth-century poetry has been content to exploit this theme almost exclusively is one of the chief weaknesses of our poetry. . . . It is all related to the horrors of Progress, the puritanism of hard work, the failure of success, the betrayal of the social character, and so on. We are a very social minded bunch of poets, carrying a burden of historical guilt which is way out of proportion to our sins. . . . It is instilled in the American poet at a very early age that something is antipoetic in the state of America. Some poets pin it on the social system; some on the economic system; some on the failure of spiritual belief; some on the religion of science; but all use the Way of Life as a target.

To the airconditioned nightmare or the Way of Life try to apply the Sikelianos standard. Try it also with Louis Sullivan's "as your buildings are, so are you." I have the same relation to Chicago's buildings as Sikelianos has to his high blood pressure. The dizzy spells, the fits of faintness, are *his*. The streets of Chicago are *mine*.

In one of his journal entries, Seferis writes that he thinks he has suffered the worst that could have happened to him in these times—the murderousness of Europe in the forties; exile; intimate knowledge of slaughter; the extermination camps. He says: "a flood of sensitivity makes me feel as if, stripped of protective skin, I'm wandering about with open wounds. Dust, flies, awkward gestures—all very painful. From deep down I long for the days when I could sometimes control this sensitivity with grace."

Now, against this background, bearing in mind the hints drawn from Sullivan, Shapiro, Sikelianos, Seferis, I go about Chicago this winter, considering the city as it is and remembering what it was like more than forty years ago. There are cities where change is slow; a Florentine can dismiss a mere forty years with a shrug. But here centuries of change can be crammed into a few years, and then and now can be as far apart as Stonehenge is from a computer. A bakery I knew in the days of wood-burning ovens, when cursing, good-natured bakers worked over the vats with their fists or brought loaves from the oven with the long wooden peel, is now automated. The workers look like research assistants. Then Petrush the watchman, the one who had lost a finger in a machine, slept drunk on the flour sacks, and the rats hopped over his feet; now there isn't a sack in sight. Machines fill the hoppers. The rats, once unwillingly tolerated, have been wiped out. The streets surrounding the new plant are not greatly changed. The Polish bungalows and six-flats still stand. Puerto Ricans are moving in; the Polish population is under siege.

The Poles were devoted to their property. They kept their bungalows in splendid repair, the brickwork pointed up and covered with waxy red, chocolate, or green paint. Employees of Dole Valve Co. or the casket factory on Carroll Avenue, warehouse and packing plant workers, locksmiths, electricians, press operators, came home after work to paint their fences of threaded pipe after work, to prune the trees or repair the wooden steps. The housewives wore frilly white transparent caps as they tended flowers growing in old washtubs on the lawn. I remember dull summer afternoons when whole blocks crackled with the baseball broadcast and golden houseflies slept in the privet hedges. (I wonder why these hedges became fly dormitories.) I am thinking, of course, of the twenties and thirties, when Chicago was a city made up of such neighborhoods. On warm Sundays in the prohibition era, the streets smelled of home-brewed beer and homemade sauerkraut. Weddings went on for three days, with stamping and roaring, and there were fistfights in the alleys. Nor because you made your own sauerkraut and drank home-brewed *piva* and swore Polish or Ukrainian oaths were you necessarily a foreigner. Polish veterans of the First World War gathered on Kościuszko Day with a band playing American tunes and carried banners of the Polish National Alliance as they marched patriotically in Humboldt Park. The marchers spoke either Polish or the English-based lingua franca, American. For they were Americans. To be American was neither a territorial nor a linguistic phenomenon but a concept—a set of ideas, really. This collective effort (seldom conscious) to do what was utterly untraditional and historically anomalous had been accurately described by Abraham Lincoln in phrases like "conceived in liberty" or "dedicated to the proposition that all men are created equal." I call your attention to words like "proposition" and "conceived." The Americanism of immigrants was to some degree conceptual and involved mental choices. It cannot be unimportant that a most significant historical development begins in choices among abstractions. At no stage of development can human beings in the present age avoid abstract choices. Marxism, too, made an offer of concepts to the cultureless, traditionless working class, but thinking was not to continue after you had joined the revolutionary party. Now, this is dangerous stuff. The necessary critical intelligence may not be forthcoming in the U.S., but it has not been proscribed by law; it has only been discouraged by the conditions of life.

It has always been my opinion—the opinion of an amateur "urbanologist"—that the Immigration Act of 1924 entirely changed the character of the city. No more carpenters, printers, mechanics, pastry cooks, cobblers, sign painters, street musicians, and small entrepreneurs entered the country from Greece, Serbia, Pomerania, Sicily. Such trades were infra dig for the children of immigrants. They improved themselves and moved upward. The neighborhoods they left were repopulated by an internal immigration from the South and from Puerto Rico. The country people, black or white, from Kentucky or Alabama, brought with them no such urban skills and customs as the immigrants had. Assembly-line industries had no need for skilled labor.

What we have now taken to calling "ethnic neighborhoods" fell into decay long ago. The slums, as a friend of mine once observed, were ruined. He was not joking. The slums as we knew them in the twenties were, when they were still maintained by European immigrants, excellent places, attractive to artists and bohemians as well as to WASPs who longed for a touch of Europe. The major consequences of the devastation of these neighborhoods, invariably discussed on these occasions—the increase in crime, the narcotics addiction, the welfare problem, the whole inventory of urban anarchy—I will spare you. I will appease the analytical furies by mentioning only three side effects of the change: the disappearance of a genial street life from American cities; the dank and depressing odors of cultural mildew rising from the giant suburbs, which continue to grow; the shift of bohemia from the slums to the universities. But I shall stop with that.

I sometimes think of Sullivan the prophet as I go about Chicago looking at its bungalows and six-flats. Architects tell me that the three-story six-flat extends the bungalow principle to the apartment house. After fifty years, one is reconciled to these brick shapes. You get the builder's *idea*. You see what sort of man *he* was, and you take his some-times lamentable work to your heart. In the entry of a typical six-flat are the brass mailboxes and the bells, three to a side, and a short flight of stairs. Indiana limestone or Vermont marble, pleasingly worn, leads to the glass door that brings you to the main staircase. There are sometimes more imposing entrances. Some six-flats have a pair of Doric or Ionic columns. Some have great clumsy square cement planters on pedestals, meant for geraniums or ferns but filled invari-ably with hard mud and ancient litter. More pretentious buildings had a pair of carved lions in front, now reduced by erosion and the beating of the years to lamblike figures. Six open porches at the front were common in Chicago, the coarse brick laid ornamentally, looking a lit-tle out of plumb. The elms have succumbed to blight. The commonest shade trees are cottonwoods. Few streets are well paved, but there is plenty of space. Land was cheap, and the government was liberal with it. There were grass plots between the sidewalks and the curbs, cement passages between the buildings, and then there were large backyards, which faced the alley with its line of small garages. Chicago's back porches are wooden, and the stairs are open to the weather, crudely built, trussed with planks that are hammered to the beams in long X's. These are what you still see when you ride the elevated trains. I was taken aback on my first trip to New York in the thirties to find the tracks of the Third Avenue El so close to the parlor windows of the tenements. There was always plenty of space in Chicago; it was ugly but roomy, plenty of opportunity to see masses of things, a large view, a never entirely trustworthy vacancy, ample grayness, ample brown-ness, big clouds. The train used to make rickety speed through the vi-olet evenings of summer over the clean steel rails (nothing else was clean) through the backyards of Chicago with their gray wooden porches, the soiled gray stairs, the clumsy lumber of the trusses, the pulley clotheslines. On the South Side you rode straight into the stockyard fumes. The frightful stink seemed to infect the sun itself, so that it was reeking as well as shining.

But I was speaking of the six-flats with their simple symmetry, like six-pack bungalows, economically built from the simple plans of hack architects, kitchen above kitchen, bathroom above bathroom, sun par-lor above sun parlor, the strict regularity making the plumbing, heat-ing, and wiring cheaper to install. In this mass production there were nevertheless trimmings, nifty touches, notes of elegance and aspiration. In each front room (no one ever called it a drawing room) was a dummy fireplace with artificial logs; an electric bulb was concealed within, and the heat of this bulb fluttered a pleated disk, which revolved and threw flickering shadows. At each end of the dud fireplace were bookcases with art nouveau glass doors. Above these, at each end of the mantelpiece, were two small hinged windows, also leaded. The fleur-de-lis was the commonest ornament. There might be a pane or two of stained glass even in the toilet. The dining room was separated from the front room by china cabinets, waist high. On top of these a pair of hollow wooden columns (serving no purpose) occasionally stood. In the dining room was a built-in buffet in the same style, often with a beveled mirror. These fixtures, turned out by the hundreds of thousands, were designed to be quickly and cheaply installed.

And this was how most of Chicago lived. You heard little through the six-flat walls. Occasionally a water pipe stuttered, jerking noisily, when a tap was turned on. It was through the ceilings that you heard your neighbors playing the piano or fox-trotting; you heard the tired, short-tempered breadwinner raging or the comfortable murmur of kitchen conversation on a winter night; or, on the first floor, the janitor's shovel gritting in the furnace room below. A commonplace good dullness. It was all uneventful, in the same sense that in the physical universe subatomic particles are uneventful, or the unseen explosion of stars is uneventful. Events too small or too large to be comprehended occurred, during which people sat in their parlors or on their porches.

The other day, toward the end of the short winter afternoon, I sat with one of my friends in his third-floor apartment, one of the usual six, looking out at the frost-hardened snow and the sunny smoke dragging, slow to rise when the thermometer has sunk below zero. We were having a drink in his dining room, which faces the rear of the building, the back stairs and the porches, blunt woodwork clapped together by literal-minded carpenters—the same rails, the same slats, treads, risers, floorboards, almost as familiar to a Chicagoan as his own body, seconding his physical existence. Beside all this lumber, a hibernating cottonwood, the big, sooty, soft, graceless tree in crocodile bark, just the sort of organism that would thrive in an environment like this. The cottonwood makes out, somehow, under the sidewalks and successfully transacts its botanical business with the summer murk. In April, it drops its slender sexual catkins, and the streets are fragrant for a day or two; in June, it releases its white fluff; by July, its broad spearhead leaves are as glossy as polished leather; by August, everything is fibrous and brown.

In Hyde Park, near the University of Chicago, the faculty lives peacefully enough in its six-flats, but a few blocks away in either direction are the black slums. A different sort of life, in Woodlawn and Oakwood, tears apart the six-flats and leaves them looking bombed out. They are stripped of salable metals, innards torn out, copper cable chopped to pieces and sold for scrap, windows all smashed, and finally fire and emptiness. Sometimes there is no one at all in these devastated streets—a dog, a rat or two. The grass-plot fences are torn up. True, they were inelegant, shapeless lumber, four-by-four rails set on an angle, the sharp edge upward to discourage lounging. But even these have been stolen, burned. The grass plots themselves have been stamped into solid clay.

If you want to know what happens in devastated Chicago, you must look into the welfare system, inquire in the grammar schools and high schools, read the sociologists, talk to the police and the firemen, visit the eviction court, the youth court, the violence court, the hospitals, clinics, the Audy "Home" for juvenile offenders, the county jail. The first fact that strikes you in courtrooms is that so large a part of Chicago's black population is armed—men, women, children, even, go into the streets with handguns. When the police make an arrest for illegal possession of guns, they have to justify themselves under questioning by defense lawyers who throw the Fourth Amendment at them. Stop and frisk. "How did you know the defendant was carrying a weapon?" "His jacket was open, and I saw it stuck in his belt." Or the prosecution says, observing the clumsy formalities of the courtroom, "Directing your attention, Officer, to the night of January 4, when you entered those premises on South Lawndale—tell the court why you did it." "Because we received a radio call at 1:15 A.M., instructing us to investigate a report that unlicensed liquor was being sold at this address. This was a burned-out condemned building, where we found sixteen men consuming unlicensed liquor and a pair of guns lying on the plank with the bottles. The defendant said they were his guns. He had no permit for them. I arrested him." A small-businessman, Puerto Rican, driving a van, was stopped by the police because he was weaving in traffic. He was carrying a gun. "I was taking my money to the bank, Your Honor—twelve hundred bucks. If they rob me, I close my business. I got to protect myself." His honor understands this, and a great deal more. His honor, a man in his late forties, is himself a product of these streets, so altered in the last decades. He served in Korea with the Marine Corps. Badly wounded but not crippled by an exploding land mine, he still plays handball and spends his virile holidays out West, breaking horses. After Korea he became a cop, he went to law school at night and, with a little political help, became a magistrate. The political connection is indispensable. And, in Chicago, entirely normal. Chicagoans used to prefer machine appointments to civil service procedures. They preferred the pols to the bureaucrats. The politicians know their constituents, and they are right to put a man like R. on the bench rather than a technician or a trained administrator. We know by now what these highly trained specialists are like. The need is for common sense, street experience, and sympathy, and Judge R. has all of these. He has had to defend himself now and then from attackers in the courtroom. A few months ago, a defendant who went at him with a knife was dragged away to a cell and chained to a bench. "So freaked out," said the judge, "that he tore the bolted bench out of the floor." I know that the judge himself, when he was in night court at Eleventh and State, carried his service revolver in his belt because it wasn't safe, at four in the morning, to walk to a parked car within a block of Chicago's police headquarters.

The hookers who hold up their tricks, the pushers who post bond from huge rolls of fresh bills, the rapists, the security guard at the shopping center who cracks a man's head for stealing a package of Certs, the schoolgirls who are caught lifting blue jeans, the senseless shootings and stabbings and ridiculous thefts, endlessly appear before the bench. We take away their guns, says the judge, and they buy more—send them to the house of correction, they come back.

Among schoolchildren, you look in vain for resemblances to the past. The schools are now almost entirely black and Puerto Rican. Chicago's teachers have the highest salary scale in the country, but they are not paid to keep order. That, in theory, at least, is the business of the security system. There is no security. What teachers teach is hard to determine, and *whom* they teach is even more mysterious. I have entered classrooms in which the pupils wandered about knocking out rhythms on the walls, absorbed in their transistors. No one seemed to grasp that the room had a center. No one heeded the teacher when she spoke. In this disorder you felt the ungrasped despair of the children. It pressed on your heart and viscera.

Some of the kids are like little Kaspar Hausers—blank, unformed; they live convulsively, in turbulence and darkness of mind. They do not know the meaning of words like "above," "below," "beyond." But they are *un*like poor innocent Kaspar in that they have a demonic knowledge of sexual acts, guns, drugs, and of vices, which are not vices here.

The young men and women as they stand before Judge R.'s bench are unreachable, incomprehensible. You will never know what they are thinking and feeling. I am speaking, please notice, of what sociologists call the underclass, not of black Chicago as a whole, the orderly, churchgoing black working people or members of the growing middle class. These struggle to maintain themselves in a seemingly disintegrating city and to protect their children from beatings in school corridors and assaults in hallways and toilets, from shootings in the playgrounds. No one goes out carefree for a breath of air at night.

It takes a gun in the waistband to give you freedom of the streets. If you are one of those dudes for whom it is a necessity to button up into a long coat of patchwork leather, to put on a fancifully swelling peaked cap , to wear clacking platform shoes and Berber, Polynesian, American Indian ornaments, to be bearded like the pard, you are ready for display. So you go out carrying a gun, a knife.

You see costumes of powerful originality in the Loop, where many of the shoppers are junior civil servants who work in the skyscrapers built by the federal government. The Loop streets at noon are a fashion show. And in courtrooms and detention cells, men charged with mugging are also dressed in high style, soiled but elegant, in suede and velveteens, hair teased out in saffron or henna puffballs. Dudes in torn shirts but with coat sleeves that pucker ingeniously at the shoulders wear blunt boots in four colors with red or yellow laces that crisscross up the leg.

Norman Macrae in *The Neurotic Trillionaire* lists our main institutions, in reverse order of importance, as the business corporations, the government, and the mechanisms for living together. What are these mechanisms? "A sense of community"; "values held in common." The

U.S.A., the most productive country in the industrial world, has apparently begun to put to itself curious questions, such as: "After production—what?" Or: "Why not begin to make use of commodities with gypsy vigor and, right now, in a setting of squalid glamour, use the miracle of productivity for 'camp' purposes and, day in, day out, turn street life into theater?"

The not-so-well-meaning friend who needled me about Success had not kept up with the times. Success today is in junk bonds, in hype, in capturing the presidency itself with the aid of spin doctors. When William James denounced the Bitch Goddess, he had in mind the bad strong men who had wounded and recklessly wasted the country, justifying themselves by the fortunes they had earned and their contribution to the growth of the nation. Simple old-fashioned stuff.

Perhaps the economic historian Schumpeter was not mistaken in suggesting that the bourgeois order no longer makes sense to the bourgeoisie and that the bourgeoisie can no longer really *care*.

From this one can only conclude that the cost of all the great successes—economic, technical, organizational—may be the abasement of man, the degradation one finds in Chicago (or New York, or Rome, or Kiev). We have to go back to the Bible, to Plato, to Shakespeare, to see what man once was.

What remains to be considered is the story of how this came to pass. And there is no reason why "the end of history" and the humiliation of man's pride should impose silence on the artist. Humankind goes on thinking or fantasizing about itself, and while it prefers grandeur, it can be fascinated by misery as well. Nietzsche warned us that modernity, the time of the Last Man, was upon us. But the mind to which this warning was addressed was inevitably assumed to be capable of grasping his meaning, his historical message—his tale.

Now, Nietzsche died in 1900.

Toward the end of *The American Scene*, written in the early years of our century, shortly after Nietzsche's death, Henry James devoted some pages to the future of Beauty in the United States. For he did not see why Beauty should not have a future here. He speaks of the "ground so clear of preoccupation, the air so clear of prejudgment . . . you wonder why some great undaunted adventure of the arts, meeting in its path none of the aged lions of prescription, of proscription, of merely jealous tradition, should not take place in conditions unexampled."

Are we here to illustrate those unexampled conditions? Is it possible that James gives a new twist to Hegel's "end of history," interpreting it as a fresh opportunity, a new clearing of the ground?

He seems to have been aware that the world had used America as its dump. Like Henry Adams et al., he thought that Europe had disposed of its human refuse here. And we must suppose that it would astonish him to learn that Europe in its deadly crises was saved in this century by American intervention, by the descendants of its "rejects."

When he visited the Lower East Side, James was alarmed by the Jewish immigrants he saw, appalled by their alien, ill-omened presence, their antics and their gabble.

There is no end to the curious ironies all this offers to an active imagination—and, in particular, to a descendant of East European Jews like myself.

THE DISTRACTED PUBLIC

(1990)

*O*ur schoolteachers, when I was a boy in Chicago, were something like missionaries. They earnestly tried to convert or to civilize their pupils, the children of immigrants from every European country. To civilize was to Americanize us all, and to Americanize was in no small part to Anglicize. We were to learn what America owed to English history, English law, and English literature. We were required to commit to memory speeches from *Julius Caesar, Macbeth,* and *Hamlet.* Coleridge, Wordsworth, and Shelley also were in the curriculum, and I memorized many of Wordsworth's poems. "The World Is Too Much with Us" may, for all I know, have been my introduction to the subject of distraction, for Wordsworth's warning not to lay waste our powers by getting and spending was not lost on me (although I had so little to spend). Nor did I miss his point about emotion recollected in tranquillity—or his emphasis on the supreme importance of a state of attention or aesthetic concentration that would put the world of profit and loss in its place.

Adolescents in the streets of industrial-commercial, getting-and-spending Chicago after the Great War had their heads filled with English Romantic poetry. More intoxicating than Shelley and in my case more influential than Wordsworth was the Coleridge of "The Ancient Mariner." The Mariner, you will remember, stops a guest on his way to a wedding and compels him to listen to his story. "Hold off, unhand me, greybeard loon!" cries the guest. Physical restraint is unnecessary. The Mariner's power is hypnotic: "He holds him with his

Romanes Lecture, Oxford University, 10 May 1990.

glittering eye." The wedding guest beats his breast. He cannot choose but hear. When I think of the power of a tale-teller to obtain attention, I remember that glittering eye.

The event, the festival to which the guest has been invited, the wedding, is now an affair on a world scale, and the Mariner would need an eye with the force of the sun to keep us from the feasting, the drinking, from the music of the bassoon and the beauty of the rosy bride. But then, few distractions today are as innocent and charming as a country wedding two centuries ago. Wedding invitations now are apt to bring to mind divorce statistics, thoughts of sexual instability, reflections on the sexual revolution and on venereal disease, on the effects of herpes and AIDS on marital fidelity. Children would also figure in our thoughts, concerns about their care and nurture, anxieties about their molestation by adults, the problems of subsidy for day-care centers where kids are dumped so that parents may be free to pursue their careers or celebrate the full equality of the sexes. It is no longer shades of the prison house that surround the growing child, but the terrors of a drug-addicted and criminal future. Your contemporary wedding guest has been transported by modern forces of malign magic into a sphere of distraction where instead of hearing village musicians he is blasted by a great noise—the modern noise.

Shakespeare's view of marriage is closer to the modern one than it is to Coleridge's idyll. Hamlet tells Horatio that the baked meats served at his father's funeral reappeared at his mother's wedding feast, and he asks Ophelia: "Why wouldst thou be a breeder of sinners?" Dying, he tells Horatio: "Absent thee from felicity awhile, / And in this harsh world draw thy breath in pain / To tell my story." Today Horatio would have to wait for an opportunity to get a word in edgewise. He wouldn't have an easy time of it. It's no simple matter to get people to listen, for it is increasingly difficult to make them heed or get them to agree. There are many Horatios with stories to tell, and rival Horatios and false Horatios bidding for your time and promising to be more innovative, more exciting, more startling, and more bloody than the other guys. And by now we, the listeners, have learned to hear and not to hear, to be both present and absent. We know a trick or two ourselves.

In the tone and in the slant of these words of mine you will quickly identify the modern theme, also known as the contemporary crisis or the apocalypse of our times, and you will have begun to brace or to deaden yourselves, as I myself am apt to do when lecturers wheel their big guns into position and prepare to lay down a barrage. I shall do my best here to avoid words like "the transformation of human consciousness" or "the new urban universe" or "the last man" or "mass societies." These are not necessarily meaningless, but they do, eventually, paralyze thought, and writers instinctively avoid them. They are distracting, and distraction is the word by which I designate the main difficulty. If you are in a trade that depends on your ability to obtain and hold attention, distraction is the hostile condition (massive and worldwide) that you are called upon to overcome.

I thought it only fair to trace the history of my preoccupation with this subject back to my adolescent Romanticism, to Wordsworth's contrast between factories, desk jobs, commerce, the wealth of nations, and the poet's "sea that bares her bosom to the moon." By Wordsworth and others I was made aware in adolescence that there were higher things and that these high things were under siege, were in trouble—their ground was diminishing. It was decades later that I began to realize how quixotic and comical it was in an age of technology, in the broad noon of industrial capitalism, with steel mills on one side and stockyards on the other, to be mooning over Lucy, "a violet by a mossy stone, / Half hidden from the eye."

But my own mental history is not my topic. I propose to examine a certain common phenomenon, an affliction from which no one can be immune and which obviously originates in the endless crises of this century. Distraction is the barrier through which a writer must force his way. Distraction is a term for the ordeal of getting people to attend to what is essential—to what writers, speakers, teachers, journalists, or advertisers believe to be essential.

The attention of the public (and there are thousands of publics in every large nation, but we must begin somewhere) is something like a continent penetrated, invaded, overrun by a variety of forces—political, commercial, technological, journalistic, agitational. Vast enterprises described as the communications industry inform, misinform, or disinform the public about politics, wars, and revolutions, about religious or racial conflicts, and also about education, law, medicine, books, theater, music, cookery. To make such lists gives a misleading impression of order. The truth is that we are in an unbearable state of confusion, of distraction.

We are now face-to-face with the Information Revolution, a subject that has come to horrify us all and that we would willingly avoid, if it were possible. But George Orwell warned us some time ago: "We have now sunk to a depth at which the restatement of the obvious is the first duty of civilized men." The obvious is that all minds are drawn toward a common field. To enumerate the forces that draw them would land us at once in this vast field or swamp of obviousness. For my purpose it is enough to point out that the common field is a scene of extraordinary excitement and agitation. Wordsworth, when he tells us that poetry comes from emotion recollected in tranquillity, is speaking from a world that has gone forever. I suspect that if you went to the Lake Country now to find tranquillity, you might have to dig for it like an archaeologist. In an age of enormities, the emotions are naturally weakened. We are continually called upon to have feelings—about genocide, for instance, or about famine or the blowing up of passenger planes—and we are all aware that we are incapable of reacting appropriately. A guilty consciousness of emotional inadequacy or impotence makes people doubt their own human weight. This is not to say that fundamental feelings, the moral sentiments so long bred into civilized peoples, have been wiped out altogether, but the sentiments have obviously been unable to keep up with the abominations that have been visited upon us, with the cruelties and crimes of this century. That the old feelings would survive the First World War was probably too much to expect. Their decline had already been observed and described long before 1914. The Second World War did the rest. One of the most powerful of modern philosophers has called what overtook us in this century "the night of the world." He saw Washington and Moscow as twin evils, in all significant respects identical. Urbanization and technology indisputably dominate the planet. A world society quite different from the one anticipated by Marxists has materialized, and we are looking for ways to come to terms with it.

Much of this is common knowledge, the Orwellian "obvious," yet we can't take it for granted that its meaning is entirely clear. The media (this unattractive American term can't be avoided) are supposed to keep us informed about these new developments, and of course they don't know what is happening. It is clear that, to use another American expression, they haven't got a clue. The technology at their disposal is one of the world's wonders—sublime, from an engineer's viewpoint—but the minds in charge are far behind the computers and the satellites.

A professor in California has estimated that on an average weekday the *New York Times* contains more information than any contemporary of Shakespeare would have acquired in a lifetime. I am ready to believe that this is more or less true, although I suspect that an educated Elizabethan was less confused by what he knew. He would certainly have been less agitated than we are. His knowledge cannot have lain so close to the threshold of chaos as ours.

What good is such a plethora of information? We have no use for most of the information given by the *New York Times*. It simply poisons us. I can't imagine that anybody would want to read every single page of a national paper like the *Washington Post*, the *Wall Street Journal*, *USA Today*, or the *Times* (some eighty percent of a local paper like the *Chicago Tribune* is taken up by advertisements). I grant that an obsessive reader might, if he were in the hospital or in great despair, read the daily *Times* from end to end. With the Sunday edition, this would be impossible. I shun the Sunday papers; the very look of them deadens my mind. Newspapers must be read cautiously, cannily, defensively. You know very well that journalists cannot afford to tell you plainly what is going on. There are dependable observers who believe that the press cannot give Americans anything like a true picture of the world. The written word is untrustworthy and the spoken word (radio and TV) irresponsible. The political analyst Michael Ledeen maintains that "many of the current media stars fully believe that they should define the national agenda." The power of the media, he says, is power seized from government. The Washington press corps has shown that it can destroy national leaders, and it is therefore greatly feared. The government does not seem able to understand or to explain its authority, the grounds for its decisions. Its antagonist, the press, interprets the government's operations in such a way as to destabilize public judgment. The jargon used by both antagonists excites, it thrills, it bewilders, it frightens, it confuses, it annihilates coherence, it makes comprehension utterly impossible. Nightly the anchorpersons preen, and while they deliver the news of the day they also pressure the public to take a progressive line. They want their listeners to come to the right conclusions about South Africa or Lithuania or unwed mothers—or the drug crisis, education, or race relations. They discuss confidently matters of which they knew nothing at all last week. In a word, they are showmen or entertainers; they are expected by their networks to look intelligent and to advance enlightened views. In public life everybody uses the same formulas—presidents, former presidents, senior statesmen, secretaries of state, leaders of the legal and other professions, celebrity financiers, talk-show hosts, university presidents, disc jockeys, leaders of the various liberation movements, star athletes, rock musicians, artists, singers, Hollywood personalities, publishers, the clerics of all churches, environmentalists. All these are indistinguishable in vocabulary and syntax from junk-bond brokers, public relations men, and lobbyists. Sportscasters, rap musicians, university rightists, university leftists, all employ the same language, the same rhetorical devices. Here is a list of some of the words most commonly used: "consensus," "sensitivity," "creative," "role model," "entitlement," "empowerment," "impacted," "quality time" (the time a working mother wishes to give her children in "day care"), "concerned," "the excluded" or "the marginalized" (Jesse Jackson's Rainbow Coalition might be described as a majority formed out of excluded or marginalized minorities). Some of these terms come from psychology, from the social sciences, or from schools of divinity (the theologians have contributed words like "compassion" or "situated"—as in "spiritually situated"). Others come from higher intellectual quarters. "Charisma" is borrowed from Max Weber. "Concern" is probably a translation of Heidegger's *Sorge*.

At a recent postmodernist convention of professors, held at the University of Utah last March, one of the speakers promoted a concept called "resistance postmodernism": "We want to see whether these discourses [postmodernist ideas] can be used for political and social change. We want to know how we can deal with oppression, inequality and exploitation that exists not only in the United States but globally" (*New York Times*, April 8, 1990, as reported by Richard Bernstein). What the professor really meant is hard to say, but unless you talk this sort of nonsense, the educated public will not take you seriously. In today's *Chicago Tribune* I learn that the American Catholic bishops have hired, at a fee of five million dollars, a public relations firm to direct their anti-abortion campaign: to "practice paid persuasion," says the writer of this *Tribune* article. Evidently the Church itself is unable to preach against mortal sin and is forced to turn to experts who better understand mass culture and the mind of the public. The company hired by the American bishops successfully conducted one of Ronald Reagan's campaigns for the presidency. So the doctrines on which the Church stands are apparently considered intransmissible. You must persuade or hypnotize the public, or influence it by symbolic manipulations, by magical substitutes for fact and thought. Obviously—to turn again to George Orwell and the duty of civilized men to restate the obvious—the Church, too, must bow to the power of television.

People are understandably bored and irritated, tormented (distraction *is* a torment) by discussions of TV. I, too, dislike this sort of punditry, but if distraction is your theme, there is no way to avoid TV. I shan't be asking this time what can be done about lust and violence on the tube. Nothing can be done. Television has proved that millions of people passionately love lust and violence. I am concerned here with the contribution TV makes to the mass of our distractions. It is the principal source of the noise peculiar to our time—an illuminated noise that claims our attention not in order to concentrate it but to disperse it. Watching the tube, we are induced to focus on nothing in particular. Can we find nothing good to say about TV? Well, yes, it brings scattered solitaries into a sort of communion. TV allows your isolated American to think that he participates in the life of the entire country. It does not actually place him in a community, but his heart is warmed with the suggestion (on the whole false) that there is a community somewhere in the vicinity and that his atomized consciousness will be drawn back toward the whole. But through the promise of unity it leads us into wild diversity. And perhaps what we really look to it for is distraction—distraction in the form of a phantom or an approximate reality. Pointless but intense excitement holds us in TV dramas. We hear threatening music. A killer with a gun steals into the room of a sleeping woman. More subliminal sounds of danger, pointlessly ominous. The woman wakes and runs to the kitchen for a knife. The cops are on the case. We watch as the criminal is pursued through night streets; shots, a death; a body falls from a roof. Then time is up, another drama begins. Now we are in a church. No, we are in a lecture hall; no again—a drawer opens in a morgue. A woman is looking for her kidnapped child. Then that ends, and we are on the veld with zebras and giraffes. Then with Lenin at a mass meeting. And suddenly we flash away to a cooking school; we are shown how to stuff a turkey. Next the Berlin Wall comes down. Or flags are burning. Or a panel is worrying about the drug crisis. More and more public themes, with less and less personal consciousness. Clearly, personal consciousness is shrinking.

Remote-control devices permit us to jump back and forth, mixing up beginnings, middles, and ends, alternating Westerns with gamblers in Chinatown or talk shows. This hopping from channel to channel is, according to a survey conducted by the Nielsens, a popular game among adolescents. Mastery belongs to the holder of the switch who diverts himself with inconsequence, and his willful switching is something like an assertion of independence, or a declaration of autonomy, of supreme immunity. Each separate intelligence at its separate command post declares itself free from all influence. The kid with the clicker is the Boss. He can cope with any amount of randomness or inconsequence—with anything you can throw at him. This is clowning, of course, but it is also a sort of triumph for personal consciousness. Here consciousness emptily asserts itself. The emptiness of the assertion makes it akin to autism, a word defined in my dictionary as a state of mind characterized by daydreaming, hallucinations, and disregard of external reality.

Of course, the ceaseless world crisis, otherwise known as the chaos of the present age, is not the work of the communications industry and its Information Revolution; but for our peculiar pseudoknowledge of what is happening, for the density of our ignorance, and for the inner confusion and centerlessness of our understanding, for our agitation, the communicators are responsible. Intellectuals and universities, from the ideological side, also have much to answer for.

"Teach us to care and not to care, / Teach us to sit still," T. S. Eliot wrote, and when I was young I read these lines as a prayer for poise under threat of dissolution, but I have wondered in later years whether Eliot really believed that we might ever be able to sit still. He also said, perhaps half jokingly, that he couldn't bear to read the newspapers: "They are too exciting." Was he really able to kick the habit? I confess that like millions of others, I still need my news fix daily. Civilized people evidently find it necessary to maintain, inwardly, a high level of excitement and are apt to feel that their vital forces must be replenished by headlines.

So it's politics and murder, famine, planes exploding in flight, drug wars, hostage taking, the latest developments in the superpower drama. The average duration of a scandal or a disaster is not long, and since terrible events are presented by networks whose main focus is diversion, entertainment, quick change, we are always en route to the next shock. It is the agitation level that matters, not this or that enormity. And because we can't beat distraction, we are inclined to join it. A state of dispersed attention seems to offer certain advantages. It may be compared to a sport like hang gliding. In distraction we are suspended, we hover, we reserve our options.

Now, when a writer, a novelist, offers such a description, the democrat in him, the citizen, demands to know what he is going to do about all this, and as the heir to the literary moralism of the last century, he may be tempted to weigh, to measure, to analyze, to prescribe, to call for clarity, for justice, to edify. And of course he may also feel a contrary urge and refuse absolutely to weigh, to measure, to analyze, to prescribe. This sometimes amounts to the same thing; there are white edifiers and black ones. Many excellent contemporary writers feel that edification in any form is a mistake, that it is a great sin to write novels with long discursive or analytic passages, à la Thomas Mann or André Malraux. Is cognitive activity the cure for distraction? Will ideas cure this sickness?

Increasingly, I find myself agreeing with Vladimir Nabokov. A work of art, Nabokov argued, detaches you from the world of common travail and leads you into another world altogether. It carries you into a realm of aesthetic bliss. Can there be anything more desirable than aesthetic bliss? Nothing can be more desirable, and it is especially so when the massed powers of cognition (among which vain cognitions and false cognitions are prominent) oppress and restrict the free imagination.

If Freud was right in saying that happiness is nothing more than the remission of habitual suffering, then it may be legitimate to say that art, in bringing relief from the absurd strivings of consciousness, from the enslaving superego, frees us for aesthetic bliss. Endless cycles of crisis have made us superserious theorists of modernism and postmodernism, definers and redefiners of culture and tradition. It is demanded of us that we place ourselves historically. To illustrate this I shall quote (as briefly as possible) from a recent book on modern literary culture: "The term *postmodernism* had not been coined, but the atmosphere of *The Loved One* is aftermodernist. Something has died—that, above all, is clear. In the aftermath, the Muse of poetry has a new vocation prepared for her servants. . . . As *The Loved One* neared completion, *Waiting for Godot*, the emblematic work of postmodernism, was in preparation. . . ." It is implied here that important modern writers have to place themselves and place themselves appropriately in this joint project and make an appropriate statement about the burden of modern civilization. But why should we demand emblematic works of ourselves or our contemporaries? Isn't aesthetic bliss nicer? Why should writers pump intellectual iron together with historians, philosophers, religious thinkers, and psychologists—the Nietzsches, the Spenglers, the Heideggers, or the Jungs? They *will* naturally take an interest in these muscular giants, but what do they add to literature by themselves accepting heavy theoretical labor? I really don't care to think about the inevitable succession of modernism by after- and postmodernism. I will grant you the "night of the world" and accept the fullest listing of the charges: emptiness of life, the unity of mankind on the lowest level, the increasing vacuity of personal existence, the victory of urbanization and technology—in short, the prevalence of nihilism, the absence of the noble and the great.

All the more reason, I think, to embrace aesthetic bliss when you can get it. For when it is available in modern form, as it is from time to time, we have reason to be profoundly grateful to its creators.

As for the classy world-historical all-embracing work aforementioned, with its modernism, aftermodernism, postmodernism, dense with authoritative names like Vico or Foucault or Eliot or Quine or Bradley, with metaphilosophers and metacritics, such work makes its own contribution to distraction. The distraction of sophisticates is even harder to dispel than the distraction of proletarian mobs. When their attention is solicited, these metacritics give it grudgingly. To sway them you have to display prestigious credentials. "What is most distinctively modern in modern literature," Professor Richard Rorty says, "depends for its effect upon straight-men, and especially upon philosophers." Rorty also observes that many critics apparently wish to speak in philosophical tones and apparently think that "literature can take the place of philosophy by *mimicking* philosophy." This does not simplify the tasks of the aesthetic-bliss people and the would-be delight-givers.

Since no path in modern life can possibly lead to a rose-garden sanctuary, there are difficulties about aesthetic bliss too, about the means by which it is generated. In *Lolita*, Nabokov's narrator, Humbert Humbert, is an enchanting Mariner. We willingly surrender and gladly give up a dozen weddings to go across the U.S.A. with Humbert and his nymphet. True love, ideal love, can have only one single object, but in an age as defective as our own, Eros, too, is inevitably kinky. We cannot refuse Humbert our fullest attention, but often he also grates us. He is not in all respects a pleasant patrician. Many of his judgments are madly arbitrary. His snobbery is particularly disagreeable. He can be very cutting about minor errors in conversational French, and he occasionally abuses the attention we so wholeheartedly give him. But these are petty objections, when you think what a great gift he makes us: Eros the comedian, a bit tatty here and there, but nonetheless a child of the gods—godlike. Still, the aesthetic bliss Humbert affords is uneven, and the cause of its fluctuation lies in the curious modern intricacy of Humbert's character and also the character of his perverse enemy, Quilty. Nabokov does not want us to make character analyses in the modern style, but his hero's character leads us toward the abysses created by the modern cognitive habit, for which Nabokov has a deadly loathing. These modern cognitive operations bring us back to the heart of distraction: the curious instability of disorderly consciousness.

What I call distraction may also be described as the dispersion of themes. It is this dispersion of themes that agitates and confuses us. Naturally, my point of view in a discussion such as this is that of a writer, so it is as a writer that I ask whether the difficulties caused by this dispersion or distraction can be surmounted. By a writer fit for the job, yes. Such a writer can obtain the attention of the tormented. He must be a fit person to entrust with the hoarded and guarded attention of someone who has actually been waiting to be asked.

My task has been, for some time now, to take my bearings and stay on course. I am a performer and speak as a performer. But for about two centuries, performers have also felt it necessary to vindicate themselves while performing. Someone has written about William Blake that his work was "one prolonged vindication of the cause of all the artists in the world." In these modern centuries, the writer becomes the embattled artist at war with society, with the power of money, with tyranny, etc. I need not and will not go into all that now. But when I think back on my life as a performer, I often recall a sentence from one of Samuel Butler's essays: "Life is like playing a violin solo in public and learning the instrument as one goes on," and then I add that there is a drunken riot in the concert hall, and nobody at all is minding the music.

The simile is exaggerated, of course; it is a caricature. The grain of truth in it is that when you are at last ready to play, you cannot be sure of your listeners. They will predictably be tormented by a plethora of alternatives. Why should they be here, not elsewhere? And why should they listen to you, not to somebody else? A craving to make the best possible use of their time may turn them fretful, even feverish. "As well him as another," Molly Bloom said to herself when Leopold wooed her. She might as easily have said, "As well another as him."

In short, the performer must have the power to impose himself. It helps if he is a Nabokov and speaks with the natural authority of an artist-patrician, a boyar, a hereditary autocrat. This, however, gives an ideological color to the problem, and people have indeed begun to protest and to denounce exploitation by tyrannical traditionalists, misogynists, racists, imperialists—those dead white males whose works, called classics, are imposed upon us. Not everybody can be seduced by the promise of bliss. For some, liberation (perhaps pseudoliberation) is the higher aim. Or the shattering of icons. Or restlessness without limits. As the writer Leonard Michaels has recently put it: "We have been abandoned to the allure of non-specific possibility, or the thrill of infinite novelty." He also says, in the same paragraph, that "value has fled the human particular."

Now, writers are naturally attentive; they are trained in attentiveness, and they induce attentiveness in their readers (without a high degree of attentiveness, aesthetic bliss is an impossibility). "Try to be one of those people on whom nothing is lost," was Henry James's advice to apprentice novelists. And Tolstoy in his essay on Maupassant said that a writer should write clearly, take a moral view of his subject, and be capable of giving the most intense attention to his subject and his characters. In no uncertain terms, Nietzsche tells us that the modern age concerns itself primarily with Becoming and ignores Being. And so perpetual Becoming preys on us like a deadly sickness.

Without being a licensed philosopher, I grant myself permission to associate distraction with Becoming and Becoming with progress and to observe that we have made rapid (so rapid that it appears magical) progress toward a technological world society. And whether a world society can be human is a question writers (performers) are obviously not capable of answering but evidently cannot avoid putting, since fictional characters, together with the rest of mankind, are involved in this transformation. Already observers like Mr. Michaels have warned that value is fleeing (or has already fled) the human particular.

Well, the writer cannot make the seas of distraction stand still, but he can at times come between the madly distracted and their distractions. He does this by opening another world. "Another world," I am fully aware, carries suggestions of never-never land, and people will be asking themselves how seriously any man can be taken who still believes that the moronic inferno can be put behind us, bypassed or quarantined by art. It isn't as though the champions of art had won any great victories. Madame Bovary dies of arsenic, but Flaubert the artist-chronicler is dangerously wounded too. Tales of love and death can be mortal to the teller. Yet for many people (certain Russian artists of the Stalin period, for instance), the abandonment of art cannot happen. Dictatorships did not succeed in frightening artists to death, nor has democracy done them in altogether, although some observers consider democracy to be by far the greater threat. In the West, Stalinism is sometimes seen as a political disaster but, to artists, a blessing in disguise. It kept them serious. They died, leaving us great works. With us, the arts sink into the great, soft, permissive bosom of basically indifferent and deadly free societies: and so goodbye. A gulag death is obviously superior to a Hollywood or Manhattan one. So it's damn braces, bless relaxes. "Relaxes" denatures and dissolves. The acid by-products of well-being and distraction eat us up. Wicked, murderous state stepmothers are better for the little princesses of art than the Lady Bountiful, quality-time vulgarians whose slovenly and ignorant toleration is death.

Civilized opinion was divided in this century by the revolution of 1917, which promised mankind everything it had ever hoped for, and it was tenaciously supported by advanced thinkers long after it became apparent, even to the less advanced, that the Russia that brought an end to the imperialist war of 1914 was great only in the extent of its economic and political disasters. Marxist Leninism, which contributed so much to the unpleasant distraction of the world for seven decades, while it still has passionate followers in Africa and Asia, is largely discredited in the West (and a portion of the East). Though it gives us nothing to exult over or brag about, we may as well face the ambiguous complex of facts suggesting that not Russia but the U.S.A., a country ideologically drab and insignificant, has made the real revolution of this century. You need not take the word of a mere writer (performer) for it. Grave scholars, like the Hegelian Alexandre Kojève, have made this argument. "One can even say," Kojève writes, "that from a certain point of view, the United States has already attained the final stage of Marxist 'Communism,' seeing that practically all the members of a 'classless society' can from now on appropriate for themselves everything that seems good to them, without thereby working any more than their heart dictates."

He continues: "Now, several voyages of comparison made (between 1948 and 1958) to the United States and the USSR gave me the impression that if the Americans give the appearance of rich Sino-Soviets, it is because the Russians and the Chinese are only Americans who are still poor but are rapidly proceeding to get richer. I was led to conclude from this that the 'American way of life' was the type of life specific to the post-historical period, the actual presence of the United States in the world prefiguring the 'eternal present' future of all humanity. Thus Man's return to animality appears no longer as a possibility that was yet to come, but as a certainty that was already present."

These sentences may surprise but they will not astonish us. The "return to animality" is a bit of a shock, but we will quickly see that no insult is intended. Modern life meets every creaturely need. History is in the main (if we accept Kojève's view) the struggle to meet the creaturely needs of humankind. Everything we ever wanted is here—except, from the Hegelian standpoint, transcendence. Now, the final or systematic account of transcendence and Spirit is not my cup of tea. I have invoked M. Kojève primarily to support my flimsy novelist's notion that the people I write about are the beneficiaries and, in part, the victims of a revolution more extensive and permanent than the revolution of 1917. The realization of these perennial desires of the species will naturally take some time. Such realization is not like the mental act of grasping an idea. It must all be lived through, and we cannot expect to live long enough to see the outcome.

I have said enough to bring us fully to the heart of distraction—the subject of my seemingly endless sermon. Can our distraction (Wyndham Lewis called it "the moronic inferno") be induced to yield to attention? I have suggested that distraction is a mental and emotional counterpart to revolution and world crisis, that it is probably a by-product of nihilism. I have observed also that it is inviting. It can be seductive. It is often flattering. Pascal, a great observer of such things, said that the happiness of highly placed persons was due to their having a crowd to amuse them. "A king," he wrote, "is surrounded by men who take wonderful care never to let him be alone and think about himself." So in a sense we are all highly placed persons—kings even—or treated as such by those who control (but is control really the word for it?) the electronic instruments that disseminate information-entertainment-opinion in hypnotic words and images.

Writers, poets, painters, musicians, philosophers, political thinkers, to name only a few of the categories affected, must woo their readers, viewers, listeners, from distraction. To this we must add, for simple realism demands it, that these same writers, painters, etc., are themselves the children of distraction. As such, they are peculiarly qualified to approach the distracted multitudes. They will have experienced the seductions as well as the destructiveness of the forces we have been considering here. This is *the* destructive element in which we do not need to be summoned to immerse ourselves, for we were born in it.

If the remission of pain is happiness, then the emergence from distraction is aesthetic bliss. I use these terms loosely, for I am not making an argument but rather attempting to describe the pleasure that comes from recognition or rediscovery of certain essences permanently associated with human life. These essences are restored to our consciousness by persons who are described as artists. I shall speak here of artists who write novels and stories, since I understand them better than poets or dramatists. When you open a novel—and I mean of course the real thing—you enter into a state of intimacy with its writer. You hear a voice or, more significantly, an individual tone under the words. This tone you, the reader, will identify not so much by a name, the name of the author, as by a distinct and unique human quality. It seems to issue from the bosom, from a place beneath the breastbone. It is more musical than verbal, and it is the characteristic signature of a person, of a soul. Such a writer has power over distraction and fragmentation, and out of distressing unrest, even from the edge of chaos, he can bring unity and carry us into a state of intransitive attention. People hunger for this. The source of their hunger is found in the aforementioned essences. In our times, those essences are forced to endure strange torments and privations. There are moments when they appear to be lost beyond recovery. But then we hear or read something that exhumes them, even gives them a soiled, tattered resurrection. The proof of this is quite simple, and everyone will recognize it at once. A small cue will suffice to remind us that when we hear certain words—"all is but toys," "absent thee from felicity," "a wilderness of monkeys," "green pastures," "still waters," or even the single word "relume"—they revive for us moments of emotional completeness and overflowing comprehension, they unearth buried essences. Our present experience of anarchy does not destroy this knowledge of essences, for somehow we find ways to maintain an equilibrium between these contradictories, and others as well.

But this is why the artist competes with other claimants to attention. He cannot compete in the athletic sense of the word, as if his object were to drive his rivals from the field. He will never win a clear victory. Nothing will ever be clear; the elements are too mixed for that. The opposing powers are too great to overcome. They are the powers of an electrified world and of a transformation of human life the outcome of which cannot be foreseen.

Tocqueville predicted that in democratic countries the public would demand larger and larger doses of excitement and increasingly stronger stimulants from its writers. He probably did not expect that public to dramatize itself so extensively, to make the world scene everybody's theater, or, in the developed countries, to take to alcohol and drugs in order to get relief from the horrors of ceaseless intensity, the torment of thrills and distractions. A great many writers have done little more than meet the mounting demand for thrills. I think that this demand has, in the language of marketing, peaked. Can so much excitement, so much disorder, be brought under control? Such questions must be addressed to analysts and experts in a variety of fields. Prediction is their business. The concern of tale-tellers and novelists is with the human essences neglected and forgotten by a distracted world.

THERE IS SIMPLY TOO MUCH

TO THINK ABOUT

(1992)

*A*sked for an opinion on some perplexing question of the day, I sometimes say that I am for all the good things and against all the bad ones. Not everybody is amused by such a dinner-table joke. Many are apt to feel that I consider myself too good for this world, which is, of course, a world of public questions.

Was President Kennedy right to tell us, "Ask not what your country can do for you; ask what you can do for your country"? In the ordinary way of life, what can one do for one's country? One can be preoccupied with it. That is, one can hold enlightened opinions. Most people conclude that there isn't much, practically speaking, they can do. A few become activists and fly around the country demonstrating or remonstrating. They are able to do this in a free and prosperous America. I speculate sometimes about the economics of militancy. There must be a considerable number of people with small private incomes whose lifework is to march in protest, to picket, to be vocal partisans. At this moment the *Roe* v. *Wade* issue has attracted demonstrators to Washington and to Buffalo. Atomic energy, environmentalism, women's rights, homosexual rights, AIDS, capital punishment, various racial issues—such are the daily grist of newspapers and networks. The public is endlessly polled, the politicians and their advisers are guided in their strategies by poll statistics. And this, let's face it, is "the action." This is where masses of Americans find substance, importance, find definition through a combination of passion and ineffectuality. The level of public discussion is unsatisfactory. As we become aware of this, our hearts sink. The absence of articulate political leadership in the country makes us feel that we are floundering.

What are we, today, in a position to do about the crises chronicled daily in the *New York Times*—about the new Russia and the new Germany; about Peru and China and drugs in the South Bronx and racial strife in Los Angeles, the rising volume of crimes and diseases, the disgrace of the so-called educational system; about ignorance, fanaticism, about the clownish tactics of candidates for the presidency?

Is it possible to take arms against a sea of troubles so boundless?

Wherever it is feasible, arms, of course, should be taken. But we must also consider what it requires to face the trouble-sea in its planetary vastness—what an amount of daily reading it demands of us, to say nothing of historical knowledge. It was brave of Karl Marx to assert that the time had come for thinkers to be doers. But to consider what his intellectual disciples *did* in the twentieth century will send us back to our seats. It is, after all, no small thing to correct our opinions frequently, and when you come right down to it, the passivity imposed upon us forces us to acknowledge how necessary it is to think hard, to reject what is mentally dishonorable.

We feel heavy when we recognize the limits of our effectiveness in the public sphere, when we acknowledge the weight of the burden laid upon us and the complexities we have to take into account—when we become aware of the impoverished state of public discussion. Reading and hearing what most editorialists and TV commentators tell us about the Los Angeles crisis, for instance, forces us to recognize that few opinionmakers are able to think at all. To leave matters in their hands is an acute danger.

"The Good are attracted by Men's perceptions, / And think not for themselves." William Blake, who wrote this about two hundred years ago, did not really believe in the goodness of the nonthinking good. He meant that the nonthinking good were inclined to surrender their mental freedom to the cunning—the sharpers and con artists—who would eventually show "their private ends."

It is apparent to experienced observers that well-meaning people emphatically prefer the "good" things. Their desire is to be identified with the "best." The more prosperous and the "better educated" they are, the greater the effort to identify themselves with the most widely accepted and respected opinions. So they are naturally for justice, for caring and compassion, for the abused and oppressed, against racism, sexism, homophobia, against discrimination, against imperialism, colonialism, exploitation, against smoking, against harassment—for all the good things, against all the bad ones. Seeing people virtually covered with credentials, buttons, badges, I am reminded of the layers of medals and campaign ribbons worn by Soviet generals in official photographs.

People who have the best of everything also desire the best opinions. Top of the line. The right sort of right thinking, moreover, makes social intercourse smoother. The wrong sort exposes you to accusations of insensitivity, misogyny, and, perhaps worst of all, racism. As the allure of agreement—or conformism—grows, the perils of independence deepen. To differ is dangerous. And yet, as we all must know, to run from the dangers of dissent is cowardly.

So much for the first part of Blake's proposition: "The good are attracted by Men's perceptions." Now for part two: "And think not for themselves."

To illustrate what this may mean, one need go no further than the daily papers. As I write, the *Chicago Tribune* reprints a piece on Michael Jackson, the pop music prodigy, by Charles Burress, a staff writer for the *San Francisco Chronicle*. Michael Jackson's video "Black and White" attracted a worldwide audience of half a billion youngsters. Jackson, Mr. Burress says, has achieved "monumental prominence in the cultural landscape." To what is this prominence due? Jackson frolics over the boundaries of race and sex, Burress writes. "We've told our children that race shouldn't matter, that boys and girls are equal and that many sexual roles are arbitrary. Could youngsters be enthralled at seeing these ideas made flesh?

"The refrain in the 'Black and White' video is 'It doesn't matter if you're black or white.' Most riveting is a computer-enhanced segment where a person changes ethnicity and sex in rapid succession. Jackson seems to be saying we are first of all human, and secondarily male or female, one race or another. He urges us toward human unity and away from prejudice."

And finally: "In a world threatened by racial tensions and overpopulation, the survival instinct could summon a new human, one who has no single race and who, by being most asexually androgynous, is less subject to the procreative urge."

Readers may feel that I have gone far out of my way to find such a bizarre example. But no. Those of us who read widely in the popular press and watch the flakier channels of cable TV know that views like Burress's are not at all uncommon. The language he uses identifies him as a college graduate—possibly, though not necessarily, a California product. Besides, his preoccupation is with what appears to have become a national project—namely, the fashioning of a new outlook, a new mind. The mind of this "new human" is synthetic, homogeneous, improved. It transcends the limits of heredity, nature, and tradition, goes beyond all limits and all obstacles. "How do we object to [Jackson's] changing his appearance when we tolerate many body alterations, from shaving and bodybuilding to face-lifts and sex-change operations?" Burress asks.

Now, a term widely understood to signify not thinking for oneself is ideology. Ideology for Marx was a class-induced deformation, a corruption of reality by capitalism. Ideology, to make it short, is a system of false thinking and nontruth that can lead to obedience and conformity. In putting Mr. Burress in the high company of Marx, my sole purpose is to throw light on the attempted invention of an altogether new human type. This new and "more desirable" American will be all the good things: a creature of no single race, an androgyne, free from the disturbing influence of Eros. The idea is to clobber everything that used to be accepted as given, fixed, irremediable. Can it be that we are tired of whatever it is that we in fact are—black, white, brown, yellow, male, female, large, small, Greek, German, English, Jew, Yankee, Southerner, Westerner, etc.—that what we now want is to rise above all tiresome differences? Perhaps gene fixing will eventually realize this utopia for us.

But the rejection of thinking in favor of wishful egalitarian dreaming takes many other forms. There is simply too much to think about. It is hopeless—too many kinds of special preparation are required. In electronics, in economics, in social analysis, in history, in psychology, in international politics, most of us are, given the oceanic proliferating complexity of things, paralyzed by the very suggestion that we assume responsibility for so much. This is what makes packaged opinion so attractive.

It is here that the representatives of knowledge come in—the pundits, the anchormen, the specialist guests of talk shows. What used to be called an exchange of views has become "dialogue," and "dialogue" has been invested with a certain sanctity. Actually, it bears no resemblance to any form of real communication. It is a hard thing to describe. Two or more chests covered with merit badges are competitively exposed to public view. We sit, we look, we listen, we are attracted by the perceptions of hosts and guests.

When I was young, the great pundits were personalities like H. G. Wells or George Bernard Shaw or Havelock Ellis or Romain Rolland. We respectfully read what they had to say about communism, fascism, peace, eugenics, sex. I recall these celebrities unsentimentally. Wells, Shaw, and Romain Rolland brought punditry into disrepute. The last of the world-class mental giants was Jean-Paul Sartre, one of whose contributions to world peace was to exhort the oppressed of the third world to slaughter whites indiscriminately. It is hard to regret the passing of this occasionally vivid spirit.

On this side of the Atlantic, our present anchormen are the successors of the Arthur Brisbanes, Heywood Brouns, and Walter Lippmanns of the twenties, thirties, and forties. Clearly, figures like Peter Jennings, Ted Koppel, Dan Rather, and Sam Donaldson, with their easy and immediate access to the leaders of the nation, have infinitely more power than those old wordmen their predecessors. Rather odd-looking, today's tribunes (not magistrates chosen by the people), with their massive hairdos, are the nearest thing observable to the wigs of Versailles or the Court of St. James's. These crowns of hair contribute charm and dignity but perhaps also oppress the brain with their weight. They make us aware, furthermore, of the study and calculation behind the naturalness of these artists of information. They speak so confidently and so much on such a variety of topics—do they really know enough to be so fluent? On a talk show not long ago, a prominent African-American declared that the Roosevelt administration had closely supported Hitler until the Pearl Harbor attack. The journalists on his panel made no objection to this. Had none of them heard of Lend-Lease, hadn't they read about FDR, were they unaware of

Nazi hostility toward the United States? Can these high-finish, well tailored and hairstyled interviewers know so little about history?

America is, of course, the land of the present; its orientation is toward the future. That Americans should care so little about the past is fetching, even endearing, but why should we take the judgments of these splendid-looking men and women on public matters seriously? That they have had "backgrounders" or briefings we may take for granted. One is reluctant to conclude that their omniscience is a total put-on. But this, too, may be beside the point. The principal aim of these opinionmakers is to immerse us again and again in a marinade of "correctness" or respectability.

What is it necessary that we Americans should know? When is ignorance irrelevant? Perhaps Americans grasp intuitively that what really matters to humankind is here—all around us in the capitalist U.S.A. Lincoln Steffens, playing the pundit in Russia after the Revolution, said: "I have been over into the future, and it works." Some secret wisdom! As a horseplayer he would have lost his shirt. Sigmund Freud, visiting the U.S. before World War I, said America was a great experiment that wasn't going to work. Later, he called it a *misgeburt*— a miscarriage. This was the judgment of German high culture on us. Perhaps the death camps of World War II would have changed Freud's mind.

That America is an experiment has been said often enough (probably more often said than understood). Consistent with this—in a small way—Charles Burress on Michael Jackson is advocating experimentation. "Suppose Jackson were seen," he writes, "not as a freak, but as a brave pioneer devoting his own body to exploring new frontiers of human identity." The underlying hypothesis seems to be that we human beings, considered as material, are totally plastic and that the material of which we are made will take any (improving) shape we choose to give it. A less kindly word for it is "programming." The postulate is that it is necessary to reject what we are by nature, that the given, the original, the creature of flesh and blood, is defective, shameful, in need of alteration, correction, conversion, that this entity, as is, can contribute nothing, and that it would be better to remake us totally. In my youth, the civilized world was taken aback by the Stalin model of Soviet Man as pictured in newspapers and textbooks, in art and literature. Stalinist falsification, we called this. Now we, too, seem to have come up with a synthetic man, a revised, improved American. What this implies is that the human being has no core—more accurately, that his personal core, if there should be one, would be undesirable, wicked, perverse, a lump of prejudices: no damn good at all.

We are beginning to feel the effects of this project. Perhaps the personal core, or what we are by nature, is becoming aware that what lies behind this drive to revise us is tyranny, that consciousness raising and sensitivity training are meant to force us to be born again without color, without race, sexually neutered, politically purified, and with minds shaped and programmed to reject "the bad" and affirm "the good." Will the real human being become *persona non grata?* No wonder so many of us are in a blue funk.

A self-improving lot, Americans have a weakness for this kind of thing: the idealist holding aloft a banner with a strange device. Huck Finn had no use for the nice bright clean New England boy advancing under the motto *Excelsior.* When Aunt Sally threatened to "sivilize" him, he decided to "light out for the territory ahead." There was a time when it was normal for American children to feel that "self-improvement" propaganda would lead us not up the mountain but into the sloughs.

In the matter of opinion, Americans are vulnerable to ideologues, "originators," trendsetters, heralds of better values. Lacking the sustaining traditions of older cultures, we cast about for prescriptions, we seek—in our uncertainty—the next necessary and "correct" step. I can't at the moment remember who it was who said (it sounds like Elbert Hubbard, or perhaps R. W. Emerson), "Invent a better mousetrap and the world will beat a path to your door." Revised and updated, this would go: "Invent a new cliché and you will make it big."

Perhaps the worst thing of all is the language used by these "originators," these heralds of the new. Can anything palpably, substantially, recognizably human be described in words like theirs? It was perhaps in reaction to the degradation of this newspeak—the very latest—that I instinctively turned to William Blake:

The Good are attracted by Men's perceptions,
And think not for themselves;

Till Experience teaches them to catch
And to cage the Fairies & Elves.

And then the Knave begins to snarl
And the Hypocrite to howl;
And all his good Friends shew their private ends,
And the Eagle is known from the Owl.

PART FOUR

Thoughts in Transition

SPANISH LETTER

(1948)

*T*he police come first to your notice in Spain, taking prece-
dence over the people, the streets, and the landscape: The Guardia
Civil in their wooden-looking, shiny, circular hats, brims flattened at
the back, hats that are real enough, since they are worn and seen, but,
unlike the tommy gun that each *guardia* has in the crook of his arm,
lacking in *real* reality. Next, gray-uniformed police with the red eagle
on their sleeves and rifles hanging on their backs. Even the guard in
the park, an old man in the costume of a Swiss chasseur, with a drag-
gled feather, leather jerkin, and shabby leggings, holds a rifle by the
strap. Then there are the secret police; no one knows how many kinds
there are, but you see a great deal of them. On the Irún–Madrid express, our passports were examined by one who swung into the compartment and reversed his lapel, showing us the badge of blue, gold,
and red enamel. He was quiet, equable, and unsystematic, sighing
while he wrote some of the passport numbers into his notebook and
ruffling the pages as if wondering what to do next with his authority.
He murmured *Adios* and withdrew. The train labored on toward the
flower-blazing villas of Santander, the wooden walls of the car quiver-
ing. The seats were long and seignorial, each headrest covered with
lace, and in one of them sat a Spaniard who, as we were passing the
harbor, engaged us in conversation, not casually, by design, preventing
me from looking at the ships in the silver, coal-streaked evening water.
He gave us a lecture on the modernity of Santander and invited us to
ask questions on Spanish life, Spanish history, geography, industry, or

Partisan Review, 15 February 1948.

character, and without being asked, wrinkling his narrow forehead and shooting forward his palms like a photographer ordering you to hold still, he began to speak of hydroelectric power, very minute in his details about turbines, wiring, transmitters, and whatnot. We were American and therefore interested in mechanical subjects. I was not an engineer, I told him. Nevertheless he finished his speech and sat as if waiting for me to propose a subject closer to my interests. He was a small, nervously mobile, brown man with measuring, aggressive, melancholy eyes. He wore a gloomy brown gabardine suit, shiny with dirt, and shoes that were laced through only half the eyelets. Already we were climbing into the thickening darkness; farms appeared below, remote in the steep green valleys. "You are on a holiday?" he said. "You will see many beautiful things." He enumerated them: the Escorial, the Prado, the Alhambra, Seville, Cádiz, *la taza de plata.* He had seen them all; he had been everywhere; he had fought everywhere. "In Spain?" I asked. In Spain, of course, and in Russia and Poland as a member of the Blue Division against the Reds. Essentially he was a soldier; he came of a military family; his father was a high-ranking officer, a colonel in the air force. He threw his hand open to me, displaying a white scar in the palm—his souvenir of Albacete. Just then a young *guardia,* lanky and sunburned, began to roll back the refractory door, and he sprang from his place, seized the handle, and held it. He spoke a few rapid words in an undertone to the *guardia* and rattled the door shut. Someone, certainly not one of the Spaniards in the compartment, said, "*Hay sitio.*" There was room enough for two more passengers. But the colonel's son kept his counsel, and stepping over legs to his own seat, he resumed his conversation—with me alone this time, confidentially; and for a while something of the expression with which he had dismissed the *guardia* lingered on his face, the roused power of his office. Yes, he belonged to the police and made three trips a week between Irún and Madrid. He liked the job. Being an old campaigner, he did not mind the jolting or the noise—there was singing accompanied by rhythmical clapping and stamping in the next compartment; in his own good time, he put a stop to that. The pay was not enough for his style of life, but he was expecting a good *enchufe,* or sinecure, to which he felt himself entitled. Fortunately, he could add to his income by writing. He wrote fiction, and at present he was busy with a long historical novel in verse. His eyes grew hot and visionary as he began to talk of the poets he admired and to quote, somber and reverent. I reflected that it was probably appropriate, since so many European writers were ambitious to become policemen, that the police should aspire to become writers.

Meanwhile the sky had grown dark, and the train threaded its weak light among the trees and rocks or stopped briefly at stations as weakly lighted as itself. Crowds waited in the mist, and the passage was filling. No one made a persistent effort to get into the compartment; everyone was turned away by the colonel's son. We, the Americans, were in his charge, and he was determined that we should have a comfortable night, with space enough to stretch out and sleep. But somehow, by pressure of numbers, the vacant places were filled, and sensing our disapproval of such a thing, he did not try to evict the new occupants. He continued to be as solicitous as before. When I broke off a piece of the loaf I had bought in Hendaye, he was horrified to see me eat such inferior bread. I must have a slice of his tortilla. He dragged down his valise, touched the lock, and it sprang open. The tortilla was in a round tin box. Under it lay copies of *Green Hornet*, *Coyote*, and other pulp magazines. He cut a thick gray slice of the cake. I ate what I could of it, excused myself from finishing, and went into the corridor. Most of the people there were traveling between local stations, a crowd of *gente humilde*, sad, shabby, and world-worn, resting between the walls, leaning on the brass rods along the windows, with gloom-deepened eyes and black nostrils; in muffling shawls or berets that flattened their heads and made a disproportion in their long, brown faces; melancholy, but with a kind of resistance to dreariness, as if ready to succumb so far but no farther to it—the Spanish *dignidad*.

The passengers in the neighboring compartment had become very boisterous, and now the colonel's son came out and subdued them. I returned to my seat and he to his. Immediately he opened a new topic. Tired of his conversation and of humoring him, I refused to respond, and at last he was silent. Then the shades were drawn, someone turned off the light, and we tried to sleep.

By morning the passage was bare, swept clean. The colonel's son said, "We will pass the Escorial soon, where the tombs of the kings are." I was stony to him. We were running downslope in a rush of smoke. The shallow fields, extending on either side to the mountains, looked drought-stricken, burnt, desert, mere stubble and dust. We burst into the suburbs of Madrid and into the yards. On the platform the colonel's son was at my back, and in the sooty arcades and the hell's-antechamber turmoil of the station he hung on, rueful and anxious at my speed. Presumably he had to know where I was staying in Madrid to complete his report. From the hotel bus I saw his brown face in the spectator throng of porters, cabbies, and touts for hotels and *pensiones*, watching the baggage being lifted to the roof, hot-eyed, avoiding my glance, and looking on at the work. Successful!

First and last, the police. In every hotel there are police forms to fill, and passports have to be registered at the station. To obtain a railroad ticket you must make out a declaration stating the object of the journey, and you cannot travel without a *triptico*, a safe-conduct. No consulate or embassy is permitted to grant a visa without the police *salida*. The broad face of Seguridad, near the place where the first shots were fired on Napoleon's troops, dominates the Puerta del Sol with barred and darkened windows. The police license radios. The police go through your suitcase in a provincial rooming house. The woman living in the cave dug in the bluff near the Manzanares is quick to tell you, "We are here with the permission of the *policía*." Everywhere you hear that the jails are full. There is regular bus service for visitors from Cibeles, at the center of town, to the Carabanchel prison. On a trolley car near the Toledo Gate, I saw two arrestees, an old man and a boy of about eighteen, being taken there. They were handcuffed and in the custody of a pair of *guardias* with the inevitable machine guns. The boy, with thick hair that grew sturdily down his neck and with prematurely deep creases beneath his eyes, had the precarious nonchalance of deep misery and deep hatred. There was a loaf of bread sticking out of his pocket. The old man was one-armed, filthy, and scarred. His feet were coming through the rope-soled *alpargatas*. He was nearly bald, and the lines of a healed wound spread under his thin gray hair. I looked at him, and he gave me a gentle shrug of surrender, not daring to speak, but when I got down in Mataderos, among buildings demolished during the civil war, he ventured to lift his hand and wave it as far as the steel cuff permitted.

These were probably common criminals, not *Rojos*. Hundreds of the latter are arrested every month, and the trials at Alcalá de Henares continue endlessly. Political prisoners released from the overflowing jails are on conditional liberty and show you the cards on which they must have a current official stamp. Most of them are not granted work permits and live as they can in the streets, shining shoes, opening taxi doors, peddling lottery tickets, and begging.

At the center of Madrid you occasionally notice shot-scarred buildings, but on the whole there are few reminders of the civil war in the better *barrios*. On Gran Via the shops are almost American in their luxury, and the early-evening café crowds that sit looking down the broad curve of the street at the mass of banks, churches, and government buildings resemble those in New York and Washington bars. Hollywood pictures run in all the better theaters, and the craving for American good things—Buicks, nylons, Parker 51 pens, and cigarettes—is as powerful here as in the other capitals of the world, and as in most of the capitals, there are no dollars and the black market thrives. The police do not interfere with it. Peddlers go among the tables offering pens and cigarettes. Some of these, especially the pens, are obvious counterfeits; the Lucky Strike packages are beautifully done; the blue tax stamps are perfect; the cigarettes are filled with dung and crumbled straw. A boy comes with a huge gold ring to sell. He gives you glimpses of it in his cupped hands with exaggerated furtiveness, his face frantically thievish. It is a heavy, ugly, squarish ring, and you wonder who would ever buy it. He whispers, "It's stolen," and offers it for two hundred pesetas, one hundred, fifty, and then he gives you up with a sad, bored look and tries another table. Women flap their lottery tickets and beg tenaciously. Some of them carry blind or crippled infants and exhibit their maimed or withered legs. One, with a practiced movement, turns the child and shows me a face covered with sores and a pair of purulent eyes. Juanita, my Basque landlady at the pension, tells me that most of these children are hired out by the day to the professional beggars. It's all business, she contemptuously says.

In the dining room of the pension, the conversation is mainly about movie stars. The commandante's wife is equally attracted to James Stewart and Clark Gable. The Sanchez sisters, who were born in Hong Kong and speak English well, are for Brian Aherne and Herbert Marshall, British types. Even the commandante has his favorites and adds his dry, nervous, harsh voice to the rattle of the women. The commandante is lean, correct, compressed, and rancorous and has a pockmarked face, a shallow pompadour, black eyes. He and the señora do not eat our ordinary bread. A black-market white loaf is delivered to them daily, and at noon he carries it under his arm like a swagger stick. There is a little military rush when they enter, she with small, pouncing steps, wagging her fan, he blind to us all but inclining his head. Even on the hottest days his tunic is buttoned to the throat. I offend him by coming to the dining room in a T-shirt and slippers. He sits down grimly to his meal, taking the señora's fan to cool his soup. His is the *dignidad* of gnawing hauteur and dislike, the hateful kind.

There is an important person in the pension, an admiral stationed at the ministry, who never eats in the dining room and who often, in the afternoon, blunders through the dark, curtained rooms in his pajamas. Juanita enters his apartment without knocking, and they are obviously on terms of intimacy. The Sanchez girls explain in an embarrassed way that the admiral is under a great obligation to Juanita, who, during the civil war, concealed and nursed his sick son, or perhaps his nephew, and he swore to reward her. The Republic was unjust to the admiral. He taught at a very low salary in the naval academy. The commandante served under Franco in Morocco and is now head of a military school. He has the reputation of being a great disciplinarian, the sisters inform me rather proudly. They themselves were educated in a convent.

The rest are middle class, people who must be well connected to be able to afford a pension as good as this one, beneficiaries of *enchufismo* or civil service patronage—literally, the *enchufe* is an electric socket. An ordinary civil service job—and one must be, politically, as faultless as a sacrificial lamb to get it—carries a salary of five or six hundred pesetas a month, or roughly twenty dollars, and since *desirable* things are approximately American in price (higher, in many cases; a pound of black-market coffee costs two and a half dollars), a man needs *enchufes* to live comfortably. If, through family influence or friends high in the church or the army, he has several jobs, he makes the rounds of the ministries to sign in and sign out. Occasionally he may be required to do a little work, and he does it *para cumplir*, to acknowledge the obligation, but as hastily as possible. This is in part traditional. All Spanish regimes have used the same means to keep the educated classes from disaffection. "Modern" government programs receive great publicity. Recently a social security system modeled on the Beveridge plan was announced, and Sir William himself was invited for consultation. But the real purpose of these programs is to extend *enchufismo*, for the actual benefits to the sick or unemployed worker under this insurance scheme amount to about three pesetas a day, hardly enough for a loaf of bread. Franco has great-state ambitions, like Mussolini's, but Spain is too poor; the cost of staying in power is too high for him to realize them. The buildings called the New Ministries, which were to have gone up monumentally at the foot of the Castellana, stand in scaffolding, uncompleted and apparently abandoned.

For middle-class families without *enchufes*, the difficulties are terrible. One must wear a European suit, a shirt that costs two hundred pesetas, a tie, and to appear in the rope *alpargatas* of the people is inconceivable. It is essential to have a maid. And then one's wife has to be properly dressed, and the children clothed and educated. One must cling to one's class. The fall into the one below is measureless. Its wretchedness is an ancient fact, stable, immemorial, and understood by everyone. The newer wretchedness, that of keeping one meager suit presentable, of making a place in the budget for movies in order to have something to contribute to polite conversation when *The Song of Bernadette* is discussed, of persisting to exhaustion among the stragglers in the chase after desirable things, the images of the earthly kingdom reflected in every casual American, is nevertheless not *the* wretchedness. That you see in the tenements and the inhabited ruins, old kilns and caves, the human swarms in the dry rot of Vallecas and Mataderos.

Summer is arid in Madrid, and cloudless. The sound of thunder is very rare. When it is heard, the maids cry out, *"Una tormenta!"* and dart through the pension, slamming the windows. Across the air shaft, the blond Bibi calls "A storm!" to me in her tense, warlike voice, wavers behind the smoky glass, and leaves the thick drapes trembling like the curtains of a stage on the last cry of a tragedy. Then the rain begins with a plunge, falling with the heaviness of drops of mercury.

In ten minutes it is over; ten minutes more, and it has dried. On the hottest days the streets and the locust trees are watered morning and evening. The parks are divided by irrigation ditches and are grassless. The only grass I saw in Madrid, that before the Prado, was kept alive by continual sprinkling. As one goes out from the center of the city the green becomes more and more thin until, from the blank, sun-hardened flats of the outlying districts, overlooking the trenches that have sunk and are grown over with brown weeds and brown wires, there is only the scattered green of gardens on the immense plain, each garden with the diagonal pole of a well sweep rising above the Indian corn.

The Manzanares River is almost empty, yet on Sunday, in the section called the Bombilla, where, in places, the water has collected to a depth of several inches, there are hundreds of bathers and picnickers in throngs at the working-class cafés for miles along the shores, the *gente humilde*, choking the streets and bridges and lying on blankets on the dusty banks under the scanty acacias. It is like a vision of the first moments of resurrection, seeing those families lying in the smothering dust and milling in the roads. On the city side there are homes in the ruins, fenced round with the wreckage of bombardments and rolls of barbed wire. A few gypsies live in the Bombilla, in wagons. They are not like the Andalusian gypsies; they have a citified, depressed air; the women, filthy and gaunt, sit by their iron pots; the children lie naked on sacking. Goats are tethered to the wheels and axles, and under one wagon I saw two apes crouching spiritlessly. A factory that makes concrete tubes rises on the other side—a long, proudly lettered, modern industrial wall against which there are always a few men relieving themselves. Behind are the usual unfinished public works, and miles away, far upland, is the intricate earthen blue of the Sierra, which sends down the trickle of the Manzanares, more like the idea than the actuality of a river. It appears to be the idea, the *hope* of a river that attracts the gigantic crowd from the desert African dryness of the slums. The boys leap high into the air, as if the water were measured in feet, not inches, and the dust clings to their legs when they clamber up the bank. The river flows in a dirty green vein from shallow to shallow; gangs run yelling up and down the sand islands of its bed. A man leads his infant daughter, hardly old enough to walk, down to the water. She has soiled herself, and he washes her with a certain embittered tenderness while she clings screaming to his lanky, hairy legs.

Among the trees, surrounding the kiosks that sell wine and beer, the huge multitude is dancing, jogging up and down. Three young

boys, self-contained, professional, indifferent to the dancers, play sax-
ophone, guitar, and drum, imitating the downtown version of American chic. Two drunken men are blowing the *gaita*, the hairy Galician
bagpipes, for a group of drunken-looking friends. Madrid is said to be
overrun with Gallegos; Franco himself is Galician, and in the old-fashioned Spanish belief in provincial loyalties, they come to the city by
the thousands for jobs.

The soldiers in the crowd look thickset and short in their coarse
jackets, gaiters, and big boots. They bump against the wheeling pairs
of girls and try to force them apart. This is done seriously; there is little friskiness or gaiety, and you see few smiles. The dancers tramp and
shuffle but, though excited and sweating, keep a straight-browed,
straight-lipped formality of expression and hold themselves apart with
rigid heads and shoulders.

The kiosks and the cafés do not sell food. The people bring their
own bread and chick peas. You can buy a meal at middle-class prices in
the bowery beer gardens set apart behind lattice walls and bushes
growing in tubs. In one of these places, where I stop for a bottle of
beer, there is a huge, time-eaten barrel organ that produces martial-
sounding dances with missing notes, clanging bells, and queer, mechanical birdcalls. The man who winds it has the pride-bitten look of
someone who has come down in the world and gives me a glance of
"too good for my destiny and every bit as good as you are." His wife
sits beside him, evidently to give him support in his humiliation, for
she does not spell him at the organ. The brass drum inside catches the
late sun on its short spines as it revolves. He is bald and small, and his
cheeks are taut and hard as he faces me, his mouth is bitter. His wife is
passive and sits with quietly folded hands.

People complain rather freely on very short acquaintance about
the regime: the shortness of the rations, the inferior bread, the black
market, the army, the police, the Falange, and the church. Madrileños
speak of the recent referendum on the law of succession as *el reveren-
dum*, a priests' affair. It was conducted with the familiar, heavy-handed
efficiency of fascist elections. Workers in the unreliable *barrios* of
Mataderos, Vallecas, and Cuatro Caminos received ballots beforehand
with a printed *Sí*. Ration books that were not stamped at the polling
place to show that their holders had voted were invalid after election

day. Nevertheless many people, monarchists as well as republicans, abstained, and even government figures acknowledged that a considerable number had voted *no:* 132,000 in Barcelona, 117,000 in Madrid, 36,000 in Seville. The socialists interpret the referendum as an attempt by the regime to convince the United States of its stability in order to obtain a loan. Franco has become very confident since the weeks after V-E Day, when it was thought that he had lost together with Hitler. The Germans did as they liked in Madrid during the war, and everyone was therefore greatly surprised that Franco was allowed to remain in power after their defeat. But Britain and the United States did not stop selling him the gasoline without which his army, estimated at seven hundred thousand men, would have been paralyzed. And now, with the air of future allies, Spanish fascists tell you that no other country on the continent is so safe and convenient a base for the coming war with Russia. France and Italy are, or soon will be, communist. Spain is a strategic center owing to Gibraltar, and Franco's reliability as an old fighter against communism is appreciated by America. Besides, everybody knows what magnificent soldiers the Spanish are. It is curious how much national pride is mingled with the cynicism of the people who tell you this. Everyone, whether communist or socialist, has a touch of this pride, and fascists and socialists alike joke explosively about the Italian disaster at Guadalajara: "The order was '*a la bayoneta,*' and they thought it was '*a la camioneta*'"—"To the trucks!" instead of "Bayonet charge!"

There is, judging from the number of political arrests and the frequency and violence of the attacks in the press on Prieto and other exiled leaders, a great deal of underground activity. Several republicans told me that between November 1946 and April 1947, ten thousand people were imprisoned. CNT, UGT, and communist newspapers circulate in Madrid and other large cities, but there is little organized resistance except in isolated mountain districts in the north and in Andalusia. From abroad, both the socialists and the communists claimed leadership in the short Asturian coal strike, which occurred in May 1947, but little is actually known about it. Many socialists and republicans admit that the communist underground is growing, mainly because the international situation favors it. Of the Western countries, only France has boycotted Franco, and it is believed that the border was closed by the French government as a concession to the communists. The victory of the Labour party did not change Britain's policy, notwithstanding the pledges of support made by Attlee to the Loyalists when he visited Spain during the civil war as his party's representative.

Alcalá de Henares, where I saw one of the political trials, is an ancient, decayed town, the birthplace of Cervantes and, in the fifteenth century, famous for its university. Ten men, tramway employees from Cuatro Caminos charged with distributing the communist paper *Mundo Obrero*, were the defendants. I was told by the son of one of them that they had been arrested sixteen months before. Such trials are theoretically public, but they are never announced; embassies and the foreign press are notified by the underground or by relatives of the accused. I came with one of the embassy secretaries, in a resplendent green embassy car before which soldiers and Guardia Civil gave way in the antique streets. *Diplomáticos*, we went unchallenged past the sentries and under rifles up the staircase into the long hall of the courtroom. It was lined with *guardias* and their machine guns. We sat down at the rear among the families of the accused.

The court was a tribunal of officers, for members of illegal political parties are in the category of criminals endangering public safety and come under the army's jurisdiction. Looking toward the narrow windows, we could see only dimly. The prisoners were on benches, with their backs turned to us. The members of the tribunal had the light behind them, and their faces, too, were obscure. In profile at either side of the room were the prosecutor and the officer appointed for the defense. Boots and scabbards shone under the tables.

A clerk hurriedly reads the depositions of the ten. On such and such a night, Fulano de Tal met another conspirator in such and such a place and received or handed over money, instructions, papers. One by one the accused, called on by court or prosecutor, rise and acknowledge the confessions. Only one balks at a detail. He does not recall it. He is ordered to look at the signature of the deposition. Is it his? It is, but he cannot remember making the statement in point. Again, more impatiently, does he recognize the signature as his own? He does. Obviously, then, the statement is his. He is ordered to sit, and he stiffly obeys. All the prisoners with the exception of two elderly men rise and stand with a military bearing, infected by the manner of the tribunal. To see them play the soldierly game and stand like *hombres honrados* to verify confessions extracted, everyone knows, in the cellars of the Seguridad affects me painfully, like the injection of a depressant that thickens the heartbeat. No doubt it is very *castizo*, purely and essentially Spanish, that the prisoners should conduct themselves like captives in an honorable war, and probably it also sustains them to stand at attention, but I have a horror of this game as I do of the commandante's bouncing and pivoting game in the pension, his peevish chivalry.

Each of the prisoners answers questions. The defense does not cross-examine them, no evidence is introduced, and there are no witnesses. You become aware, when the prosecutor stands up, of his large hands and powerful body; they give an effect of incongruity to the meticulousness of his uniform. He makes a neat prosecutor's packet of the depositions: "It is admitted . . . it is admitted . . . according to the statements of Fulano de Tal . . ." Not until he concludes does he become bullish and exhortatory. He puts forth his strong voice suddenly. In cold blood, lifting up his chest, he begins to thunder that crimes "in a foreign spirit" against a whole people cannot be pardoned, and he asks that the leader of the ten be given a twelve-year sentence and the rest four years each. W. whispers that this is relatively lenient. Then the defense lawyer reads a short statement to the effect that in the Christian democracy of the Caudillo's government there is room for differences of opinion when the expression of those differences is temperate. These words cause a sighing stir in the gloomy end of the room where the families sit. The prosecutor speaks for another half hour in reply, his showmanship at times becoming perfunctory. This is a very minor trial. He towers before the window in the clear morning light of Castile and makes his last summation, reads from notes, and repeats his demand for twelve years and four. The time served awaiting trial does not count. The president of the tribunal now asks each of the prisoners in turn whether he has anything to say before sentence is passed. Six do not. The seventh, however, the leader of the ten, starts to speak; the president says loudly, "*Cállese!*"—"Shut up!" The prisoner persisting, he rises and shouts, "*Cállese!*" startling everyone. "*Nada de la política!* Sit down!" He sits. "Stand up!" The prisoner rises. "You have been heard on the evidence. Nothing else is relevant. There will be no politics here. Be seated." There is no other disturbance. The trial is over, and we file down under the guns with the silent relatives. I see the grieving face of a boy on the stairs, and I talk to him. His father is one of those who received four years. Will he be allowed to see him? He does not know; since the arrest he had not seen him till this morning. He is now the eldest at home. There was an older brother, but he disappeared in the last days of the war. He has another brother, eight years old, and two sisters. "How do you live?" I ask; he does not reply. Thin and tall, he stands pigeon-toed beside me on the street, drawing his long hands out of his pockets and thrusting them back. His face is narrow, and his soft eyes seem almost without whites: all center. I make a low-voiced comment on the barbarousness of the trial. W. has meanwhile taken down the names of the condemned for his report and wants to leave, so I say goodbye, and we get into the car.

The uselessness of it afflicts me. Poverty and the harshness of the dictatorship make resistance inevitable, and the relations of powers outside the country make it vain, perfectly useless. The Spanish problem will not be settled within Spain. Franco wants to bargain with America, and the communist leaders, were they in power, would represent Russia. But people continue to struggle in the political spirit of past times when they were still free within national boundaries to make revolutions and create governments. There is no such freedom now, as a growing number of Europeans are aware. "We liberated ourselves from Napoleon in 1812," a Spanish acquaintance said to me, "and we manifested the same spirit in 1937 when we fought Hitler. Against him, however, we were powerless. And perhaps we might have been swallowed by Stalin if we had succeeded in defeating him. I dread another civil war here, for it would inevitably turn into the conflict of greater powers. The doctrines of 1789 are for us like the morals of Christianity: pieties. We are not strong enough to enjoy the Rights of Man. If Russia does not dominate us, your country will. We must resign ourselves to remaining subjects and withdraw our hopes of independence from the realm of politics to another realm."

Nearly every conversation in Madrid eventually turns to the subject of national character, and more than once I was referred by other foreigners to Unamuno's essay on Spanish envy and was quoted Quevedo's line, used as an epigraph by Unamuno: "Envy is lean; it bites but cannot swallow." An Italian explained to me that the Spaniards were half Moorish and that I would not understand them if I forgot it for an instant, and according to a German lady who has lived in Madrid for many years, the great fault of the Spaniards was that they had no real feelings. After her brother's death, several Madrileño friends came to visit her. "They did not console me," she said. "They sat and talked of their *marmotas* [maids] and their children. They knew I was in mourning. They really are heartless." On the other hand, Pio Baroja, with whom I had a conversation, found the German character inexplicable. "At first I could not believe that they were burning their captives in ovens. But then I met a young man who had lost his mother and a sister in that way. And to tell the truth, I found Germany a queer place when I visited it in the twenties. In Hamburg, a nudist family got on the streetcar: father, mother, and little ones all as naked as my hand, a family of petit bourgeois carrying bundles and packages like any petit-bourgeois family that has been shopping. And the parents weren't even handsome. The father had a huge *tripa*, like a barrel."

All these discussions of national character were occasions of resentment, and the resentment was particularly strong when it was the American character that was discussed. A traveling salesman said to me, his eyes aswim with poetic heat behind thick lenses, "America is still looking for a soul; our soul is very old." Others spoke of "American emptiness," "unhistorical Americans who live only in the future," etc.

But people, of course, feel the sway of American strength and American goods and the loss of their own liberty and strength. Until 1898, Spain still considered itself an empire, and for a nation of traditionalists, 1898 is by no means the distant past. The emphasis on national character is an emphasis on value. Take away the ignorant nonsense, and there is still something left—namely, an assertion of worth in a world in which worth is synonymous with power, and power has passed to featureless mass societies for which the past has little meaning, and machinery, wealth, and organization topple the old dignity to replace it with contempt and discontent.

Between Málaga and Granada, at the railroad junction of Bobadilla, shivering under the heat that darkened the stone hills and olive fields, I went into the station restaurant. It was a buffet, doing a feverish business in bread, grapes, tortillas, ham, boiled eggs, jelly sausage and blood sausage, salami, cheese, chicken, a huge abundance without boundaries, spread on thick paper and shining with fat. There were two women and a man behind it. The man was middle-aged, gray-faced, and he coughed continually. Three or four strands of hair were arranged with elegant care over his bald head. He behaved toward me with iron *dignidad*. I was an American, therefore he refused to speak Spanish. He addressed me in a kind of French acquired, probably, in a restaurant in Madrid or Barcelona or in a luxury hotel on the Mediterranean and ripened during many isolated years in the desert wilderness of Bobadilla. *"Les oeufs son' a cinq cad' un, m'sieu."* He kept coughing softly and could not stop, obviously consumptive. *"Y qué precio tienen las uvas?"* *"Cuat' le demi-kilo, m'sieu."* Great politeness; fiery politeness. Meanwhile he stared at me secretly with his rather vindictive eyes, the cough blurting softly through his lips so that his cheeks shook. By my accent, by the cut of my clothes, the pattern of my shoes, and who knows what unconscious attributes, he recognized me as an American, one of the new lords of the earth, a new Roman, full of the pride of machines and dollars, passing casually through the junction where it was his fate to remain rotting to death. But he faced me at least with the proper *dignidad*, like the bitter organ grinder in the Bombilla.

The commandante's dignity is something else again. The commandante is, after all, the tyrant's friend, and the tyrant, too, believes in organization and is trying to trade his way into the new imperium. The señora wears nylon stockings, and the commandante owns a marvelous cigarette lighter, and I am sure he has a large supply of American flints.

ILLINOIS JOURNEY

(1957)

*T*he features of Illinois are not striking; they do not leap to the eye but lie flat and at first appear monotonous. The roads are wide, hard, perfect, sometimes of a shallow depth in the far distance but so nearly level as to make you feel that the earth really is flat. From east and west, travelers dart across these prairies into the huge horizons and through cornfields that go on forever: giant skies, giant clouds, an eternal nearly featureless sameness. You find it hard to travel slowly. The endless miles pressed flat by the ancient glacier seduce you into speeding. As the car eats into the distances, you begin gradually to feel that you are riding upon the floor of the continent, the very bottom of it, low and flat, and an impatient spirit of movement, of overtaking and urgency, passes into your heart.

Miles and miles of prairie, slowly rising and falling, sometimes give you a sense that something is in the process of becoming or that the liberation of a great force is imminent, some power, like Michelangelo's slave only half released from the block of stone. Conceivably the mound-building Indians believed their resurrection would coincide with some such liberation and built their graves in imitation of the low moraines deposited by the departing glaciers. But they have not yet been released and remain drowned in their waves of earth. They have left their bones, their flints and pots, their place names and tribal names, and little besides except a stain, seldom vivid, on the consciousness of their white successors.

The soil of the Illinois prairies is fat, rich, and thick. After spring

Holiday, 22 September 1957.

plowing it looks oil-blackened or colored by the soft coal that occurs in great veins throughout the state. In the fields you frequently see a small tipple or a crazy-looking device that pumps oil and nods like the neck of a horse at a quick walk. Isolated among the cornstalks or the soybeans, the iron machine clanks and nods, stationary. Along the roads, with intervals between them as neat and even as buttons on the cuff, sit steel storage bins, in form like the tents of Mongolia. They are filled with grain. And the elevators and tanks, trucks and machines, that crawl over the fields and blunder over the highways—whatever you see is productive. It creates wealth, it stores wealth, it is wealth.

As you pass the fields, you see signs the farmers have posted telling, in code, what sort of seed they have planted. The farmhouses are seldom at the roadside but far within the fields. The solitude and silence are deep and wide. Then, when you have gone ten or twenty miles through cornfields without having seen a living thing—no cow, no dog, scarcely even a bird under the hot sky—suddenly you come upon a noisy contraption at the roadside, a system of contraptions, rather, for husking the corn and stripping the grain. It burns and bangs away, and the conveyor belts rattle. A double flame twists and roars within the generator. Three broad women in overalls stand at the hoppers and toss the ears of corn upward. A dusty red mountain of cobs is growing under the small dinosaur's head of the conveyor, and the chaff dazzles and trembles upward. The hard kernels, red and yellow, race down the chutes into the trucks.

When you leave, this noise and activity are cut off at one stroke; you are once more in the deaf, hot solitude of trembling air, alone in the cornfields.

North, south, east, and west, there is no end to them. They line roads and streams and hem in the woods and surround towns, and they crowd into backyards and edge up to gas stations. An exotic stranger might assume he had come upon a race of corn worshipers who had created a corn ocean; or that he was among a people who had fallen in love with infinite repetition of the same details, like the builders of skyscrapers in New York and Chicago who have raised up bricks and windows by the thousands, and all alike. From corn you can derive notions of equality, or uniformity, massed democracy. You can, if you are given to that form of mental play, recall Joseph's brethren in the lean years and think how famine has been conquered here and superabundance itself become such a danger that the government has to take measures against it.

The power, the monotony, the oceanic extent of the cornfields, do indeed shrink and dwarf the past. How are you to think of the small bands of Illini, Ottawas, Cahokians, Shawnee, Miamis, who camped in the turkey grass, and the French Jesuits who descended the Mississippi and found them. When you force your mind to summon them, the Indians appear rather doll-like in the radiance of the present moment. They are covered in the corn, swamped in the oil, hidden in the coal of Franklin County, run over by the trains, turned phantom by the stockyards. There are monuments to them here and there throughout the state, but they are only historical ornaments to the pride of the present.

In the northwestern part of the state, the Black Hawk country near Galena, the land is hilly and the streams have a steeper gradient. This is the region in which Chief Black Hawk, in 1832, made his last resistance.

The principal city of that portion of the Mississippi is Galena, once a great center of trade but now a remote place beside a shrunken river. There is no historical mood about the flourishing towns. Prosperity wipes out the past or, in its pride, keeps the relics dusted, varnished, polished—sentimental treasures like the Lincoln residence in Springfield. Entering such houses, you feel the past undeniably; only you feel the present much more. Ulysses S. Grant lived in Galena, and his house is a museum, but it is a museum within a museum, for the town itself is one of the antiquities of Illinois, and it has a forsaken, tottering look.

Galena is not deserted; it is inhabited and its houses are not in bad repair, yet they blink, and lean on their tall hillside in the peace of abnormalcy. The streets are empty under the stout old trees. Of course, even the streets of thriving towns are vacant five days a week. The emptiness of Galena, however, will never be filled. The long street of the lower town resembles that of a Welsh village when everyone is down in the pit. On the main street, the store windows have no luster except the dull one given by rock samples. Lead enriched Galena in the first half of the nineteenth century. Its harbor was filled with steamboats. The boom started in the 1820s and continued about forty years.

Now if you lift up your eyes from the drab streets at the waterfront you see on the hill something that confusedly resembles the antebellum South, old mansions of brick and stone, a few of them still handsome, ornamented with wrought iron in something like New Orleans style. Galena is an old, cracked, mossy place, and looks a little crazy. An invisible giant tent caterpillar has built over it, and the sun comes through the trees as through frayed netting. From an upper street you stare four narrow stories downward into a spinsterish backyard where a cat, in the easy way of all cats, is lying on a small plot of green. Within the long rooms are Franklin stoves, recamier couches, ornate wallpaper, and on the rooftops stand television antennae.

There are many towns in Illinois that have been thus bypassed, towns like Cairo and Shawneetown in the south. They flourished until the railroads made the steamboats obsolete, and now they sit, the fortresses of faithful old daughters and age-broken sons who do not go away.

An old resident of Galena said, "The young folks leave. And they don't come back. Not alive, at least. Lots of them ask to be buried here, but whilst they live there's nothing for them in Galena."

Some twenty miles away, across the river, is Dubuque, Iowa, full of vigor and enterprise. The diesel trains run through there with deep, brazen cries, like the horns of the Philistine army, and the city rejoices. There is success, and here is its neighbor, failure. The inhabitant of the failure city bears a personal burden of shame. The old resident would leave too, if he were younger; but what could he do now in Chicago or Los Angeles? Here he can live on his old-age money, his Social Security income. Elsewhere it wouldn't make ends meet.

The residents of the failure town are often apologetic. They talk of history and tradition, fusty glamour or the unrecorded sins and tragedies of the place, as though these were all they had to offer. By and by, the old man points out a high hill in the distance and says, "There was a man lynched over there long ago. The whole town of Galena turned out and did it. Afterwards they found out he was innocent."

"Is that so? Who was he?"

"They don't know. They killed him over there. Then they found out they were wrong. But it was too late to make it up to him then. It was before my time. I only been here fifty years. I came from Wisconsin when I was a young fellow. But they hanged that innocent man. Everybody knows about it here. They each and every one of them do."

When Illinois was a frontier state, it attracted men of strange beliefs from everywhere, dissidents and sectarians, truth seekers and utopians. Those who did not depart were assimilated.

On the Mississippi a few hours south of Galena, the Mormons built a city at Nauvoo in 1839 and erected a temple. After the murder of the prophet Smith and his brother in neighboring Carthage, the Mormons emigrated under the leadership of Brigham Young, leaving many empty buildings. Into these came a band of French communists, the Icarians, led by Étienne Cabet. Their colony soon failed; discord and thefts broke it up. Cabet died in Saint Louis, obscurely. And after the Icarians came German immigrants, who apparently sobered up the town.

Now, unobtrusively but with steady purpose, the Mormons have been coming back to Nauvoo. They have reopened some of the old brick and stone houses in the lower town, near the Mississippi; they have trimmed the lawns and cleaned the windows, and set out historical markers and opened views on the river, which here, as it approaches Keokuk Dam, broadens and thickens with mud. Sunday speedboats buzz unseen below the bend where the brown tide, slowly hovering, turns out of sight.

Nauvoo today is filled, it seemed to me, with Mormon missionaries who double as tourist guides. When I came for information I was embraced, literally, by an elderly man; he was extremely brotherly, hearty and familiar. His gray eyes were sharp, though his skin was brown and wrinkled. His gestures were wide, ample, virile, and Western, and he clapped me on the back, as we sat talking, and gripped me by the leg. As any man in his right mind naturally wants to be saved, I listened attentively, but less to his doctrines perhaps than to his Western tones, wondering how different he could really be from other Americans of the same type. I went to lie afterward beside the river and look at Iowa on the other bank, which shone like smoke over the pungent muddy water that poured into the southern horizon. Here the Mormons had crossed, and after them the French Icarians. The Icarians held together for some years after leaving Nauvoo. But they were absorbed, as everything eventually was absorbed that could not be reconciled with the farm, the factory, the railroad, the mine, the mill, the bank, and the market.

Some process of absorption is going on in Shawneetown, on the other side of the state from Nauvoo, where the Ohio and the Wabash rivers meet. This is the country called Egypt, the southernmost portion of Illinois. Its principal city is Cairo (pronounced Cayro), at the southern tip of the state. Cairo is not so thriving as it once was, but Shawneetown has changed even more profoundly in the course of a century. They will tell you there how representatives from a little northern community called Chicago once approached the bankers of opulent Shawneetown for a loan and how they were turned down because Chicago was too remote a village to bother with.

"Well, look at us now," my informant said to me.

We stood in the midst of wide dirt streets from which the paving had been washed out. About us were deserted mansions, dilapidated huge buildings, with falling shutters, their Greek Revival pillars gone gray.

Such is old Shawneetown, in its time one of the great cities of the state. With the disappearance of the keelboat and the steamboat, it would gradually have withered anyway, but its ruin has been made complete by the flooding of the Ohio.

A strange, Silurian smell emanates from the mud and the barren houses. The scene is Southern. Whittlers sit on boxes, and the dogs roll in the potholes; the stores sell fatback, collard greens, mustard greens, and black-eyed peas. The flies wait hungrily in the air, sheets of flies that make a noise like the tearing of tissue paper. People in the river bottoms tell you that old Shawneetown is a rip-roaring place on a Saturday night; it swallows up husbands and their paychecks. The bars near the levee burst into music, and the channel catfish fry in deep fat, and the beer flows.

On higher ground to the west, a new Shawneetown sits under the hot sky of Egypt. It is like many another Illinois town, except newer. The state and the WPA created it beyond the river's reach. It is high and dry, spacious and rather vacant. For many of the diehards refuse to leave their old homes. Half ghost, half honky-tonk, old Shawneetown has a fair-sized population of traditionalists. Like old campaigners, they name the years of disaster with a ring of military pride—" 'eighty-four, 'ninety-eight, nineteen and thirteen, nineteen and thirty-seven." The 1947 edition of the Illinois *State Guide* says that the flood of 1937, which rose six feet above the levee, "marked the end of Shawneetown's pertinacious adhesion to the riverbank." Reasonable people, the authors of the *Guide* have spoken prematurely. The pertinacious adhesion continues in spite of reason and floods.

Between the new and the old Shawneetowns there is a deep rivalry; the two factions express pity and contempt for each other. Old Shawneetowners tell of many who are held against their will up there, people whose children prevent their return. Some have moved back from the new town, bored by its newness and aridity. Nothing is happening up there. Sensible new Shawneetowners reply, as a fine portly woman with spreading short blond hair did, "If they want to degenerate down there and play hero"—a strange combination of terms—"that's their own fool business. I have cleaned house after floods too many times. And if you saw what it looked like after the water has been in it! Six inches of silt on the carpets, and just like a swamp. I sat down and cried."

In old Shawneetown a retired railroad man whom I met on the levee said that his wife was old enough to recall how the victims of '84 were laid in rows on the sitting room floor. "Right in here," he said, and showed me the red, ancient house. It had belonged to the first president of Shawneetown's bank, the very bank that had refused Chicago's request for a loan.

"We live here in the summer now," the railroad man explained. "This here is our little grandboy. We raised him up ourselves." And raised him all too well, I should have said, for at the age of eight he must have weighed about a hundred and fifty pounds. He looked at me with precocious significance, as if the manitou of this place had entered his fat little body.

The trodden earth of the levee makes you feel safe. Below, the river is fire blue. The summery Kentucky shore is green. The banks look supple and full as they decline toward the water. A new bridge of orange steel hangs in the air. The child says, "Three guys fell off it and got kilt."

"Oh, mercy." His grandfather laughs. "Only one was, because he hit a barge. The others went into the water and was saved. Three falling is not bad for as big a bridge as this one is."

From this old man I heard the first sensible explanation of the stubbornness of the old Shawneetowners. He said, "When you have grown up here and see the river every day of your life, it isn't so easy to move away and do without. And especially only a few miles away."

Between the Ohio and the Mississippi, Egypt lies low and hollow. Its streams are sluggish, old, swampy, and varicose. Spring floods bring fresh topsoil to many areas, and the corn is thick. Toward Cairo the farmers make good cotton crops. We are here farther to the south than Richmond, Virginia. To a Northern nose, the air is slightly malarial. People's faces and their postures are Southern, and you begin to see things for which no preparation is possible. A young Negro woman, her head tied up in a handkerchief, drives by in a maroon convertible; on her shoulder sits a bull terrier. That is a pleasant thing to see and all the better because of the slight start it gives you. In a river town, a place whitened by the local lime-burning, is a small bar and restaurant. You enter on a calm Sunday afternoon and see what appears to be a clan of working people eating and drinking. Anyone who wants beer may work the pulls for himself. Sliced bread and ham are on the bar, and a woman is drinking beer while her baby nurses. North of Vandalia you are not likely to see a child at breast. And yet this is a sight which has no business to be remarkable.

On a road in Egypt a warm wind was booming across the flashing sky and turning the white clouds round, the corn leaves were streaming, and I saw a roadside marker that read Old Slave House. An arrow pointed, as roadside arrows sometimes will, skyward. It said Equality. Two spring-breaking and stone-embedded ruts under low willow branches led finally up to a bald hill on which a corn crop sadly petered out in gullies, ashes, old flivver bodies, and various cast-iron relics. On the summit of the hill stood the old mansion or slave house, once the property of John Crenshaw: a brown structure, formerly white.

Because you know it is a slave house it looks evil, dangerous; it also looks trashy; its brown color is disheartening. The evil is remote because slavery is dead. A sort of safe thrill passes through the liberal heart. But then, the evil is not altogether remote, because nothing has been done to make the house historic. There are no exhibits in glass cases. In a great vacant room, the slaves' shackles lie on the linoleum-covered floor. The white form of a washing machine stands in the background. Its present owners live in the old mansion, and it is both domicile and museum.

Slaves were imprisoned at the top of the house, in narrow cells no larger than closets. Runaways or freed slaves were kidnapped by Crenshaw, so the story goes, and resold in the markets of the South. Long sheets of foolscap framed on the walls give the history of the place. The writing is old-fashioned, the ink faded; the details are sinister. Crenshaw tortured his captives on crude devices made of heavy beams. These still lean against the walls. This is a dismal, chalky, low-pitched, aching garret. Many hands have left signatures on the plaster. The wind drives against the walls; the corn stoops in the bald, runneled clay.

The lady of the house has a great deal to tell about it. She is a Southerner and evidently a lover of legend. Mr. Crenshaw, she says, was a fearsome man. It is possible that he had to leave England for his sins, and he became a great power in Illinois. His abuses of the black people were so horrible he was attacked by one of his own slaves and wounded in the thigh. The slave was cast alive into a furnace, said the lady, but Crenshaw lost his leg. Her catalogue of horrors is very long; possibly endless. Crenshaw bred his captives. Made pregnant by studs, the slave girls brought higher prices. And yet, she said, Abe Lincoln was a guest in this house. She told me this with an air of triumph. When he campaigned against Douglas he came to visit Crenshaw, who was a Democrat. "Politics!" she said.

"And did he know what sort of a man Crenshaw was?" I said.

"Everybody knew. And he was waited on by slaves. But he was here to get the votes. Now looka here at the family pictures." Brown and yellowed people seemed to return my gaze from the framed portraits. Their hair and garments were heavy, their faces long, severe. In our day we have learned something about charm, the art of self-presentation, and are told to look sunny when we are photographed; but there is nothing to mitigate the austerity of these slave owners. They were masters and looked like masters; they scorned to enliven the expression of their eyes, the sullenness of their mouths. But why should they, the overlords, have looked so dull and sullen? "Now, here," said my guide, "is Crenshaw's daughter. She was waited on hand

and foot, and never even had to brush her own hair until after the Civil War was over." I must say that she sounded a little envious. Was she not the present lady of the house?

Egypt belongs not merely to the South but to the Deep South. Cairo is as Southern a city as Paducah, in Kentucky across the river. But even in Lincoln's own county of Sangamon I heard things said against him. In Sangamon the pioneer village of New Salem has been restored. New Salem was Lincoln's home before it was abandoned circa 1840. He had already moved to Springfield, eighteen miles away. In 1837, he helped to establish Springfield as the state capital.

There is a residue of old grievances still in Sangamon County, for North and South meet here. Northern Illinois was settled by New Englanders, the southern part by Kentuckians and Virginians. Slavery and its enemies, Union and Secession, struggled here. Sangamon County may be said to have been at the very center of this conflict, and despite the public worship of Lincoln's memory you meet people who say, the feuding blood still running strong in them, "We knew him here. Yes, they called my granddad Copperhead hereabouts, but what of it? Lincoln was for the big cities and the banks." But it is nothing but a residue. Most of the old differences have long since been composed; it is mainly the historical (feuding) sense that preserves them.

ISRAEL: THE SIX-DAY WAR

(1967)

In Israel's Eyes, It's a Crazy World

*T*el Aviv, 12 June 1967—Day and night the armored columns came down the main street of Tiberias, turned left at the Lake of Galilee, and continued northward past the Mount of the Beatitudes, where Jesus preached.

From the mountains on the Syrian side, the road was often shelled at night. One could see the fields blazing, set afire by artillery, and hear the deep growling of bombs. Tiberias was blacked out. People sat by the water and listened to the news, exchanging rumors and predictions.

Nasser had resigned, the Egyptian announcer had sobbed, but the Egyptians were free weepers. Nasser had not resigned, said someone else. By then he no longer mattered; his army had been torn to pieces in the Sinai Desert. It was the Syrians who mattered now. The invasion had begun that morning. The Israeli armies appeared to be on their way toward Damascus. The Russians were threatening to break off diplomatic relations. No one seemed much disturbed by this.

Apparently Israelis decided that they need not concern themselves with the great powers since the great powers had apparently decided to let the Arabs have their way.

The great powers had allowed Nasser, Hussein, and the Syrians to mobilize and to threaten to run the Israelis into the sea, to drown them like rats, to annihilate everyone. Now, Nasser, one Israeli told me, was clearly a lunatic. Yet the Americans had given this lunatic wheat, and the

Russians had given him arms and military advice. The French courted him; the Yugoslavs believed that he headed the progressive elements of the Middle East; the Indians sympathized with him. Though shrewd, he was perhaps also crazy. Therefore these leaders who let him lead the world to the brink of a wider war shared his dementia.

These views at this moment do not appear to be farfetched. On Saturday morning, northern Israel was filled with troops, armor, and artillery. The tanks were decorated with flowers and photographs, captured flags and female dummies modeling the latest Arab fashions. In the mountains, the shelling and bombing continued. The jets screamed by invisibly, and shortly afterward one heard the thump and saw the smoke on the mountaintops. But in the kibbutzim, parents now felt that it was safe to bring their kids out of the shelters where they had been kept for days.

The Syrians had been shelling the frontier settlements heavily on Friday. The kibbutz I visited had also been attacked. The attackers had left some of their dead in the orchards. But now Israeli troops were here, and the settlers carried their kids up from the shelter. At seven in the morning, Kibbutz Resem resembled a community-service working-class camp in New Jersey, with baby buggies and playthings in the shabby sandy yard and small children in Denton pajamas and fleece slippers. But there are shell holes and corpses in the woods, and now and then one smells explosives and burned oil; and just below the trees there is an armored column. The soldiers are picking apples from the trees, and this—soldiers, apples, kids in sleepers, tricycles—is what the war looks like on Saturday morning.

The soldiers want to chat with foreign journalists. One, with studious thick specs, fought the Jordanians two days ago. With another, to my surprise, I find myself speaking in Spanish. He comes from Málaga, has lived eleven years in "the land," is a welder by trade and at present slightly wounded. His head is bandaged.

With great satisfaction the Israeli-Spaniard points below to the first Syrian prisoners. They are squatting in a gravel pit, slight brown men in high boots looking up at their guards. "The first," says my Jewish Spaniard. He spoke of them as though they were minnows. The big fish yet to come.

Then, grinning at my seersucker coat, he said I must be an American. Who else would be so oddly gotten up at the front? Some of the

European correspondents were in full jungle camouflage. My seer-sucker was like the Denton sleepers, but it has all been like that. From the comfortable veranda and the smooth grounds of the King David Hotel in Jerusalem, guests watched the violent fighting last Monday in the Old City. One eyewitness told me that he had just finished his breakfast when he went to look at the battle. He saw an Israeli service-man hit by a mortar, blown out of his boots; just a moment before, the man had been reading a newspaper.

Later, within sight of Mount Hebron, I stood with a party of journalists looking down into the valley where armored columns ma-neuvered. We could hear artillery and heavy machine guns and see the bombs exploding. Accompanying one of the foreign cameramen was an English chick in purple slacks, Carnaby Street boots gladdening her feet. It was, of course, no fault of hers that men were being killed be-low. The boyfriend had said, "Come along," so she came.

In Tel Aviv, there are ultramodern buildings, but in Gaza, within a few miles there are Arab tents that look like the moulted husks of dung beetles. They are patched with dirty sheets of plastic and pieces of cardboard. One rides through rich orchards, and suddenly the irri-gation ends. Waves of sand gush across the road. One leaves a tourist hotel with every modern luxury and an hour later sees Egyptian sol-diers swollen in death along the roads of the Sinai Peninsula, black and stinking in the desert sun, and all about them are the most mod-ern machines—Russian—burned out and useless. But these puzzling contrasts will not affect an Israeli at this moment. To him the ques-tions are clear. His existence was threatened, and he defended himself.

Sinai's Savage Sun Fits Its Scenery

Somewhere in Sinai, 13 June 1967—A concrete emplacement built by the Egyptians in the square of Gaza is now manned by an Israeli with a machine gun. Tanks control the main avenue and, from the rooftops, soldiers are watching.

Hot. Dull. The streets stink with fermented garbage. Corrugated roofs are weighted with rocks and old truck tires. Elderly women in black cover their somber, mannish faces with black veils, and some of the men go about in striped pajama trousers, suggesting sleep. The

Arab music, too, induces torpor with its endless sweetish winding and its absurd insinuations and seductions. One not only hears it but feels it distressingly in the bowels, like a drug.

The rubble is being swept from the sidewalks near Israeli headquarters by men in drooping white trousers, and an Egyptian doctor tells us that he has been given plenty of food and medical supplies by the army. He has a Nasserish look, even the Nasser mustache, and he smiles, but his mouth turns down at the corners, and when he is silent his face is heavy.

Leaving Gaza, we see the first of the tanks, vehicles, guns, and supplies abandoned by the Egyptians—some smashed and burned, but most of them intact. The lettering on the new trucks informs you that they were made in the Gorkvsky Autozavod. A fine investment for the Russians. It gives you confidence in the judgment of great powers when you see the Sinai Peninsula filled with millions of dollars' worth of machinery run off the roads into the sand and the dead bodies of Egyptians alongside.

Many of the dead are barefooted, having thrown off their shoes in flight. Only a few have helmets. Some wear the headdress. After leaving Gaza, I saw no live Egyptians, except for a group of captured snipers lying bound and blindfolded in a truck. The tent dwellers had run off. Their shelters of old sacking and tatters of plastic were unoccupied, with only a few dogs sniffing about and the flies, of course, in great prosperity. The jackals would be along presently, someone said.

A veteran of the 1956 Sinai campaign told me that the Egyptians had done much better this time. They had prepared their positions skillfully. They had extensive trenches. Their Russian or Nazi teachers—for there are, said my informant, a good many Germans in Egypt who settled down to a useful life after World War II—had some reason to feel encouraged, but without air cover, the Egyptian army was helpless, and Israel had knocked out the Arab airfields, even those supposedly out of range, blasting the runways, then returning to shoot up the planes. If they had not done this, the war would have been long and bloody.

No military expert, I know nothing of the caliber of guns or the thickness of armor. What I am aware of is the enormous scale of the victory and the wreckage, the heavy strength of the sun and the heavy odor of death. Burned trucks overturned, artillery shells spilling from boxes, clothing, shoes, bedsprings, smashed furniture, letters, Arab newspapers, stretchers, bandages, duffel bags, and a scattering of gas masks.

I particularly observed the destruction of automobiles. For an American, the car is something of an icon, and the fate of cars in war therefore has a singular interest. The hood and the trunk of a struck car flap open as if in surrender, and what is left of the glass becomes opaque. Some of the grayish cars left behind by the UN force are flattened and dismembered.

The Egyptian dead lie where they have fallen. No attempt has been made to gather them. The first dead Egyptian I saw was on his belly, raised from the ground by bloat. Legs spread taut, the swollen bodies resemble balloon figures in a parade. Faces blacken and are obliterated by the sun. Corruption is rapid in this heat, and the skull soon stares through. One feels the bristling of horror, not pity. The sour-sweet, decayed-cardboard smell becomes a taste in the mouth.

For once, as a nonsmoker, I am glad to have people about me puffing cigarettes. Some of the corpses lie charred and curled up near their tanks. Others, in groups, are seen in the trenches on hillsides, in the hollows. Presently one stops looking. You simply know by the slant of the figures that they are there.

Near the airport of Al Arish, the Israeli boys are playing soccer, performing calisthenics, resting. Two have found easy chairs and are lounging, chatting, eating rye bread. Behind them at a siding are burned-out railroad cars, black metal plates loosened from their rivets and springing out. One looks, trying to find relief from omnipresent death.

A Look o'er Jordan

16 June 1967—You pass from the Israeli sector of Jerusalem to the Jordanian along improvised corridors of brown Jerusalem dust; through coils of figure-eight barbed wire, steering around oil-drum barriers at the checkpoint where the fighting was heavy.

New Israeli apartment buildings were shelled. From some windows, inexplicably, dangle baby strollers and tricycles. Out in the dry weeds, soldiers in bush hats are digging up mines. They prod the ground lightly with metal rods and mark out safe lanes with white tapes.

This is touchy work. The Arabs were generous with their mines in this neighborhood around the United Nations relief warehouse. The UN building was shot up, but roof and walls are intact, and so are the sacks and cases of U.S. flour and rice, Swiss powdered milk, the cakes of soap, the beans, the Argentine corned beef, and the blended ground vegetable matter sent from America for the Arab refugees. The dried milk is labeled "Gift of the Swiss Confederation."

We—that is, Sydney Gruson, the representative of the *New York Times*, the Israeli liaison officer, the driver, and myself—are going down into the Jordan valley, territory taken last week. We are bound for Ramallah and will be going as far as Nablus, which the Bible calls Shechem. In Shechem, a passionate prince fell in love with Dinah, the daughter of Jacob, and took advantage of her. In revenge, her brothers killed all the young men of the town. Someone briefly mentions this piece of ancient history as the convoys pass.

Tanks and cannon are still going down toward the river ("I looked o'er the Jordan, an' what did I see"). Toward us come trucks, heavily loaded. The day is hot; the parching dusty wind, the khamsin, is blowing. New automobiles damaged by shrapnel and crumpled by tanks are a common sight. The trucks coming up the road carry British and American munitions. Enormous quantities of these have been found in storage dumps cut into Jordanian mountainsides. No one is surprised.

We Americans examine these exports curiously. The wooden cases, containing more than a hundred tons of munitions, are quite new. They bear a proud sticker—stars, stripes, red, white, and blue— and come from the Anniston Army Depot in Alabama. On the U.S.A. sticker two strong hands are joined in a heartening symbol of unity and friendship. One of the friends is unnamed. It might be anybody— anybody, that is, able to use 4.2-inch mortars or 106-mm ammunition for recoilless rifles, capable of launching W-20 grenades or of firing artillery shells. The caves in which this stuff was stored are two miles from biblical Shiloh and are very spacious, cool and airy. Ventilators are visible on the cliff above.

A soldier, British by birth, bare head, bare dusty chest streaked with sweat, says a few things to us about our country and our President, which I cannot reproduce. He says, "You bastards are awfully nice to us. You let us have tractors. And you give the peaceful natives all this other stuff." In fairness it should be added that some of the supplies are British.

There are also large cans of potatoes from Poland, neatly peeled, there are peas from Holland, and there is canned meat from Nigeria. Over the meat an Orthodox sergeant raises his arms in interdiction. The Israeli army keeps a kosher diet. Some of the soldiers, however, fix a hungry eye on the cans. But who knows, says someone, what the Nigerians are canning?

In Ramallah, before curfew, the Arab population is in the streets, the shops are open, and although one informant tells us there is nothing to eat, nothing to drink, we see meat in the butcher shops, bananas on the carts. Crews are repairing electrical lines.

The military governor here is Colonel Orial, a reserve paratroop officer. There are twin cities here, he tells us. Fibira is largely Moslem. Ramallah's Arabs are Christians. In addition to the combined population of 32,000, there are 25,000 Palestinians in the refugee camp. Several thousand Jordanian villagers took refuge in the town when the fighting began. There are two mayors, one from each community, who are cooperating with the colonel. Water will be in short supply until the electrical repairs are completed. The pumping is staggered, but no one is dying of thirst. There is no danger of epidemics. The Jordanian casualties are being buried. An Israeli medic supervises public health. The UN Relief and Works Agency for Palestine Refugees in the Near East continues to feed refugees.

Colonel Orial says that we will probably be interested as Americans in the plight of eighty or ninety American citizens of Arab birth visiting here and caught by the war. Since they are now in Israeli territory but with passports showing no Israeli entrance stamp, they are temporarily unable to leave. Himself a lawyer, Colonel Orial thinks this a nice point in law. "But we will solve it," he says. The colonel does not appear to be the sort of man who finds it hard to solve problems.

Going down, we meet an elderly couple from Chile visiting their old Ramallah home and have a Spanish chat with them. We have in common the Western hemisphere and are soaring above all local questions. The itinerary they show us ranges from Cairo to Spitzbergen.

The old gentleman wears Arab cloth on his head, bound with a braided plush cord, but he is quite an American in spirit. He is in his seventies. About the neck he is somewhat crumpled, but he does not seem weak or frightened.

Others, waiting to talk to the colonel, are near tears. Two soldiers in a jeep, leading us to the large refugee camp, lose their way and ask us to wait at the Ramallah Hilton while they make inquiries. There we talk with other soldiers and prowl about the empty hotel.

The Ramallah is not one of the classier Hiltons. It has a truncated look, as if severed from something much grander.

I get into the kitchen—always drawn to kitchens—and admire the great saucepans and cleavers, grinders, the chopping block a piece of tree trunk with the bark still on it. Nothing edible here—not that one has much appetite in the Holy Land while the khamsin blows and the hot mountains glitter. Shade and water count much more. Investigation, not hunger, is my motive.

I look into old gravy in a sauceboat covered with a crust of mutton fat. The deep freeze, unfrozen, is empty and smelly. A lily-pad pool has a coat of slime. "Our garden," the hotel's publicity reads, "6,800 sq. meters, is a relaxation to all. And during summer, Oriental delicious with the local 'arak' is served in folkloric presentation—an experience not to be missed. The cuisine blending west and eastern food will satisfy the most exacting appetite."

We are informed also that the hotel is five minutes from the airport. That is indeed so. The terminal and the runways are now in the hands of the Israelis. They seemed from the road to be intact. We drive up to the Kalandia camp and are at once surrounded by Arabs.

Young men in shirtsleeves come running from all directions. Two soldiers with submachine guns stand apart. Five deep, the stocky young men crowd in on us. At the center is someone speaking English. Three or four days unshaven, he has large fillings in his front teeth. Arms crossed, his eager nose and his eyes dilated, he is here to deliver the goods to the foreign press, the goods being a tale of hunger and grief.

The claim that people are starving is a little hard to support. We see bread everywhere and know that there is plenty of flour. The UN may not offer a varied diet, but there is no hunger. In tiny corners of soil near their stone warren, the refugees have tomato plants, squash vines, and a few small fig trees.

Less propaganda-conscious, the older people, the men in their pillow-ticking coats and the wives busty and comfortable in coarse white, ask us into their houses with elaborate courtesy. The tiny, sunken, windowless rooms have a few scraps of carpet, a stool, a bedroll, a piece of broken mirror. I look into the latrine—the cement floors with slots for the feet are washed down. There is water.

The men study trades at the UN schools but do little with them. It was impossible to find out how many of these Palestinian refugees had actually fought against Israel. Some—a considerable number, probably—had taken off and crossed the Jordan.

Israelis say that the Jordanians armed the entire population two days before the war. Guns are now being surrendered. Some sniping has occurred in Ramallah. But snipers are far more active in Gaza, where the refugee problem is acute. In Gaza, the UN is trying to feed 300,000 people, who are in an explosive state. I have been told that not even UN officials are safe among the Gaza refugees.

A Jordanian report says that 70,000 people who fled from Jericho and from the Syrian borders are in the Zerka area, near Amman. The Jordanians are now supposedly turning refugees back. And defeated Egyptians in the Sinai Desert are trying to make it back to Suez without food or water. Nasser does not want these survivors to spread details of the disaster. In rumor-happy Tel Aviv, people are saying that Egyptian soldiers emerging from the Sinai have been shot on Nasser's orders, and a French newspaper this morning has put this in print.

That Nasser, endorsed by Marxist leaders like Tito as a progressive and by the Russians and the Chinese as a true enemy of imperialism, might order a massacre of the survivors is not inconceivable. In any case, more men are dying at this moment of hunger, thirst, and exposure than were killed in battle.

An editorial in the London *Times* urges the great powers to send emergency help. Their fleets are still in the eastern Mediterranean. It seems to have taken Israel some time to realize that in disarming the Egyptians and allowing them to go free, "they were in fact sentencing them to death," says the *Times*.

Obviously the refugee problem requires an international solution. No one can reasonably claim that right is entirely on the Israeli side, and although some Arab leaders exploited the misery of the refugees to intensify hatred of Israel, the Israelis might have done more for the Arabs. It should have been possible, for instance, to set aside money for indemnity and reconstruction. Part of the money paid to Israel by West Germany might have been used for this purpose. Now the number of refugees has increased enormously, and if the old system is followed, the UN will be supporting more dozens of rotting slums in which demoralized, idle young men can concentrate on "politics."

Only Arab extremists can profit from this. A negligible percentage of the oil royalties of Kuwait would have paid for the rehabilitation of the Palestinian Arabs. So would the billions spent on two campaigns in the Sinai. So would the Suez Canal tolls.

A big Arab crowd in Nablus waits for gas or kerosene rations. Curfew has been advanced to 6:00 P.M., according to the military authorities. It is now 2:00 P.M. The streets are filled. The light comes down sharply, with a stony glitter from the Judean hills. Under this parching heat, I begin to sag somewhat.

I am glad to sit down in the thick-walled HQ building. An Israeli sergeant pours us a slug of whiskey. When we get our second wind, we venture into the heat again. The sun hits you at the back of the neck, and you get an odd thickening sensation in the skull.

We go down the street, looking into shops. We can buy nothing. Israeli currency is not accepted. Half a dozen Arabs stare at us from a barbershop and seem to be inviting us to enter. All the customers but one wear Western clothes. The exception, an elderly gentleman, has a tarboosh covering his head down to the sad brows. His chin is puckered with many emotions, but it is curiosity that wins out. He stands near us listening, a hookah tube (as near as I can make out) hanging from his pocket like a stethoscope.

The mirror is straight from a Coney Island funhouse. We all look very wide, with squash noses, split grins, and distorted eyes. Here, too, there is a spokesman. Very handsome, dark-browed, he has a furious nonsmile, and as the old barber, engrossed and even doting, cuts steadily at his black hair, the spokesman tells us, to begin with, that the Americans are spies. No, he does not believe that the Americans flew air cover for Israel. But Americans did spot the Egyptian airfields for the Israelis. Come, come, says the *New York Times* representative.

The hair snipping continues, and the spokesman tries to be pleasant but has too many passions to manage. His grin is bitter. Still, he wants to talk. Speaking to correspondents, he feels that his truth will reach the world. He is a dairy farmer, he says. He has sixty cows to milk. He can't get the gas to go to the relief of his suffering cows. They need their hay, and the children need milk. It occurs to me that the job might be done with donkeys. There are plenty of people here listening to music, being shaved, passing the time of day, and the farm is only two miles up the road.

Instead we go on about the future, Arab unity, hints of vengeance. "But you declared war on Israel," says the *Times*. "We had a treaty," says the gentleman dairy farmer. He adds, "King Hussein was pushed, outsidely, and pulled, insidely." Then he is silent and looks at us from under his brows, like the late John Gilbert playing an Arab role.

It is instructive to see what Middle Eastern poster artists do with the faces of Hollywood stars, the feelings they impart to them. Robert Mitchum Arabized is strong, honorable, but his features are twisted with foreknowledge of defeat. Fate is dead against him. We know that he is not going to make it. Our gentleman farmer is like that.

Now, having his neck trimmed with a Schick electric razor, he sits with stilted suffering pride. I am unable to give a T. E. Lawrence/Freya Stark interpretation to this look. In my cruder Midwestern judgment, it seems all wrong. What good are these traditional dignities? No good at all if they lead to the Sinai roads with their blasted Russian tanks, the black faces of the dead dissolving, and the survivors fighting for a sip of ditch water.

NEW YORK:

WORLD-FAMOUS IMPOSSIBILITY

(1970)

*H*ow do Americans think of New York? That is perhaps like asking how Scotsmen feel about the Loch Ness monster. It is our legendary phenomenon, our great thing, our world-famous impossibility. Some seem to wish that it were nothing more than a persistent rumor. It is, however, as human things go, very real, superreal. What is barely hinted in other American cities is condensed and enlarged in New York. There people feel themselves to be in the center of things. That is certainly true, and it is certainly odd.

In New York, as in all great capitals, people often behave symbolically and try to express the spirit of the place. A visiting diplomat writes a letter to express gratitude to the anonymous person who discovered his wallet and returned it intact to a lost and found. Off Times Square, a blind man has been assaulted, his Seeing Eye dog stolen, he is bleeding and weeping. A cop mutters, "This could only happen in New York." Impulses can be released here that in calmer environments are restrained. On every street, people are taught "what life is like."

New York is stirring, insupportable, agitated, ungovernable, demonic. No single individual can judge it adequately. Not even Walt Whitman could today embrace it emotionally; the attempt might capsize him. Those who want to contemplate the phenomenon are well advised to assume a contemplative position elsewhere. Those who wish to *feel* its depth had better be careful. For fifteen years I lived in and with New York. I now reside in Chicago.

The New York Times Book Review, 6 December 1970.

In other cities and regions, local pride has subsided. The old naive self-confidence is gone. After the events of the last decade, Texas no longer brags, Mayor Daley's Chicago does not boost. At the turn of the century, Chicago was a regional capital. In 1893, it dreamed of being a world city. Scholars, architects, poets, musicians, came up from Indiana, down from Wisconsin, east from Nebraska, but by the end of the twenties the cultural life of the Midwest was dying. Trains leaving Chicago carried poets as well as pork, and the city rapidly sank into provincialism.

Several generations of young Americans, seeking a broader and deeper life, abandoned Main Street to the businessmen and yokels and went to Paris or Greenwich Village. America's great aim was not, after all, to encourage painters, philosophers, and novelists. To live as a painter or an intellectual, one had to go "somewhere else," away from Detroit, Minneapolis, or Kansas City. As bohemians and expatriates, these emigrants hoped to find the dream states and the special atmospheres on which art thrives.

Bohemian life in the Village was, in the twenties, quite elegant—even patrician, for it attracted the rich as well as writers, painters, and radicals. The old Village was a grand success, and for a time New York really was the center of the country for certain rare and valuable qualities. Its free versers, free lovers, elegant boozers, its rich ninnies and eccentrics, its artists and revolutionists, charmed and heartened the younger generation, strengthening their resistance to the ugliness and philistinism of the hometown.

All that, of course, is over. New York is now the business center of American culture, the amusement or frivolity center, the excitement center, the anxiety center. But it has no independent and original intellectual life. It provides no equilibrium, it offers no mental space to artists. Ideas are no longer discussed here. Meeting an old Village intellectual, now gray-bearded and hugely goggled, I find him as densely covered with protest buttons as a fish is with scales. He has become a former intellectual.

For better or for worse, the intellectual life of the country has found sanctuary in the universities. Bohemian manners and notions have also spread over the continent. New York is the principal processor and distributor of the mental goods consumed by the American public. The present leaders of culture in New York are its publicity in-tellectuals. These are college-educated men and women who have never lived as poets, painters, composers, or thinkers but who have successfully organized writing, art, thought, and science in publishing houses, in museums, in foundations, in magazines, in newspapers (mainly the *New York Times*), in the fashion industry, in television, and in advertising. All these things have been made to pay and pay handsomely.

No less an authority than Mr. Jason Epstein of Random House has told us in the *New York Review of Books* that New York can be a splendid place—if you are making fifty thousand dollars a year. He might have added that what Mr. Theodore Roszak has called the "counterculture" and Professor Lionel Trilling the "adversary culture" is the Dick Whittington's cat that brings in this sort of wealth; that the sale of radical ideas (some of them quite old, but people have been too busy to read Baudelaire, Proudhon, or Marx for themselves) is prof-itable; and that criticism, or even open hatred of society, is no impedi-ment to success in this glittering city.

But I do not think anyone will fly in today from Boise, Idaho, ea-gerly seeking in New York other writers whose love of poetry is pure or who are waiting on the steps of the public library like Athenians to discuss Existence or Justice. The publicity intellectuals have little in-terest in such matters. They read little, and they don't gather to talk about literature. Cultural New York founds its prosperity on the for-mer presence of these great things and keeps up the illusion that they are still present. New York is a great marketer of echoes. The past is profitably translated into Village rentals and real estate values, into meal prices and hotel rates. New York seems to thrive also on a sense of national deficiency, on the feelings of many who think themselves sunk hopelessly in the American void where there is no color, no the-ater, no vivid contemporaneousness, where people are unable to speak authoritatively, globally, about life.

We have no holy places in America, so we make do with the pro-fane. Inquire in Rockford, Illinois, what is happening there. The com-monest answer will be: "Nothing. The action is all in San Francisco, Las Vegas, and New York." When you return to Chicago from a trip to New York, you are asked: "What did you see? Of course you went to the theater." But what can one see in the New York theater now? People's sexual organs. The aim is perhaps to celebrate one's emancipation from puritanism and to mark our redemption from sexual bondage. But *Oh! Calcutta!* is really a play within a play, for New York itself is the theater of the nation, showing strange things. Outsiders—the rest of the country—do not tire of watching.

THE DAY THEY SIGNED

THE TREATY

(1979)

*T*he gray skies opened as the historic hour approached, the wind blew the clouds out, the sun shone on the great crowd of guests and journalists who had come to watch the signing of the Egyptian-Israeli peace treaty on the North Lawn of the White House.

Despite the sunshine the wind was stiff; the thermometer stood at 45 degrees, a nipping and an eager air. On their platforms the TV technicians worked with great-snouted, funnel-eyed cameras, and private camera buffs by the hundreds stood on folding chairs to photograph the scene: Prime Minister Begin, Presidents Carter and Sadat, their wives. They were perhaps hoping that their lenses might capture things their own eyes weren't seeing. The Marine band played jazzy, military quick-step music. From Lafayette Park came the amplified screams of demonstrating Palestinians and their sympathizers, kept at a distance by hundreds of riot police. Saint John's Church rang its bells to celebrate the occasion and perhaps also to send ecclesiastical blessings over the noise of protest. Secret Service agents checked the papers of invited guests; on the roof of the White House were men with binoculars. From an upper window, the White House chef in his tall white hat was looking down.

Beside me, an elderly couple had gotten up on their chairs. The lady said to me with an Eastern European accent, "But I am so small —I can't see." Her husband, in his old-fashioned, voluminous, fur-collared coat, was not much taller. He would, forty years ago, have been well dressed in his conservative pinstripes and homburg. I identi-

Newsday, 1 April 1979.

fied them as Americanized refugees. Greatly stirred, they seemed hardly to hear the indignation of the working press behind the ropes, telling them to step down. Nor did they care much about the eminent persons who went about recognizing one another: Henry Kissinger, Senator Moynihan soaring pleasantly above everyone—the privilege of importance or great height.

Abraham Beame of New York City did not enjoy the same advantage but was unmistakably a "notable"—that is what cops in Chicago call people whose pictures appear in the papers. Hizzoner carries his own sharp little aura. I mistook him for Judge Charles E. Wyzanski of Cambridge, Massachusetts, and had to be corrected by a New Yorker. Arthur Goldberg was present too. About him someone asked, "Why did he let himself be wheedled out of a lifetime job? Some sweet-talker, that Lyndon Johnson."

The many celebrities embraced enthusiastically, grappling affectionately, kissing one another. There were wonderful personages to look at: gowned Coptic and Greek Orthodox priests, generals with campaign ribbons, faces familiar to us on the television screen advancing in the flesh; behind us, masses of cameramen; before us, the alert formations of the Secret Service and flags flapping over the historic table on which the treaty was to be signed.

Until the last moment Sadat and Begin had bickered over wording, Sadat insisting on the Gulf of Aqaba, Begin holding out for the Gulf of Eilat and also, I was informed, for Judea and Samaria. But here they were, differences for the moment composed, ready to sign their names.

Most of those present were moved. Some said they were moved against their better judgment. They hadn't the strength to resist the great moment. "Stupendous," said Arthur Goldberg. I spoke to other observers, however, who could not bring themselves to put aside the habit of a caveat. Well, we'll see, they said. Or, *Pourvu que ça dure.* We are all filled with warm blood; the impulse to hope is very strong in us; those who have seen a great deal of life have learned, however, the wisdom of keeping a quantity of cold blood in reserve.

But even the most reserved and cautious of the Israeli, Egyptian, and American diplomats and journalists whose opinions I sought said that this was a most significant advance, a great historic occasion, peace between enemies who have repeatedly spilled each other's blood.

Hardly a man of importance today present has escaped personal suffering. The brother of Sadat fell in the war of 1973, the son of Israeli Defense Minister Ezer Weizman has never recovered from his wounds. Israeli Foreign Minister Moshe Dayan very early suffered the loss of an eye. The families of Begin and of many of his cabinet officers and assistants were destroyed in Hitler's murder camps. One of Begin's staff, Mr. Elissar, was as a boy saved from destruction by the death of another child, whose parents had emigration papers and who took young Elissar in the dead boy's place. Elissar's own family did not survive. Such are the people who this day affix their names to the agreement.

The AP reports from Beirut: "Much of the Arab world seethes with outrage today, the day of peace for Egypt and Israel. Palestinian leader Yasser Arafat vowed to 'chop off the hands' of the 'stooge Sadat, the terrorist Begin, and the imperialist Carter.'"

The ceremony of signing is followed by the speeches of the principals. Mr. Carter announces that we must begin to wage peace. Mr. Sadat, a measured, mellowed orator, says, against waves of protest from Lafayette Park, let there be no more bloodshed and suffering. Let there be no denial of rights, he adds, adroitly referring to the Palestinians. He is an accomplished statesman, the most polished of today's speakers.

Begin, taking his turn at the microphones, is aware of his reputation as a chronic objector. "I agree but, as usual, with an amendment," he says. He tells the crowd that this is the third-greatest day of his life, the first being the day in 1948 on which Israel achieved statehood, the second that on which East Jerusalem was taken by Israeli troops.

Thus Sadat tries to assure the Arab world that he continues to represent Arab interests, while Begin still asserts that Jerusalem belongs to the Jews. He speaks of the personal sacrifices exacted by the long treaty negotiations, says that he has been abused by the world, abused by his own people; worst of all, he has been abused by his oldest friends. But he concludes with the 126th Psalm: "They that sow in tears shall reap in joy."

The ceremony ending, my wife and I return to the White House press quarters, where we find that crowds of reporters have been watching the event on color television sets. All the vending machines are empty, all the candy has been eaten, everywhere cardboard boxes are stuffed with empty cans and paper plates and cups and sandwich wrappings and cigarette butts.

A weary young woman in slacks and white sneakers is curled up in her paper's cubicle, eating Fritos from a package. The elderly correspondent of the *New Republic* unlocks his confidential file, then with another key unlocks his telephone, pulls out the plug of a lock, and dials a number. Egyptian and Israeli newsmen confer in separate groups. One Middle Eastern journalist, a big man, limps by. The look on his face is the look of Androcles' lion before the thorn was removed.

On a day like this, one naturally regrets not being an expert or one of those insiders who thoroughly understand. It's hell to be an amateur. A little reflection calms your sorrow, however. The experts in their own little speedboat, the rest of us floating with the rest of mankind in a great barge—that is the picture. We must do what we can to grasp whatever it is possible to grasp of all these treaties, SALT talks, Iranian revolutions, Russian maneuvers in Yemen, Chinese visits.

President Johnson used to say that *he* knew what was happening in Vietnam; *he* had information he couldn't share with us and without which we had no opinions worth considering. But he, too, turned out to be just another amateur. And we non-knowers have our rights. "No annihilation without representation," as Arnold Toynbee once put it. You dare not give up the struggle to form an opinion.

There are moments, certainly, when you feel like Mother Goose's pussycat who goes to London to see the queen. But at other times you refuse to concede that the keenest of professionals and specialists have the right to dismiss any considerable investment of mind, feeling, and imagination. When I supported the Israeli Peace Now Movement last summer, I, together with the other signers, was denounced as a meddler and an ignoramus who had no right to a viewpoint. "The notion—how can we criticize when we do not live in Israel—has been a remarkably powerful slogan," writes the Chicago sociologist Morris Janowitz. From our side we might argue that Israel, for its survival, is obliged to understand certain matters of which we as Americans have some firsthand knowledge.

One need not be a professional superstar to understand the fundamentals. Israel's Arab neighbors have until now refused to recognize its legitimacy, its right as a sovereign state, and to this day speak of it as the "Zionist entity." Sadat, for a price, of course, has given Israel this indispensable recognition. Moreover, Israel has until now had to depend for survival entirely on its strength, but it is plain to everyone that the military effectiveness of Israel must eventually reach its limit, perhaps has already reached it.

There are those who question whether Israel won a decisive victory in 1973. They question also whether it can continue to stand the economic and social strains of preparedness, the strain of internal disputes provoked by garrison conditions, the mobilization of reservists, the anxieties and the expenses of siege life, the prospect of further wars and of greater casualties, and the last and most terrible of alternatives—namely, the "nuclear option."

What is fundamental, therefore, and beyond argument, is the need for a political solution—a political-military solution. Israel is in no position to reject this. Begin could not of course publicly state what he assuredly knew about the increasing futility of relying on military strength alone. It would be both demoralizing and dangerous to make such statements.

But since the revolution in Iran, the facts are clear for all the world to see. A complete victory of radical extremism in the Arab world would mean the defeat of all Jewish hopes, the end of Israel. According to President Carter's national security adviser, Zbigniew Brzezinski, with whom I talked briefly after the ceremony, this would present the greatest danger also to Western Europe. What he had in mind, I take it, is what people have begun to call "the Finlandization of Europe." He did not himself use this phrase.

I had met Mr. Brzezinski about a decade ago, at a meeting of some sort. (How many meetings of some sort there have been! You can measure your life out with them, as if they were Mr. Prufrock's coffee spoons.) Mr. Brzezinski has a pleasing face, a narrow aristocratic Polish nose in which I, raised among Poles in Chicago, can identify a characteristic irregularity of line, the Slavic eye frame, and a whiteness of the skin more intense than that of Western Europe—not a pallor but a positive whiteness.

Mr. Brzezinski, a fluent and willing talker, necessarily guarded but not dragging his feet, said he was immensely pleased by the treaty—

pleased but not exuberant. Brzezinski did not believe the Saudis would discontinue financial support to Egypt although they declared that they would follow the policies laid down in the Baghdad conference last November, and these include economic sanctions against Egypt. He opined also that the Israelis would prove flexible enough to deal with the Arab problem. He cited in evidence the liberal traditions of Judaism and, more to the point, a recent speech in the Knesset by Shimon Peres, the leader of the opposition.

Mr. Peres, in his desire to come to terms with the Palestinian Arabs, took positions his party would have rejected only a few years ago. Golda Meir refused to acknowledge that there was any such thing as a Palestinian at all. Mr. Brzezinski did not think that Peres was merely sounding off. Peres is a tough politician who expects to return to power, and a softening of his views reflects a change in opinion in the country. Mr. Brzezinski evidently believes that responsible Israeli politicians do not intend, cannot afford, to let the treaty unravel and that they understand quite well what the seizure of power by radicals in Egypt would mean for them.

Less guarded officials, off the record, tell you that Sadat was hardly oppressed by the great rage he had generated in the Arab world. Instead Sadat seems fairly lighthearted about it, all things considered. These officials tell you that Sadat has the most violent contempt for his enemies in the Arab world, that his untranslatable purple invectives belong to no minor branch of the art of metaphor. H. L. Mencken once published a dictionary of curses, of all the terrible things his detractors had to say about him. This was purely a local American product. It might be useful to do the same thing on a world scale.

About Jordan's King Hussein the same free-spoken officials say that his recent behavior has been unpleasant, that he complains, beefs, and reproaches the Americans. They concede, of course, that he is a man who has been living uncomfortably close to death for many years and that, unable to pursue an independent course in the Mideast, he is intensely frustrated.

Boutros Ghali, the Egyptian foreign minister, in his large hotel suite, gave us his view of some of the disputed issues. He is a diplomat whose smooth Egyptian-French surface easily deflects unwelcome questions. There are no unmannerly rejections, only an easy, practiced turning aside of things he doesn't intend to discuss. For these things he substitutes certain rhetorical preparations of his own. I have done much the same on some occasions, with less style, and not in a setting of Oriental rugs and cut flowers.

Egypt, he says, has a duty to represent the interests of the Palestinian Arabs since no stability in the region is possible until they receive satisfaction. So peace with Israel requires justice for the Palestinians and is the direct concern of Egypt. I suggest that Egypt might offer more definite plans to mitigate the hardships of Palestinians, especially those in the refugee camps. I am thinking of the camps in Lebanon. Ghali counters that the greatest hardship for the Palestinians is that they have no national base, no home to return to. But not that many would want to go back. A large number of Palestinians have prospered abroad. They are among the most advanced, the best educated and skilled, of the Arabs. Some are self-made millionaires, and it is unlikely that these would want to live in a Palestinian state, but it is necessary for such a state to exist. It is after all one of the effects of Zionism to sharpen Arab nationalism.

His comment on Dayan, with whom he has had extended discussions in this same hotel suite, is that Dayan is Begin's vizier, that between them there is the Oriental connection of caliph and courtier-statesman. Ghali sees Weizman as the crown prince and heir apparent who has the traditional mistrust of the vizier and invariably fires him.

I ask Ghali what he thinks of the anti-Westernism of the Iranian Moslems and whether the revolution is evidence that Moslem orthodoxy cannot accept modernism. He answers that Islam is able and willing to accept modern conditions. I suggest that these conditions are not universally attractive and that I can readily understand why the religious are so repelled by them. You foreigners lack the true perspective, says Ghali. There are so many factions in Iran that only time will show which will win out. I say nothing of hands lopped off and executions ordered by revolutionary councils. My wife speaks of the woman question in the Moslem world. Mr. Ghali does not choose to discuss this.

He is interested, however, in a question about Israeli businessmen and technicians in Egypt. He puts cultural relations in the first place. These, to him, are more important than business connections. The Israelis should learn Arabic, he says. He emphasizes that he does not mean the lower-class Arabic many Jews learned from their neighbors in the old days—the sort of Arabic Dayan speaks. Oriental Jews when they emigrated to Israel should not have discarded their Arabic when they began to speak Hebrew.

Israelis would be wrong to take an attitude of superiority and assume that they would naturally be called upon to improve the backward Egyptians. They must not make the mistake the French made in Algeria of adopting the superior role. I interpret him to mean that a crowd of Israelis will be attracted to Egypt by business opportunities and by the vast sums provided by the United States for the modernization of agriculture and industry. They will not be welcome; they had better proceed with infinite tact.

Ghali speaks often of France and the French, of French intellectuals. He recommends an article by Jean-Paul Sartre on Sadat's visit to Jerusalem. His friends call him Pierre, he tells us. Sadat calls him Pierre when he is pleased with him and when he is displeased addresses him as Boutros.

When we leave his suite we see through the open door of an adjoining room the Egyptian musclemen, the hulking guards, coatless, taking it easy, their leather holsters creaking as they move about. They are formidably armed. The American security gentleman sitting quietly in the corridor has a device for messages plugged into his ear like a hearing aid. Under his buttoned jacket he no doubt carries a magnum: a calm type you might meet at a ticket counter in the airport and exchange the usual inanities about fog on the runway with.

Lastly the party, the Carters' great outdoor bash, to which Joseph Alsop referred as "the President's durbar." A long line of guests waited in the sharp wind to enter the White House and made their way, through a passage walled in fluttering plastic, into the great orange and yellow tent.

The *Washington Post* reported the words of one delighted guest: "It's the first time I've seen so much of Washington's social establishment in the Carter White House." People, the *Post* added, flitted about like mayflies.

Yes, they did flit, and chat, and embrace, and exchange show-business kisses. Well-known people are ecstatic at finding one another on these great occasions. Bands played, the Singing Sergeants sang hard; no one paid much attention to them. The important guests— Vice President Mondale, Mr. Kissinger, Energy Secretary James Schlesinger (a person of monumental presence, a great pillar smoking his pipe)—shook hands, smiled, gave out their views, I presume. I listened to few conversations; there were too many distractions.

I met Mr. Ghali again; he bowed with polite charm; in his black-rimmed spectacles he looked extremely Parisian, something like the late actor Sacha Guitry. Senator Moynihan told me how greatly the afternoon ceremony had moved him. Mr. Kissinger told me nothing but coldly endured my handshake. He was very like Queen Victoria, it struck me. Some of my mischievous remarks in print apparently had displeased him. ("We are not amused.")

Our table companions were Congressman Clement Zablocki of Milwaukee, a power in Foreign Affairs; his young daughter, a student of remedial speech; a Texas businessman, one of Carter's very early supporters, his wife and daughter, all extremely good-looking, silently taking in the celebrity show; Joseph Burg, Israeli minister of the interior, a large, amiable, loose-jointed person in an Orthodox beanie, keen to have some good talk but dismayed by the volume of noise.

He did his best. He told me two very good jokes in Yiddish and reminisced about old times at the University of Leipzig, where he had studied symbolic logic. Hearing that my wife was a mathematician, he talked with animation about the great Hilbert and told us what he, Mr. Burg, had had to say in his orals about Immanuel Kant. Later, I heard him trying to interest Mr. Zablocki in Tocqueville's *Democracy in America*, suggesting that the congressman read it.

So there were, after all, serious people present who could not easily accept the gala on a day like this and were puzzled and put out by the gaudiness and the noise. But the Americans had apparently tired themselves out making statements about the great event. "Wonderful, the greatest day there's been," Averell Harriman had said. And Arthur Goldberg had told the press, "a stupendous achievement."

"Wonderful" and "stupendous" bring you to a full stop. For the moment there is nothing to do but eat your salmon mousse, sip your wine, and wait for the powers of mind and feeling to regroup themselves for a fresh start.

You tell yourself that human beings have lived for many thousands of years in the Mideast and in that time have created complex difficulties, beliefs bewilderingly similar and for that reason utterly dissimilar, hatreds and profound needs that cannot be conjured away. What footing rationality can find in these infinitely contorted desires and antipathies in our revolutionary time remains to be seen.

MY PARIS

(1983)

*C*hanges in Paris? Like all European capitals, the city has undergone changes. The most unpleasantly conspicuous are the herds of tall buildings beyond the ancient gates. Old districts like Passy, peculiarly gripping in their dinginess, are almost unrecognizable today with their new apartment houses and office buildings, most of which would suit a Mediterranean port better than Paris. It's no easy thing to impose color on the dogged northern gray, the native Parisian *grisaille*—flinty, foggy, dripping, and, for most of the year, devoid of any brightness. The gloom will have its way with these new *immeubles* too; you may be sure of that. When Verlaine wrote that the rain fell into his heart as it did upon the city (referring to almost any city in the region), he wasn't exaggerating a bit. As a onetime resident of Paris (I arrived in 1948), I can testify to that. New urban architecture will find itself ultimately powerless against the *grisaille*. Parisian gloom is not simply climatic; it is a spiritual force that acts not only on building materials, on walls and rooftops, but also on character, opinion, and judgment. It is a powerful astringent.

But the changes . . . I wandered about Paris not very long ago to see how thirty-odd years had altered the place. The new skyscraper on the boulevard du Montparnasse is almost an accident, something that had strayed away from Chicago and come to rest on a Parisian street corner. In my old haunts between the boulevard du Montparnasse and the Seine, what is most immediately noticeable is the disappearance of

The New York Times Magazine, Part 2, The Sophisticated Traveler, 13 March 1983.

certain cheap conveniences. High rents have driven out the family bistros that once served delicious, inexpensive lunches. A certain decrepit loveliness is giving way to unattractive, overpriced, overdecorated newness. Dense traffic—the small streets make you think of Yeats's "mackerel-crowded seas"—requires an alertness incompatible with absentminded rambling. Dusty old shops in which you might lose yourself for a few hours are scrubbed up now and sell pocket computers and high-fidelity equipment. Stationers who once carried notebooks with excellent paper now offer a flimsy product that lets the ink through. Very disappointing. Cabinetmakers and other small artisans once common are hard to find.

My neighbor the *emballeur* on the rue de Verneuil disappeared long ago. This cheerful specialist wore a smock and beret, and as he worked in an unheated shop his big face was stung raw. He kept a cold butt end in the corner of his mouth—one seldom sees a *mégot* in this new era of prosperity. A pet three-legged hare, slender in profile, fat in the hindquarters, stirred lopsidedly among the crates. But there is no more demand for hand-hammered crates. Progress has eliminated all such simple trades. It has replaced them with boutiques that sell costume jewelry, embroidered linens, or goose-down bedding. In each block there are three or four *antiquaires*. Who would have thought that Europe contained so much old junk? Or that, the servant class having disappeared, hearts nostalgic for the bourgeois epoch would hunt so eagerly for Empire breakfronts, recamier sofas, and curule chairs?

Inspecting the boulevards, I find curious survivors. On the boulevard Saint-Germain, the dealer in books of military history and memorabilia who was there thirty-five years ago is still going strong. Evidently there is a permanent market for leather sets that chronicle the ancient wars. (If you haven't seen the crowds at the Invalides and the huge, gleaming tomb of Napoleon, if you underestimate the power of glory, you don't know what France is.) Near the rue des Saints-Pères, the pastry shop of Camille Hallu, Aîné, is gone, together with numerous small bookshops, but the dealer in esoteric literature on the next block has kept up with the military history man down the street, as has the umbrella merchant nearby. Her stock is richer than ever, sheaves of umbrellas and canes with parakeet heads and barking dogs in silver. Thanks to tourists, the small hotels thrive—as do the electric Parisian cockroaches who live in them, a swifter and darker breed than their American cousins. There are more winos than in austere postwar days, when you seldom saw *clochards* drinking in doorways.

The ancient gray and yellow walls of Paris have the strength needed to ride out the shock waves of the present century. Invisible electronic forces pierce them, but the substantial gloom of courtyards and kitchens is preserved. Boulevard shop windows, however, show that life is different and that Parisians feel needs they never felt before. In 1949, I struck a deal with my landlady on the rue Vaneau: I installed a gas hot-water heater in the kitchen in exchange for two months' rent. It gave her great joy to play with the faucet and set off a burst of gorgeous flames. Neighbors came in to congratulate her. Paris was then in what Mumford called the Paleotechnic Age. It has caught up now with advancing technology, and French shops display the latest in beautiful kitchens—counters and tables of glowing synthetic alabaster, artistic in form, the last word in technics.

Once every week during the nasty winter of 1950, I used to meet my friend the painter Jesse Reichek in a café on the rue du Bac. As we drank cocoa and played casino, regressing shamelessly to childhood, he would lecture me on Giedion's *Mechanization Takes Command* and on the Bauhaus. Shuffling the cards, I felt that I was simultaneously going backward and forward. We little thought in 1950 that by 1983 so many modern kitchen shops would be open for business in Paris, that the curmudgeonly French would fall in love so passionately with sinks, refrigerators, and microwave ovens. I suppose that the disappearance of the *bonne à tout faire* is behind this transformation. The post-bourgeois era began when your housemaid found better work to do. Hence all these *son et lumière* kitchens and the velvety pulsations of invisible ventilators.

I suppose that this is what "modern" means in Paris now.

It meant something different at the beginning of the century, and it was this other something that so many of us came looking for in 1948. Until 1939, Paris was the center of a great international culture, welcoming Spaniards, Russians, Italians, Romanians, Americans; open to the Picassos, Diaghilevs, Modiglianis, Brancusis, and Pounds at the glowing core of the modernist art movement. It remained to be seen whether the fall of Paris in 1940 had only interrupted this creativity. Would it resume when the defeated Nazis had gone back to Germany? There were those who suspected that the thriving international center had been declining during the thirties, and some believed that it was gone for good.

I was among those who came to investigate, part of the first wave. The blasts of war had no sooner ended than thousands of Americans packed their bags to go abroad. Eager Francophile travelers, poets, painters, and philosophers were vastly outnumbered by the restless young—students of art history, cathedral lovers, refugees from the South and the Midwest, ex-soldiers on the GI Bill, sentimental pilgrims—as well as by people no less imaginative, with schemes for getting rich. A young man I had known in Minnesota came over to open a caramel-corn factory in Florence. Adventurers, black-marketeers, smugglers, would-be *bon vivants*, bargain-hunters, bubbleheads—tens of thousands crossed on old troop ships, seeking business opportunities or sexual opportunities, or just for the hell of it. Damaged London was severely depressed, full of bomb holes and fireweed, whereas Paris was unhurt and about to resume its glorious artistic and intellectual life.

The Guggenheim Foundation had given me a fellowship, and I was prepared to take part in the great revival—when and if it began. Like the rest of the American contingent, I had brought my illusions with me, but I like to think that I was also skeptical (perhaps the most tenacious of my illusions). I was not going to sit at the feet of Gertrude Stein. I had no notions about the Ritz Bar. I would not be boxing with Ezra Pound, as Hemingway had done, or writing in bistros while waiters brought oysters and wine. Hemingway the writer I admired without limits; Hemingway the *figure* was to my mind the quintessential tourist, the one who believed that he alone was the American whom Europeans took to their hearts as one of their own. In simple truth, the Jazz Age Paris of American legend had no charms for me, and I had my reservations also about the Paris of Henry James—bear in mind the unnatural squawking of East Side Jews as James described it in *The American Scene*. You wouldn't expect a relative of those barbarous East Siders to be drawn to the world of Madame de Vionnet, which had, in any case, vanished long ago.

Life, said Samuel Butler, is like giving a concert on the violin while learning to play the instrument—that, friends, is real wisdom. (I never tire of quoting it.) I was concertizing and practicing scales at the same time. I *thought* I understood why I had come to Paris. Writers like Sherwood Anderson and, oddly enough, John Cowper Powys had made clear to me what was lacking in American life. "American men are tragic without knowing why they are tragic," wrote Powys in his *Autobiography*. "They are tragic by reason of the desolate thinness and forlorn narrowness of their sensual mystical contacts. Mysticism and Sensuality are the things that most of all redeem life." Powys, mind you, was an admirer-of American democracy. I would have had no use for him otherwise. I believed that only the English-speaking democracies had real politics. In politics continental Europe was infantile—horrifying. But what America lacked, for all its political stability, was the capacity to enjoy intellectual pleasures as though they were sensual pleasures. This was what Europe offered, or was said to offer.

There was, however, a part of me that remained unconvinced by this formulation, denied that Europe—as advertised—still existed and was still capable of gratifying the American longing for the rich and the rare. True writers from Saint Paul, Saint Louis, and Oak Park, Illinois, had gone to Europe to write their American books, the best work of the twenties. Corporate, industrial America could not give them what they needed. In Paris, they were free to be fully American. It was from abroad that they sent imaginative rays homeward. But was it the European imaginative reason that had released and stirred them? Was it Modern Paris itself or a new universal Modernity working in all countries, an international culture, of which Paris was, or *had* been, the center. I knew what Powys meant by his imaginative redemption from the desolate thinness and forlorn narrowness experienced by Americans, whether or not they were conscious of it. At least I thought I did. But I was aware also of a seldom-mentioned force visible in Europe itself to anyone who had eyes—the force of a nihilism that had destroyed most of its cities and millions of lives in a war of six long years. I could not easily accept the plausible sets: America, the thinning of the life impulses; Europe, the cultivation of the subtler senses still valued, still going on. Indeed, a great European prewar literature had told us what nihilism was, had warned us what to expect. Céline had spelled it out quite plainly in his *Voyage to the End of the Night*. His Paris was still there, more *there* than Sainte-Chapelle or the

Louvre. Proletarian Paris, middle-class Paris, not to mention intellectual Paris, which was trying to fill nihilistic emptiness with Marxist
doctrine—all transmitted the same message.

Still, I had perfectly legitimate reasons for being here. Arthur
Koestler ribbed me one day when he met me in the street with my
five-year-old son. He said, "Ah? You're married? Is this your *child*?
And you've come to *Paris*?" To be Modern, you see, meant to be detached from tradition and traditional sentiments, from national politics and, of course, from the family. But it was not in order to be
Modern that I was living on the rue de Verneuil. My aim was to be
free from measures devised and applied by others. I could not agree, to
begin with, on any definition. I would be ready for definition when I
was ready for an obituary. I had already decided not to let American
business society make my life for me, and it was easy for me to shrug
off Mr. Koestler's joke. Besides, Paris was not my dwelling place; it was
only a stopover. There was no dwelling place.

One of my American friends, a confirmed Francophile, made
speeches to me about the City of Man, the City of Light. I took his
rhetoric at a considerable discount. I was not, however, devoid of sentiment. To say it in French, I was *aux anges* in Paris, wandering about,
sitting in cafés, walking beside the liniment-green, rot-smelling Seine.
I can think of visitors who were not greatly impressed by the City of
Man. Horace Walpole complained of the stink of its little streets in the
eighteenth century. For Rousseau, it was the center of *amour propre*,
the most warping of civilized vices. Dostoyevsky loathed it because it
was the capital of Western bourgeois vainglory. Americans, however,
loved the place. I, too, with characteristic reservations, fell for it. True,
I spent lots of time in Paris thinking about Chicago, but I discovered—and the discovery was a very odd one—that in Chicago I had
for many years been absorbed in thoughts of Paris. I was a longtime
reader of Balzac and of Zola and knew the city of Père Goriot, the
Paris at which Rastignac had shaken his fist, swearing to fight it to the
finish, the Paris of Zola's drunkards and prostitutes, of Baudelaire's
beggars and the children of the poor whose pets were sewer rats. The
Parisian pages of Rilke's *The Notebooks of Malte Laurids Brigge* had
taken hold of my imagination in the thirties, as had the Paris of
Proust, especially those dense, gorgeous, and painful passages of *Time
Regained* describing the city as it was in 1915—the German night

bombardments, Madame Verdurin reading of battlefields in the morning paper as she sipped her coffee. Curious how the place had moved in on me. I was not at all a Francophile, not at all the unfinished American prepared to submit myself to the great city in the hope that it would round me out or complete me.

In my generation, the children of immigrants *became* Americans. An effort was required. One made oneself, freestyle. To become a Frenchman on top of that would have required a second effort. Was I being invited to turn myself into a Frenchman? Well, no, but it seemed to me that I would not be fully accepted in France unless I had done everything possible to become French. And that was not for me. I was already an American, and I was also a Jew. I had an American outlook, superadded to a Jewish consciousness. France would have to take me as I was.

From Parisian Jews I learned what life had been like under the Nazis, about the roundups and deportations in which French officials had cooperated. I read Céline's *Les Beaux Draps*, a collection of crazy, murderous harangues, seething with Jew-hatred.

A sullen, grumbling, drizzling city still remembered the humiliations of occupation. Dark bread, *pain de seigle*, was rationed. Coal was scarce. None of this inspired American-in-Paris fantasies of gaiety and good times in the Ritz Bar or the Closerie des Lilas. More appropriate now was Baudelaire's Parisian sky weighing the city down like a heavy pot lid, or the Paris of the Communard *pétroleurs* who had set the Tuileries afire and blown out the fortress walls. I saw a barricade going up across the Champs Élysées one morning, but there was no fighting. The violence of the embittered French was for the most part internal.

No, I wasn't devoid of sentiments, but the sentiments were sober. But why did Paris affect me so deeply? Why did this imperial, ceremonious, ornamental mass of structures weaken my American refusal to be impressed, my Jewish skepticism and reticence; why was I such a sucker for its tones of gray, the patchy bark of its sycamores, and its bitter-medicine river under the ancient bridges? The place was, naturally, indifferent to me, a peculiar alien from Chicago. Why did it take hold of my emotions?

For the soul of a civilized, or even partly civilized, man, Paris was one of the permanent settings, a theater, if you like, where the greatest problems of existence might be represented. What future, if any, was there for this theater? It could not tell you what to represent. Could anyone in the twentieth century make use of these unusual opportunities? Americans of my generation crossed the Atlantic to size up the challenge, to look upon this human, warm, noble, beautiful, and also proud, morbid, cynical, and treacherous setting.

Paris inspires young Americans with no such longings and challenges now. The present generation of students, if it reads Diderot, Stendhal, Balzac, Baudelaire, Rimbaud, Proust, does not bring to its reading the desires born of a conviction that American life impulses are thin. We do not look beyond America. It absorbs us completely. No one is stirred to the bowels by Europe of the ancient parapets. A huge force has lost its power over the imagination. This force began to weaken in the fifties, and by the sixties it was entirely gone.

Young M.B.A.'s, management school graduates, gene-splicers, and computerists, their careers well started, will fly to Paris with their wives to shop on the rue de Rivoli and dine at the Tour d'Argent. Not greatly different are the behavioral scientists and members of the learned professions who are well satisfied with what they learned of the Old World while they were getting their B.A.'s. A bit of Marx, of Freud, of Max Weber, an incorrect recollection of André Gide and his gratuitous act, and they had had as much of Europe as any educated American needed.

And I suppose that we *can* do without the drama of Old Europe. Europeans themselves, in considerable numbers, got tired of it some decades ago and turned from art to politics or abstract intellectual games. Foreigners no longer came to Paris to enrich their humanity with modern forms of the marvelous. There was nothing marvelous about the Marxism of Sartre and his followers. Postwar French philosophy, adapted from the German, was less than enchanting. Paris, which had been a center, still *looked* like a center and could not bring itself to concede that it was a center no longer. Stubborn de Gaulle, assisted by Malraux, issued his fiats to a world that badly wanted to agree with him, but when the old man died there was nothing left— nothing but old monuments, old graces. Marxism, Eurocommunism, Existentialism, Structuralism, Deconstructionism, could not restore the potency of French civilization. Sorry about that. A great change, a great loss of ground. The Giacomettis and the Stravinskys, the Brancusis, no longer come. No international art center draws the young to Paris. Arriving instead are terrorists. For them French revolutionary traditions degenerated into confused leftism, and a government that courts the third world made Paris a first-class place to plant bombs and to hold press conferences.

The world's disorders are bound to leave their mark on Paris. Cynosures bruise easily. And why has Paris for centuries now attracted so much notice? Quite simply, because it is the heavenly city of secularists. *"Wie Gott in Frankreich"* was the expression used by the Jews of Eastern Europe to describe perfect happiness. I puzzled over this simile for many years, and I think I can interpret it now. God would be perfectly happy in France because he would not be troubled by prayers, observances, blessings, and demands for the interpretation of difficult dietary questions. Surrounded by unbelievers, He, too, could relax toward evening, just as thousands of Parisians do at their favorite cafés. There are few things more pleasant, more civilized, than a tranquil *terrasse* at dusk.

CHICAGO:

THE CITY THAT WAS,

THE CITY THAT IS

(1983)

*T*o be concise about Chicago is harder than you might think. The city stands for something in American life, but what that something is has never been altogether clear. Not everybody likes the place. A Chicagoan since 1924, I have come to understand that you have to develop a taste for it, and you can't do that without living here for decades. Even after decades you can't easily formulate the reasons for your attachment, because the city is always transforming itself, and the scale of the transformations is tremendous.

Chicago builds itself up, knocks itself down again, scrapes away the rubble, and starts over. European cities destroyed in war were painstakingly restored. Chicago does not restore; it makes something wildly different. To count on stability here is madness. A Parisian can always see the Paris that was, as it has been for centuries. A Venetian, as long as Venice is not swallowed up in mud, has before him the things his ancestors saw. But a Chicagoan as he wanders about the city feels like a man who has lost many teeth. His tongue explores the gaps—let's see now: Here the Fifty-fifth Street car turned into Harper Avenue at the end of the trolley line; then the conductor hurried through the car, reversing the cane seats. Then he reset the trolley on the power line. On this corner stood Kootich Castle, a bohemian rooming house and hangout for graduate students, photographers, would-be painters, philosophical radicals, and lab technicians (one young woman kept white mice as pets). Harper Avenue wasn't exactly the banks of the Seine; none of the buildings resembled Sainte-Chapelle. They were downright ugly, but they were familiar, they were ours, and the survival of what is ours gives life its continuity. It is not our destiny here to get comfort from old familiar places. We can't, we Chicagoans, settle back sentimentally among our souvenirs.

From the west, your view of the new skyscrapers is unobstructed. The greatest of them all, the Sears Tower, shimmers among its companions, all of them armored like Eisenstein's Teutonic knights staring over the ice of no-man's-land at Alexander Nevsky. The plan is to advance again westward from the center of the city and fill up the vacant streets, the waste places, with apartment buildings and shopping malls. Nobody at present can say whether this is feasible, whether the great corporations and banks will have sufficient confidence in the future of a city whose old industries are stalled, whose legendary railyards are empty. Ours is the broadest band of rust in all the Rust Belt.

A fiction writer by trade, I see myself also as something of a historian. More than thirty years ago, I published *The Adventures of Augie March*, a novel that is in part a record of Chicago in the twenties and thirties. I see by the college catalogues that my book is studied in a considerable number of schools. It is read in Yugoslavia, too, and in Turkey and China, so that throughout the world people are forming a picture of Chicago, the setting of Augie's adventures. But that Chicago no longer exists. It is to be found only in memory and in fiction. Like the Cicero of Al Capone, like Jack London's Klondike, like Fenimore Cooper's forests, like Gauguin's Pacific paradise, like Upton Sinclair's Jungle, it is now an imaginary place only. The thirties have been wiped out: houses in decay, vacant lots, the local characters—grocers, butchers, dentists, neighbors—gone to their reward, the survivors hidden away in nursing homes, doddering in Florida, dying of Alzheimer's disease in Venice, California. A lively new Latin population occupies my old ward, the Twenty-sixth. Its old houses have collapsed or been burned. The school dropout rate is one of the city's highest, the dope pushers do their deals openly. Revisiting Division Street on a winter day, examining the Spanish graffiti, the dark faces, reading strange inscriptions on shop windows, one feels as Rip Van Winkle might have felt if after his long sleep he had found, not his native village, but a barrio of San Juan, Puerto Rico. This crude, brazen city of European immigrants is now, in large part, a city of blacks and Hispanics.

The speed of the cycles of prosperity and desolation is an extraordinary challenge to historians and prophets. Chicago was founded in 1833, so it hasn't been here long enough to attract archaeologists, as Rome and Jerusalem do. Still, longtime residents may feel that they have their own monuments and ruins and that accelerated development has compacted the decades, making them comparable to centuries, has put Chicagoans through a crash program in aging. If you've been here long enough, you've seen the movement of history with your own eyes and have had a good taste of history, of eternity, perhaps.

So many risings and fallings, so much death, rebirth, metamorphosis, so many tribal migrations. To young Midwesterners at the beginning of the century, this was the electrifying regional capital. Here students from Ohio or Wisconsin studied their trades, becoming doctors, engineers, journalists, architects, singers. Here they made contact with civilization and culture. Here Armour, Insull, and Yerkes accumulated huge fortunes in pork, gas, electricity, or transit. Their immigrant employees, hundreds of thousands of them, lived in industrial villages—Back of the Yards, out by the steel mills, the Irish on "Archie Road," the Greeks, Italians, and Jews on Halsted Street, the Poles and Ukrainians along Milwaukee Avenue.

It wasn't so long ago in calendar years that Carl Sandburg was celebrating Chicago the youthful giant, the hog butcher of the world, the player with railroads. But the farm boys, seduced under streetlamps by prostitutes, have vanished (as have the farms from which they came). The stockyards long ago moved to Kansas and Missouri, the railyards are filling up with new "Young Executive" housing. And even Sandburg's language is dated. It is the language of the advertising agencies of the twenties and in part recalls the slogans that came from City Hall when Big Bill Thompson was mayor. "Boost, don't knock," he told us. "Lay down your hammer. Get a horn."

What would we have been boosting? Real power in the city belonged to the Insulls and other magnates, to La Salle Street, to the venal politicians. From his headquarters in Cicero and on Twenty-second Street, the anarch Al Capone and his mob of comical killers sold beer and booze, ran the rackets,. They bought cops and officials as one would buy popcorn. Big Bill was one of our fun politicians, like Bathhouse John and Hinky-Dink Kenna, politician-entertainers who kept the public laughing. I was one of hundreds of thousands of kids to whom Big Bill's precinct captains distributed free passes to Riverview Park to ride the Bobs and make faces in fun-house mirrors, to eat cotton candy that tickled you like a beard and disintegrated instantly on your tongue. If you had a nickel to spare, you could try to win a Kewpie doll in the shooting gallery. At the age of twelve, I was one of Big Bill's fans. Schoolchildren loved him.

The mayor liked to show himself in public, and after his retirement, in his declining years, you saw him chauffeured through the Loop in his limousine. He was solitary, glum, silent. One great paw hung through the velvet strap. Part of his youth was spent on the range, so he generally wore a cowboy hat. Under it he looked swollen and corrupted. Rouault might have liked to do a portrait of him, one of those mountainous faces he painted—this one against a background of blazing Chicago boredom.

Big Bill is as remote from us today as Sennacherib or Ashurbanipal. Only antiquarians ever think of him. But Chicago still "boosts." Under Mayor Daley (the first) we were "The City That Works." The developers who have remade the north end of Michigan Boulevard announced that they had created a Magnificent Mile. Nothing less. Here Neiman-Marcus, Lord & Taylor, Marshall Field's, Gucci, and Hammacher Schlemmer have established themselves in all their pride. A thick icing of comfort and luxury has been spread over the northern end of the business district, with its boutiques, bars, health clubs, and nouvelle cuisine restaurants. The John Hancock Tower and One Magnificent Mile are the most prestigious addresses in town. From their privileged windows you look over Lake Michigan, with its pleasure boats and water pumping stations. To the south you see the refineries of Hammond and Gary, and the steel mills, or what is left of them. Turning westward you see the notorious Cabrini Green public housing blocks, one of the many projects built for a welfare population. Actually, the slums are best seen from the elevation of a ninety-five-story skytop restaurant—a wonderful opportunity for landscape lovers.

You can't be neutral about a place where you have lived so long. You come to recognize at last how much feeling you have invested in it. It's futile to think, like Miniver Cheevy, that you might have done better in another time, in a more civilized city. You were assigned to this one, as were your parents, brothers, cousins, classmates, your friends—most of them in the cemeteries beyond city limits. Where fires, wrecking balls, and falling masonry have done so much demolition, human attachments rise in value. So I seek out my cousin the baker, I go to see an old chum try a case in criminal court. I attend city council meetings and public hearings, I talk with Winston Moore about black politics or lunch at the Bismarck with one of the late Mayor Daley's assistants. City politics are comic opera. Circuit judges are convicted of racketeering. One can only guess how many grand juries are hearing testimony and preparing indictments. On my rounds, feeling like an unofficial, unsalaried inspector, I check out the new apartment houses on the banks of the Chicago River, in my time an industrial wasteland. To call these expeditions sad wouldn't be accurate. I am not heavyhearted. I am uneasy but also terribly curious, deeply intrigued. After all, I am no mere spectator, for I have invested vital substance in these surroundings, we have exchanged influences—in what proportions I can't say.

In moments of weakness you are tempted to take seriously the opinions of those urbanologists who say that the great American cities of the North are nineteenth-century creations belonging to an earlier stage of capitalism and that they have no future. But then a *Chicago Tribune* article announces that two hundred national retailers, developers, and leasing agents have met at the Hilton to plan new stores outside the Loop. Do they see a dying city dominated by youth gangs who do battle in the ruined streets? They do not! Urban shopping strips are "creating vibrant inner-city communities," we are told. Mayor Washington and "city council stalwarts" are "selling Chicago" to dozens of prospective investors.

Like other Chicagoans of my generation, I ask myself how it's all going to come out. In the past, we watched events. We had no control over them, of course. But they were lively, they were good entertainment. The Democratic bosses—Tony Cermak, Kelly-Nash, and Richard Daley—did not take a terribly high view of human nature, nor were they abstractly concerned with justice. They ran a tight oligarchy. Politicians made profitable arrangements but governed with a fair degree of efficiency. The present administration has little interest in efficiency. The growing black and Hispanic population has made a successful bid for power. Irish, Greek, Polish, and Italian voters are vainly resisting. As conflicts widen and lawsuits multiply, property taxes go up and services diminish. Not many people mourn the disintegration of the machine, but what will replace it? Everything seems up for grabs, and everybody asks, "Will we make it?" Middle-class whites, the city's tax base, have moved to the suburbs. For suburbanites the city is a theater. From Schaumburg, Barrington, and Winnetka they watch us on their TV screens.

Will Chicago, that dauntless tightrope walker who has never yet fallen, get a charley horse in the middle of the high wire? Those of us, like myself, who have never abandoned Chicago—the faithful— tell ourselves that he's not going to fall. For we simply can't imagine what America would be without its great cities. What can the boondocks offer us? We, too, would become mere onlookers, and U.S. history would turn into a TV show. To be watched like any other program: the death of the tropical rain forests, or the history of Egypt's pyramids.

Walking on Le Moyne Street, looking for the house the Bellow family lived in half a century ago, I find only a vacant lot. Stepping over the rubble, I picture the rooms overhead. There is only emptiness around, not a sign of the old life. Nothing. But it's just as well, perhaps, that there should be nothing physical to hang on to. It forces you inward, to look for what endures. Give Chicago half a chance, and it will turn you into a philosopher.

VERMONT: THE GOOD PLACE

(1990)

*I*n 1951, while I was living in a huge brick compound in the borough of Queens, I read a book about rural New England by Odell Shepard and felt that I must go there at once. I packed my knapsack, bought a pair of hiking boots, and took the train from Grand Central to Great Barrington. Following a map copied from the book, I made my way by back roads into Connecticut. I met no other walkers. It was early October, bright and warm. The going was good at first, but the country was hilly, and I began to tire. On steep grades I was overtaken by trucks. The drivers obviously wondered what I was doing there afoot. Some of them stopped to offer me a ride. I thanked them kindly but said that I meant to hike.

"Hike? You could use a lift, couldn't you?"

"I'm here to see the sights."

My refusal puzzled them. A hiker? Here? The sun was still hot, I was obviously bushed. I must have had the look of a determined self-congratulatory crank, and the truckers, driving off, had every reason to be glad I hadn't accepted. My map showed a village nearby. When I asked a telephone lineman how far it was, he only shrugged and stepped on the gas. There was no village at the bottom of the next curve, no general store where I could buy a bottle of Nehi to drink on the wooden steps; there were only sleepy hayfields. The landmarks described by Shepard—settlements, farms, taverns, stables—were gone, wiped out.

Travel Holiday, July 1990.

When a pickup with a horse trailer pulled up for me a few miles down the road, I was grateful to get in and ease my feet. This driver had a foreign accent; he was a Danish horse trainer. The fact that he was a foreigner helped; I might not have been able to tell an American what had brought me here. The horse trainer sympathized with my romantic pilgrimage. He had done the same thing in Denmark. He pointed out, however, that America was too vast for walking. These wide open spaces were no Arcadia. The weather may have been right for fauns and satyrs, but all the other conditions were wanting. The Yankee farmers were gone. Their sons were stockbrokers, their daughters were living in Philadelphia or New York.

I spent the night in a stable, among the Dane's horses. The rats were scuffling under my cot.

But my failed expedition did not end my romance with pastures, woods, and streams, with what geographers call the Eastern Woodlands, the New England countryside; it only modernized my perspective. I was an Eastern Woodlander by birth, a native of Lachine, Quebec, on the Saint Lawrence. True, I had lived most of my life in Chicago, but the Middle West had never seemed quite right to me; its soil was different, its very molecules were fatter, grosser. I imagined, apparently, that the East was materially finer.

Millions of farmers were leaving the land; but city dwellers, among them writers, entertained visions of ease and happiness in the fields, under the trees. Edmund Wilson sometimes rusticated himself on the Cape or in upstate New York; Delmore Schwartz settled near Frenchtown, New Jersey; Mr. Salinger withdrew to New Hampshire. Clearly some of these gifted people looked to the country for relief from town-engendered troubles.

I myself, a case of nerves but trembling also with natural piety, moved to the country in the mid-fifties, investing a small legacy in a house in Dutchess County, where I lived for seven or eight years and became countrified. This grand house (fourteen rooms, a Dutch kitchen, a lordly staircase, countless fireplaces, twenty-foot ceilings) turned me into a handyman. I had no money to spend on plumbing and carpentry. I had to paint walls. I mowed and gardened. I had literary neighbors—Richard Rovere, Gore Vidal—but repairs and grounds keeping left me no time for conversation or reading and writing. Besides, I couldn't bear to think that I had squandered the money left me by a hardworking father on a collapsing river mansion—"How typical of you," he would have said. I got rid of the place.

For the last ten years (I see that I am old enough now to be prodigal with decades) I have spent much of my time in Vermont.

My guess is that the land between Great Barrington and New Canaan had become too valuable for farming. Perhaps it had been acquired by developers and it was temporarily desolate because they had not yet begun to "develop" it. The broader reason for desolation was that America had gone urban after World War II. Land had been sold or abandoned. In the Northeast, a scrubby second growth of new forests had taken over fields and pastures. If you wander in the backlands of Vermont, as I often do, climbing over wavering, dilapidated stone walls and moss-covered ledges, you come upon old foundations, heaps of red brick, overgrown water mills. Along the roads, the sites of vanished farmhouses are marked by pairs of lilac bushes that once grew beside the driveway and by apple trees surviving among the maples and yellow birches. Here you can commune, if you have a taste for that kind of thing, with the premechanized America of horse-drawn harvesters and harrows. Also locks, hinges, doorknobs, old bottles, and every sort of treasure trash. The stone walls had made relatively small fields. It takes no great imaginative effort to put in some sheep or cows or crops—Lilliputian in scale to a Middle Western eye.

But in the yard one can sit in peace under a great shagbark hickory, under a maple even greater that began its life in the eighteenth century. The size of these trees seems to give more height to the sky. Few planes pass this way. Except on weekends, the dirt roads are relatively empty. In the town itself there are no shops or taverns, no industries, no gas stations or garages. The occasional sound of a chain saw or the concussions of a hammer can be heard miles away. The nearest farm is half a mile to the east. It is operated by a widow named Verna and her son Hermie, an earnest, solid, silent, simple country laborer. Hermie is known locally as an artist in fence maintenance. He spends no money on barbed wire. His fences, acres and acres of them, are spliced with odd pieces of wire, the greater part of the work well rusted, some of the bits no longer than an inch or two. There is not a whole yard of new wire anywhere. The artist is muscular, uncommunicative, unsmiling, in farm boots, bib overalls, and a peaked cap.

I have no near neighbors here. The closest is a biologist from Yale who prefers Vermont to any college town and teaches science in a local high school. His wife designs and makes jewelry. Half a mile to the west is the house of the ingenious, extraordinarily inventive man who built my place. He and his wife, an obstetrical nurse, have become my friends. There are few townspeople out this way; most of us are newcomers or summer people. No township would be complete, I suppose, without its eccentric squatter. Ours collects old heaps—cars and trucks. His huts, plastic fluttering from their windows, are surrounded by ditched machinery of every sort. His livestock browses on weeds or eats broken rice cakes trucked in from a factory somewhere near the Massachusetts line. Enormous long-legged pigs run into the road, looking as if they were wearing high heels. They invade the vegetable gardens of the people along the road and root in them. Some say that the squatter comes of a respectable family and was well educated. In the old days he would have been called a remittance man, or a gypsy, or a tinker. The property on which he squats adjoins a dam recently abandoned by the beavers.

The Old Vermonters in this neighborhood acquired their land in the reign of George II. Virtually indistinguishable from these are the French settlers who came down from Canada generations ago—people who call themselves La Rock and worship in Protestant churches. There is an immovable, change-resisting population of Vermonters in the backcountry. Some of them claim, with partly defiant pride, that they have never visited a big city. Flossie Riley, who still gets up before daylight to milk her cows (no machines for Flossie), said that she had been to Burlington once, and that was bad enough; the noise gave her a headache, and the traffic fumes were suffocating; she wouldn't *dream* of going to New York. She knew perfectly well what Manhattan was like; she had seen it on television and wanted no part of it. Adherents of the ancient ways dig, chop, tend their animals, tap maple trees; their talk is about the roads in mud time, about frostbite or thermal underwear, the price of cordwood, or the volunteer fire department. Many of the locals hold jobs in the larger towns—in a surgical-dressing factory, for instance, or in a mill that manufactures old-looking barn board for householders who want a living room that looks rustic. Centers like Brattleboro, or Greenfield, Massachusetts, attract workers who drive in from "bedroom communities" twenty or thirty miles away. Some of the remoter villages resist the real estate developers and the temptation of high land prices. From fear of outsiders and their outside noise and restlessness, they refuse to license new shops. Rural Vermonters install TV dishes in their yards and put up aerials; their children, like children elsewhere, are absorbed in the voodoo beat of a Walkman. No part of this country can be "out of it." What is happening everywhere is, one way or another, known to everyone. Shadowy world tides wash human nerve endings in the remotest corners of the earth. Villages are nevertheless controlled by insiders. Newcomers are accepted on certain conditions. They must pay their taxes, behave decently, and follow a few quite minimal rules.

My wife and I arrive in the spring, like Canada geese, sometimes taking off again but intermittently visible until the fall. The postman and the garbage collector have hard information about our comings and goings. There are, however, other mysterious underground channels of information, for when Jack Nicholson, accompanied by William Kennedy, the Albany novelist, and his wife called on me a couple of years ago, advance word got around. Nicholson, then filming Kennedy's *Ironweed* in Albany, had come to chat about a film based on one of my novels. His white stretch limousine could not make the narrow turn between my gateposts. Silent neighbors watched from a distance as the chauffeur maneuvered the long car with its Muslim crescent antenna on the trunk. Then Nicholson came out, observed by many. He said, "Gee, behind the tinted glass I couldn't tell it was so green out here." He lit a mysterious-looking cigarette and brought out a small pocket ashtray, a golden object resembling a pillbox. Perhaps his butt ends had become relics or collectibles. I should have asked him to explain this, for everything he did was noted and I had to answer the questions of my neighborhood friends, for whom Nicholson's appearance here was something like the consecration of a whole stretch of road.

Our roads—the whole township network—were described by another visitor, a motherly old person from Idaho who came here to visit her son, as "one green tunnel after another." From the perspective of a driver, shaded roads *would* look like that. On warm days a walker is grateful for the shelter, although when the wind dies down, the blackflies, deerflies, and no-see-ums will be waiting in the hollows. When it rains, you are kept almost dry by the packed leaves, and you hear the drops falling from level to level. You will have become familiar over the years with each of the beeches, yellow birches, and maples, the basswoods, the locusts, the rocks, the drainage ditches, the birds, and the wildlife, down to the red newts on the road surface.

People whose leisure time needs to be organized are the profitable concern of professional organizers worldwide. Daily papers and monthly magazines suggest, or advertise, holidays for all seasons, in all zones. East, west, north, and south, preparations are made to receive and entertain tourists, swimmers, skiers, diners, loungers, dancers. Whole regions are organized by giant corporations for travelers in quest of new scenes. More important, perhaps, than palm trees, pyramids, beaches, the temples of Angkor Wat, is the quest for peace. Repose, quiet, peace. But the restless few, longing for singular delights, find themselves once more among the many in facilities the same the world over—room, bed, shower, TV, restaurant, and at 10:00 A.M. your party will be lectured in the Uffizi or on a woodland trail.

But in the Vermont I have been talking about, there are no such preparations. In the nearest town, yes, people will be descending from their buses to buy baskets, maple syrup, aged cheddar, and knick-knacks. But ten miles away, through the woods, you hear no engines. When the birds awaken you, you open your eyes on the massed foliage of huge old trees. Should the stone kitchen be damp, as it may be even in July, you bring wood up from the cellar and build a fire. After breakfast you carry your coffee out to the porch. The dew takes up every particle of light. The hummingbirds chase away hummingbird trespassers from the fuchsias and Maltese crosses. Grass snakes come out of their sheltering rocks to get some sun. The poplar leaves, when you narrow your eyes, are like a shower of small change. And when you walk down to the pond, you may feel what the psalmist felt about still waters and green pastures.

WINTER IN TUSCANY

(1992)

Winter in Tuscany? Well, why not. Millions of Italians do it. The modern tourist takes his winter holidays either in the sun or on the ski slopes. But business brought me to Florence in December, and I had put it to my wife, Janis, that, with two weeks free when business was done, the Sienese countryside might be just the place to restore the frazzled minds of two urban Americans. The crowds of winter would be madding elsewhere—in the Caribbean or on Alpine slopes—and we should have the whole of this ancient region to ourselves, sharing the cold with the populace.

Anticipating severe weather, we had brought our winter silks, goose downs, rabbit linings, mufflers, and Reeboks. Montalcino was cold, all right, but the air was as clear as icicles. Autumn had just ended, the new wine was in the barrels, the last of the olives were in the presses, the sheep were grazing, the pigs fattening, and ancient churches and monasteries were adding yet another winter to their tally. From the heights near Montalcino we could see Siena. In forty kilometers there was nothing to block the view. I have no special weakness for views. It was the beauty of the visibility as such, together with the absence of factories, refineries, and dumps, that penetrated the twentieth-century anti-landscape armor of my soul. To admire views, however, you need to stand still, and you had to endure the cold. The *tramontana* was battering the town when we arrived. It forced open windows in the night and scoured our faces by day.

Generations of Americans brought up with central heating can endure the cold on skis, in snowmobiles, on the ice, but they lack the European ability to go about their business in cold kitchens and icy parlors. Europeans take pride in their endurance of winter hardships. It gives them a superiority that to us seems less Spartan than masochistic.

I can remember cursing the management in grim English hotel rooms while going through my pockets for a shilling to drop in the gas meter, and as a guest in a Cambridge college I was driven once to the porter's lodge to ask for a little warmth. The gentleman porter said, "If you will look under the bed, sir, you will discover a heating device."

Under the bedspring when I lifted the coverlet I found a wire fixture holding a naked forty-watt bulb. The heat this bulb threw was supposed to penetrate the mattress and restore you to life. This austerity went with the dusty ragged academic gowns of the dons, held together, literally, with Scotch tape and staples. It pleased these scholars to be dowdy, indifferent to blue fingers and red noses, and heedless of freezing toilet seats. For the mind was its own place and made a heaven of hell. The door to this mental heaven stood open, but I was freezing.

Once freed from dependency on heating, you don't mind the cold. The Tuscan winter didn't affect your appreciation of Tuscan cheeses, soups, and wines. On your hummocky mattress you slept well enough, and after breakfast you went to visit a Romanesque church, a papal summer residence; you walked in the fields. You can sit comfortably in sheltered sunny corners and watch the sheep grazing.

The people you meet are happy to have you here; they take your off-season visit as a mark of admiration for the long and splendid history of their duchy and like to reward you with bits of information. In passing, one tells you about the deforestation of hilltops during the Dark Ages; another mentions the ravages of malaria and the Black Death of 1348; a third fills you in about exports to England from medieval Tuscany. The soils of all these fields seem to have passed through millions of human hands generation after generation. Our American surroundings will never be so fully humanized. But the landscape carries the centuries lightly, and ancient buildings and ruins do not produce gloomy feelings. Romanesque interiors in fact are a good cure for heaviness.

The region is as famous for its products—oil, wine, and cheeses—

as for castles, fortresses, and churches. A disastrous freeze killed the olive groves some winters ago—the ancient trees now furnish farms with winter fuel. The new plantings do not as yet yield much oil, but the wine reserves are as full as ever.

In the Fattoria dei Barbi, belonging to the Colombini-Cinelli family, the vats, some of them made of Slovenian oak, resemble the engines of 747 jets in size. On walls and beams there are thermometers and gauges. We are conducted here by Angela, a young woman whose pretty face rivals the wine display in interest. Clean quiet cellars, level after level—the only living creature we meet below is a cat, who seems to know the tour by heart. During World War II, false partitions were put up to hide old vintages from the Germans. The almost sacred bottles are dimly, somewhat reverentially lighted. You feel called upon to pay your respects to this rare Brunello di Montalcino. With a banner tail, the cat is an auxiliary guide and leads the party up and down, in and out, from cellar to cellar. We take to this tomcat, who has all the charm of a veteran of the sex wars.

When we return to ground level the cat leaves the building between our legs. We enter next an enormous room where white pecorino cheeses, regularly spaced on racks, are biding their time. After the cheeses come the meat-curing rooms. In spiced air the hams hang like the boxing gloves of heavyweights. To see so much meat takes away the desire for food, so that when we go into the excellent Taverna dei Barbi I am more inclined to admire the pasta than to eat it. But you can never lose your desire for the Brunello wine. Your susceptibility returns at the same rate as the glass fills. Once again it makes sense to be a multimillionaire. The Brunello fragrance is an immediate QED of the advantages of the pursuit of riches. (I never joined up.)

"Don't miss Pienza," we were many times advised, so we recruit Angela to drive us there on a sunny but very sharp morning. Pienza was the birthplace, in 1405, of Aeneas Silvius Piccolomini, later Pope Pius II. He was responsible for the handsome group of Renaissance buildings at the center of the town. It is the finest of these buildings, the Palazzo Piccolomini, that we have come to inspect.

From our parking place we ascend to the main street. The first impression is one of stony Renaissance elegance combined with the modern plate glass of shops. The temperature is a bar or two below freezing. A fine group of old gents standing outside the open door of a café acknowledge us with dignity as we move down the all-stone pavement to the palazzo. As cultural duty requires, we look into the church of Pope Pio, where we see long fissures running through the stone nave. (How to keep up with the maintenance of monuments?) Continuing to the palazzo, we are overtaken in the courtyard by the custodian. He spots us from the café *en face*, his warm hideout. Thickly dressed in wool and leather, he comes with his ring of silver-glinting keys to lead us up the stairs. We pass through the small living quarters used until not very recently by surviving members of the family. A Piccolomini Count Silvio lived in the three front rooms until 1960. We understand from our guide that a picture of an aviator atop the piano in the music room represented the last of his line. Perhaps he was Count Silvio's son and heir—exact information is hard to come by.

In the living quarters there is a framed genealogical tree weighed down by hundreds of names. We pass through the noble library and the armor room. We circle rugs so ancient, so thin, so pale, that a step might shatter them. On bookshelves are huge leather-bound volumes of the classics. I note that fifteenth-century popes were reading Thucydides and even Aristophanes, and as we enter the papal bedroom I think how difficult it would have been to handle these folios in bed. In this freezing chamber the imposing bed is grandly made and formally covered in dark green, a dire seaweed-colored fabric and sinking, sinking, sinking into decay. Perhaps it goes back to the last century. The mattress and bedding may be no more than eighty or ninety years old, but the thing carries a threat of eternity, and you feel that if you were to lie down and put your head on this seaweed-colored bolster you would never rise again. There is a fireplace, or rather a Gothic cavity in the wall big enough to accommodate eight-foot logs, but you'd have to stoke it for a week to drive out such an accumulation of cold.

We are happy to escape again into the great-windowed hall. The guide has gone out on a balcony to sun himself. Joining him, we return to Italy itself and latch onto the sun with gratitude.

We order cappuccino in an open-to-the-weather café. The great espresso machine sizzles and spits, and the cups are served on the enormous polished bar. They lose heat so quickly that you'd better down them before ice forms.

Catering to tourists, the boutiques are nicely heated. We go to a stationery shop and buy a minivolume of Petrarch and other Florentine general-issue items—classy clutter for the apartments of the well traveled. The one prize is a Venetian glass pen from Murano, an iridescent spiral.

In Montalcino I am treated for a sprained shoulder by a local herbal specialist. His nickname is "Il Barba," and he is an old man of heroic stature, more stubbly than bearded. He became a local hero by playing the part of the brigand Bruscone (popularly known as "Il Barba") at a party celebrating the new Bruscone dei Barbi wine. Evidently he fell in love with his own portrayal of the legendary bandit. Himself a man of action, he was a resistance fighter, and the walls of the narrow front room of his apartment are hung with medals and certificates of valor. There is also a fine display of guns, for he is a hunter. This giant and his small wife conduct us to the long cupboardlike kitchen, where he seats me on a high stool and like any doctor asks me solicitously how I came by this sprain. I tell him I took a header over the handlebars of a bike last summer in Vermont. It doesn't make much sense to him that the likes of me should be an intrepid bike rider. He tells me to strip. I take off my shirt, and he examines me. When we have between us located the painful places, he pours his mixture into a small saucepan and heats it on the stove. At all times the old wife is close behind him with her arms folded and held tightly to her body. While she gossips hoarsely with our Italian friends, he rubs my shoulder with his herbal remedy dissolved in olive oil. He applies the hot mixture using his hand like a housepainter's brush. At a nod from her husband, the wife steps out to the porch to fetch a salve to follow the ointment. Enjoying the massage, I begin to feel that this Barba may cure me. I have a weakness anyway for secret herbal remedies, and the treatment in the kitchen has its occult side. (Special security measures are taken.) I pull on my shirt again, altogether pleased with the occasion. The exertion of getting into my pullover causes no pain, and I tell him he is a wonderful therapist. He bows as though he already knew this. In the parlor he reaches into a cupboard next to the guns and takes down a drawstring sack containing a large number of wild-boar tusks. I should never have guessed that they were so light. Some of these trophies have been tipped with silver, and I suppose necklaces or bracelets can be made of them. Thieves would rather have these than the guns, he says.

The great bandit Barba towers over us, smiling, and holds the door open, refusing payment and telling me to come back tomorrow for another treatment. He is so tall that we don't have to duck under his arm. We go down the stairs, into the night, very happy.

Further outdoor sightseeing: Habituated to the cold, we no longer shun it. We now prefer outdoor excursions to the inspection of church interiors. There is a charcoal burners' camp nearby, and an elderly gentleman, Ilio Raffaelli, who was himself, until his twenty-fifth year, a *carbonaro*, shows us how the workers lived and how the charcoal was made. The camp, which he has reconstructed himself, is extremely primitive. The little dwelling of the burners reminds me of an American sod hut, with soil and grass stuffed into a wooden framework. The place is windowless. The workmen and their families slept on simple wooden frames, which occupied most of the space. One was for man and wife, the other for the children, as many as five or six. All worked in the woods, bringing up water from the spring or, in season, gathering berries and other edibles. There were no metal artifacts except axes and saws. The shovels were wooden, the rakes were skillfully whittled. The burners contracted with the landowners, and they camped for half a year or so till they had cut all the usable wood on the property. Then they moved to another estate, where they built a new sod house. The huts, heated by a small fire, were warm enough at night, said our guide.

Raffaelli is a sturdy short man in a cap and an open jacket. (The afternoon was not particularly warm: our noses and eyes were running; his were dry. He was evidently indurated against natural hardships.) A black thread that had worked loose from the cap hung over his face unnoticed while he gave his explanatory lecture. (With his large objectives, he didn't notice trifles.) In his description of the charcoalmaking process, he was exceptionally precise: the cutting of the wood into proper lengths, the stacking of it, the layers of leaves and soil piled on the mound, the space at the center for the fire, which had to be stoked day and night. There were wooden ladders leaning on the cone, and screens against the wind, which might drive the blaze too high, endangering the work of months.

So *this* was how people for many centuries lived upon the land, right *on* the packed earth, so to speak, so adept in the management of their pots, spoons, axes, and handmade rakes, so resourceful—to see this was a lesson worth a whole shelf of history books. I understood even better what life had been like when our guide said, "Whenever one of our boys in the army sent a letter, we gathered inside the hut and sat on the beds to listen to the reading." He laughed and added that they had all been sent to the priest to learn their letters.

His little Italian car was parked just at the edge of the woods, and he would get into it at dusk and drive to Montalcino, where he lived. You felt, however, that his real life was here, in this cold clearing. He seemed unwilling to part with the old life and was perhaps not a thorough townsman. A self-taught scholar, he had written a book about the plants and small fauna. Schoolchildren were brought to him for lessons about the woods. He taught them the names of the trees and sang them the charcoal burners' ballads and reminisced about this vanished trade. He was a modest person, without the legendary airs of Signor Barba, the herbal doctor.

Finally, we go into the woods near San Giovanni d'Asso with two truffle hunters, Ezio Dinetti and Fosco Lorenzetti, and their dogs, Lola, Fiamma, and Iori. On our arrival in San Giovanni we are received by the young dark-haired mayor of the town, Roberto Cappelli, who makes us a little speech of welcome and presents us with a heavy bronze truffle medallion.

The season for truffles is almost over. It has been an unexceptional year—slim pickings. But the dogs are no less keen, rushing from the cars as soon as the doors are opened. There is no breed of truffle hounds. Lola, Fiamma, and Iori appear to be ordinary no-account mutts, but they are in fact highly trained specialists, officially listed, with their own photo-ID license cards and tattooed registration numbers. Turn them over and you can see the numerals under the pink skin. The novice Iori, a skinny dark-brown adolescent, is hobbled with a length of chain to prevent his rushing off by himself in his enthusiasm. The added weight gives him a bow-legged gait. We set out after the dogs on a path through the poplars, tramping over dry leaves. Hurrying after them, you find yourself breathing deeper, drawing in the pungent winter smells of vegetation and turned-up soil. The experienced hunters work the dogs earnestly, with urgent exclamations and commands: *Lola, dai.* (Go.) *Qui.* (Here.) *Vieni qui.* (Come here.) *Giu.* (Down.) *Dove?* (Where?) *Piglialo.* (Take it.) They cajole, huff, threaten, praise, caution, restrain, interrogate, and reward their dogs. The animals track a distant scent. Though the ground is frozen, they will sniff out a truffle under a foot and a half of earth. Each man has an implement on a leather strap slung over the shoulder, a device about two feet in length with a sharp rectangular blade for digging and sampling the earth. With this *vanghetto*, the hunters scoop up a clod of beige-brown mud and nose it with intensity. If the soil is saturated with the truffle odor, they halloo the dogs to dig deeper.

Single file, we cross a thin bridge, a couple of logs strapped together over a gully. Lola, the gifted matriarch, has found something, and the dirt near the streambed sprays behind her. Ezio knows exactly where to intervene and, paying her off with a treat, himself unearths the smallish truffle, a mere nubbin, and slips it into his pocket.

The sun is going down, and we stop more often to chat under the chilly poplars. The afternoon has not been a grand success, for the dogs have turned up only three truffles. Ezio and Fosco insist on our taking them. As we head back through the woods, we hear a dark story. Sporting honor among the hunters is not all that it used to be, they tell us. Jealous competitors have taken to poisoning the more talented dogs, tossing out bits of sausage containing strychnine when they leave the grounds, Ezio says with anger. A promising pup of his was among the six dogs lost to the poisoners last year. Months of training wasted. In the old days it took only a year to break in a dog. Now that there are more hunters and fewer truffles, you need as many as three years of training, so that when a dog dies, the loss is considerable.

The ungloved hands of the hunters when we shake them at parting are warmer than ours, for all our leather and wool and Thinsulate. Driving back to Montalcino, we consider the mystery of the truffle. Why is it so highly prized? We try to put a name to the musk that fills the car. It is digestive, it is sexual, it is a mortality odor. Having tasted it, I am willing to leave it to the connoisseurs. I shall go on sprinkling grated cheese on my pasta.

PART FIVE

A Few Farewells

ISAAC ROSENFELD

(1956)

*I*saac had a round face and yellowish-brown hair, which he combed straight back. He was nearsighted, his eyes pale blue, and he wore round glasses. The space between his large front teeth gave his smile an ingenuous charm. He had a belly laugh. It came on him abruptly and often doubled him up. His smiles, however, kindled slowly. He liked to look with avuncular owlishness over the tops of his specs. His wisecracks were often preceded by the pale-blue glance. He began, he paused, a sort of mild slyness formed about his lips, and then he said something devastating. More seriously, developing an argument, he gestured like a Russian-Jewish intellectual, a cigarette between two fingers. When he was in real earnest, he put aside these mannerisms too. A look of strength, sometimes of angry strength, came into his eyes.

He had a short, broad figure. His chest was large. But he was round rather than burly, and he could move gracefully. His lazy, lounging manner was deceptive. He was quick with his hands and played the flute well, and the recorder superbly. He was haunted, nevertheless, by an obscure sense of physical difficulty or deficiency, a biological torment, a disagreement with his own flesh. He seldom enjoyed good health. His color was generally poor, yellowish. At the University of Chicago during the thirties, this was the preferred intellectual complexion. In the winter, Isaac was often down with the flu or

Partisan Review, Fall 1956. Reprinted as Foreword to Rosenfeld's *An Age of Enormity: Life and Writing in the Forties and Fifties*, ed. Theodore Solotaroff (Cleveland: World, 1962).

with attacks of pleurisy. He was told that his skin couldn't bear much exposure to the sun. But during the war, when he was Captain Isaac, the entire crew of a barge in New York Harbor, he had good color. He read Shakespeare and Kierkegaard on the water and found it agreed with him to be in the open air. He had friends on the waterfront. In such circumstances, Isaac would never be the visiting intellectual. He never went slumming. It was impossible not to be attracted by the good nature of his face, and I assume his ineptitude with ropes touched the hearts of the deckhands on the tugboats.

I am among his friends perhaps not the best qualified to speak of him. I loved him, but we were rivals, and I was peculiarly touchy, vulnerable, hard to deal with—at times, as I can see now, insufferable—and not always a constant friend. As for him, his power to attract people might have made more difference to him than it did. He wanted their affection, he wanted also to return it . . . but then these matters we have learned to speak of so simply have not thereby become simpler.

He had one of those ready, lively, clear minds that see the relevant thing immediately. In logic and metaphysics he was a natural. He had a bent for theology too, which he did everything possible to discourage. His talent for abstraction displeased him; he was afraid it indicated a poverty of his feelings, an emotional sterility. To the overcoming of this supposed sterility, a fault fed by his talents themselves, exaggerated by them, he devoted his best efforts, his strength. He didn't like to be praised for achievements he regarded as largely mental. Heartless abstraction filled him with dread. Originally, his purpose in coming to New York was to study philosophy. During one of his bouts of pleurisy he went through Melville, and he wrote me that after reading *Moby Dick* he could no longer be a logical positivist.

There followed a period of exaggerated "feelings." But whether he gave himself over to the Theory of Signs or exclaimed sentimentally over the poor sprouting onions in an impoverished grocery, Isaac never went very long without laughing.

He was a playful man. He loved hoaxes, mimicry, parody, and surrealist poems. He was a marvelous clown. He imitated steam irons, clocks, airplanes, tugboats, big-game hunters, Russian commissars, Village poets and their girlfriends. He tried on the faces of people in restaurants. He was great as Harry Baur in *Crime et Châtiment*, the inspector Porfiry Petrovich, smoking cigarettes with an underhand Russian grip. He invented Yiddish proletarian poems, he did a translation of Eliot's *Prufrock*, a startling X ray of those hallowed bones, which brings Anglo-Saxons and Jews together in a surrealistic Yiddish unity, a masterpiece of irreverence. With Isaac, the gravest, the most characteristic, the most perfect strokes took a comic slant. In his story "King Solomon," the magnificence of Jerusalem mingles raggedly with the dinginess of the Lower East Side. The great king, also mortal and slovenly, sits in his undershirt. He fondles children in the park. They sit on his knees and smudge his glasses with their thumbprints.

He preferred to have things about him in a mess. I have an idea that he found good middle-class order devitalizing—a sign of meanness, stinginess, malice, and anality. The sight of one of his rooms with Isaac hard at work, smoking, capably and firmly writing on his yellow second sheets, would have made Hogarth happy. On Seventy-sixth Street there sometimes were cockroaches springing from the toaster with the slices of bread. Smoky, the rakish little short-legged brown dog, was only partly housebroken and chewed books; the shades were always drawn (harmful sunlight!), the ashtrays spilled over. There was no sweeping, dusting, mopping, or laundering. The dirt here was liberating, exciting. Later, downtown, it was a little less gay. In the intricate warren of rooms called the Casbah and on Hudson Street, it was simply grim. Toward the end of his life, on Woodlawn Avenue in Chicago, he settled in a hideous cellar room at Petofsky's, where he had lived as a student. The sympathetic glamour of the thirties was entirely gone; there was only a squalid stink of toilets and coalbins here. Isaac felt that this was the way he must live. The disorder had ended by becoming a discipline. It had acquired an ascetic significance for him, which, at least to me, he never explained.

By now he had given up the Reichianism which for a time had absorbed us both. He no longer questioned people impulsively about their sexual habits or estimated the amount of character armor they wore. His homemade orgone box did not follow him in his later travels. He had at one time (in Saint Albans) experimented with tomato seeds kept in the orgone accumulator; they produced better fruit, he claimed, than seeds that had not been exposed. Friends with headaches were urged to put on the tin crown or "shooter." He treated the neighbors' sick pets in his box. But during the last years of his life, all his quaintness—incomparably charming and accompanied by brilliantly persuasive lectures and arguments—was laid aside. His wit was clearer and sharper, purged of crankiness. There had been a quality in him in earlier days, described by one of his friends as "hardheaded *Gemütlichkeit*." For eight or ten years, his mood was anything but *gemütlich*. He judged people harshly; he was not less harsh with himself.

I am convinced that in his view, the struggle for survival, in the absence of certain qualities of life, was not worth making. Without heart and without truth there was only a dull, dogged shuffle about things and amusements and successes. Single-mindedly, Isaac was out for the essential qualities. He believed that heart and truth were to be had. He tried to fix them within himself. He seemed occasionally to be trying to achieve by will, by fiat, the openness of heart and devotion to truth without which a human existence must be utterly senseless.

He was perfectly aware that in this America of ours he appeared to be doing something very odd. To appear odd did not bother him at all. Nor did he ever pursue eccentricity for its own sake, for its color. He followed an inner necessity, which led him into difficulty and solitude. During the last years of his life he was solitary, and on Walton Place, in one of his furnished rooms, he died alone.

JOHN BERRYMAN

(1973)

*H*e wrote in one of his last letters to me, "Let's join forces, large and small, as in the winter beginning of 1953 in Princeton, with the Bradstreet blazing and Augie fleecing away. We're promising!"

The Bradstreet was indeed blazing then; Augie was not nearly so good. Augie was naive, undisciplined, unpruned. What John liked was the exuberance of its language and its devotion to the Chicago streets. I had, earlier, published two small and correct books. He did not care for them. In Augie there was a Whitmanesque "coming from under," which he found liberating. I admired the Bradstreet. What he said was true: we joined forces in 1953 and sustained each other for many years.

The Princeton John was tallish, slender, nervous. He gave many signs that he was inhibiting erratic impulses. Dressed in a blue blazer, a button-down shirt, flannel trousers, cordovan shoes, he spoke in a Princeton mutter often incomprehensible to me. His longish face with its high color and blues eyes I took to be of Irish origin. I have known blue-eyed poets apparently fresh from heaven who gazed at you like Little Lord Fauntleroy while thinking how you would look in your coffin. John was not one of those blue-eyed serpents. Had you, in a word-association test, said "Devil" to him, he would have answered "John Webster." He thought of nothing wicked. What he mainly had on his mind was literature. When he saw me coming, he often said, "Ah?" meaning that a literary discussion was about to begin. It might be *The Tempest* that he was considering that day, or *Don Quixote*; it

Foreword to Berryman's novel *Recovery* (New York: Farrar, Straus & Giroux, 1973). Published in *The New York Times Book Review*, 27 May 1973.

might be Graham Greene or John O'Hara; or Goguel on Jesus, or Freud on dreams. There was little personal conversation. We never discussed money, or wives, and we seldom talked politics. Once as we were speaking of Rilke I interrupted to ask him whether he had, the other night, somewhere in the Village, pushed a lady down a flight of stairs.

"Whom?"

"Beautiful Catherine, the big girl I introduced you to."

"Did I do that? I wonder why."

"Because she wouldn't let you into the apartment."

He took a polite interest in this information. He said, "That I was in the city at all is news to me."

We went back to Rilke. There was only one important topic. We had no small talk.

In Minneapolis one afternoon, Ralph Ross and I had to force the window of a house near Seven Corners to find out what had happened to John. No one had seen him in several days. We arrived in Ross's Jaguar, rang the bell, kicked at the door, tried to peer through the panes, and then crawled in over a windowsill. We found ourselves standing on a bare gritty floor between steel book stacks. The green steel shelves from Montgomery Ward, meant for garages or workshops, for canned peaches in farmers' cellars, were filled with the elegant editions of Nashe and Marlowe and Beaumont and Fletcher that John was forever importing from Blackwell's. These were read, annotated, for John worked hard. We found him in the bedroom. Facedown, rigid, he lay diagonally across the double bed. From this position he did not stir. But he spoke distinctly.

"These efforts are wasted. We are unregenerate."

At the University of Minnesota, John and I shared an office in a temporary wooden structure to the north of the School of Mines. From the window we saw a gully, a parking lot, and many disheartening cars. Scorched theology books from a fire sale lined one of the walls. These volumes of Barth and Brunner looked as if they had gone through hell. We had no particular interest in them, but they helped to furnish forth a mental life in the city of Minneapolis. Minneapolis was the home of Honeywell, of heart surgery, of Pillsbury, of the Multiphasic test, but it was not celebrated as the home of poems and novels. John and I strolled sometimes, about a pond, through a park, and then up Lake Street, "where the used cars live!" What on earth were we doing here? An interesting question. We talked about Yeats. The forces were still joined. We wrote things:

> Drop here, with honor due, my trunk and brain
> among the passioning of my countrymen
> unable to read, rich, proud of their tags,
> and proud of me. Assemble all my bags!
> Bury me in a hole, and give a cheer,
> near Cedar on Lake Street, where the used cars live.

He was proud of the living of these cars. That, he said, was "Delicious!"—a favorite expression. My offering to him at that time was a story called "Leaving the Yellow House." This, too, he declared delicious, though he found it faulty, inconclusive. (We told each other exactly what we thought.)

Tense, he stood at his desk as I entered the office. He was greatly excited. He said, "Pal, I have written some new verses. They are *delicious!*"

When he broke a leg and Dr. Thomas was called in the middle of the night, John said, as the splint was being applied, "You must hear this new Dream Song!" He recited it as they carried him to the ambulance.

I would visit John at an institution (not the one in his novel) called, I believe, The Golden Valley. He was not there because he had broken his leg. The setting of The Golden Valley was indeed golden. It was early autumn, and the blond stubble fields shone. John's room was furnished simply. On the floor was the straw tatami mat on which he performed his yoga exercises. At a collapsible bridge table he wrote Dream Songs. He said, "As you can see, they keep me in a baby crib. They raise the sides at night to keep me from falling out. It is humiliating! Listen, pal, I have written something new. It is," he assured me, raising hands that shook, "absolutely a knockout!"

He put a finger to the bridge of his glasses, for nothing was steady here. Things shook and dropped. Inside and outside, they wavered and flew. The straw of Golden Valley swirled on the hills.

John had waited a long time for this poet's happiness. He had suffered agonies of delay. Now came the poems. They were *killing* him.

Nitid. They are shooting me full of sings.

I give no rules. Write as short as you can, in order of what matters.

Inspiration contained a death threat. He would, as he wrote the things he had waited and prayed for, fall apart. Drink was a stabilizer. It somewhat reduced the fatal intensity. Perhaps it replaced the public sanction that poets in the Twin Cities (or in Chicago, in Washington or New York) had to do without. This sanction was not wickedly withheld. It simply did not exist. No one minded if you bred poodles. No one objected if you wrote Dream Songs. Some men of genius were fortunate. They could somehow come to terms with their respective countries. Others had women, the bottle, the hospital. Even in France, far from the Twin Cities, a Verlaine had counted heavily on hospitals and prisons.

John drank heavily, and he took refuge in hospitals, but he also studied and taught. The teaching was important. His lectures were conscientiously, even pedantically, prepared. He gave them everything he had. He came in from The Golden Valley by cab to address his humanities class.

He walked up the stone stairs of the university building, looking very bad. He wore a huge Western sort of hat. Under the flare of the brim, his pale face was long and thin. With tremulous composure, shoulders high, he stalked into the classroom. While the taxi waited, he gave his lecture. His first words were shaky, inaudible, but very soon other instructors had to shut their doors against his penetrating voice. He sweated heavily, his trembling fingers turned the numbered cards of his full and careful lecture outline, but he was extremely proud of his dependability and of his power to perform. "Henry" was indeed one of the "steadiest" men on the block, as faithful to his schedule as Kant, as precise and reliable as a Honeywell product. His talk ended. Then, peanut-faced under the enormous hat and soaked in sweat, he entered the cab and was returned to The Golden Valley, to the tatami mat and the bridge table, to the penitential barrenness of the cure. No wonder that after these solitary horrors he was later grateful for group therapy, submitting democratically and eagerly to the criticisms of wacky truckers, grateful under the correction of drinking plumbers and mentally disturbed housewives. In hospitals he found his society. University colleagues were often more philistine, less tolerant of poets than were alcoholics or suicidal girls. About *these* passioning countrymen he did not need to be ironical. Here in the institution his heart was open.

It all went into his poems. His poems said everything. He himself said remarkably little. His songs were his love offerings. These offerings were not always accepted. Laid on the altar of, say, an Edmund Wilson, they sometimes were refused. Wilson, greatly respected by John, had written him a harsh letter about his later poems. The last time I saw him, John was wounded, suffering. He handed me Wilson's letter. While I read it, he sat at my table, meteor-bearded like John Brown, coughing softly and muttering that he couldn't understand— these were some of his best things. Then he snatched up the copy of *Love and Fame* that he had brought me and struck out certain poems (Berryman deleted six poems from the second, 1972 edition), scribbling in the margins, "Crap!" "Disgusting!" But of one poem, "Surprise Me," he wrote shakily, "This is certainly one of the truest things I've been gifted with."

I read it again now and see what he meant. I am moved by the life of a man I loved. He prays to be surprised by the "blessing gratuitous . . . on some ordinary day." It would have to be an ordinary day, of course, an ordinary American day. The ordinariness of the days was what it was all about.

On the visit that was to be his last—he came to give a reading— he arrived in Chicago in freezing weather. High-shouldered in his thin coat and big homburg, bearded, he coughed up phlegm. He looked decayed. He had been drinking, and the reading was a disaster. His Princeton mutter, once an affectation, had become a vice. People strained to hear a word. Except when, following some arbitrary system of dynamics, he shouted loudly, we could hear nothing. We left, a disappointed, bewildered, angry audience. Dignified, he entered a waiting car, sat down, and vomited. He passed out in his room at the Quadrangle Club and slept through the faculty party given in his honor. But in the morning he was full of innocent cheer. He was chirping. It had been a great evening. He recalled an immense success. His cab came, we hugged each other, and he was off for the airport under a frozen sun.

He was a full professor now, and a celebrity. *Life* interviewed him. The *Life* photographer took ten thousand shots of him in Dublin,

John told me. But his human setting was oddly thin. He had, instead of a society, the ruined drunken poet's God to whom he prayed over his shoulder. Out of affection and goodwill he made gestures of normalcy. He was a husband, a citizen, a father, a householder, he went on the wagon, he fell off, he joined A.A. He knocked himself out to be like everybody else—he liked, he loved, he cared, but he was aware that there was something peculiarly comical in all this. And at last it must have seemed that he had used up all his resources. Faith against despair, love versus nihilism, had been the themes of his struggles and his poems. What he needed for his art had been supplied by his own person, by his mind, his wit. He drew it out of his vital organs, out of his very skin. At last there was no more. Reinforcements failed to arrive. Forces were not joined. The cycle of resolution, reform, and relapse had become a bad joke that could not continue.

Toward the last, he wrote:

It seems to be dark all the time.
I have difficulty walking.
I can remember what to say to my seminar
but I don't know that I want to.
I said in a Song once: I am unusually tired.
I repeat that & increase it.
I'm vomiting.
I broke down today in the slow movement of K. 365.
I certainly don't think I'll last much longer.

JOHN CHEEVER

(1982)

*J*ohn and I met at irregular intervals all over the U.S. I gave him lunch in Cambridge, he bought me a drink in Palo Alto; he came to Chicago, I went to New York. Our friendship, a sort of hydroponic plant, flourished in the air. It was, however, healthy, fed by good elements, and it was a true friendship. Because we met in transit, as it were, we lost no time in getting down to basics. On both sides there was instant candor. The speed at which necessary information was exchanged was wonderfully amusing. Each of us knew what the other was up to. We worked at the same trade, which, in America, is a singularly odd and difficult one, practiced by difficult people who are not always pleased by the talents of their contemporaries. (Think of that wicked wizard the late Nabokov, who coined terms like "ethnopsychic novelists," dismissing us by the platoon.) John was not in the least grudging or rivalrous. Like John Berryman, he was fabulously generous with other writers. Yes, an odd lot, poets and writers of fiction. And to those who write novels about it, the country, too, is singularly paradoxical, very different from the "normal" America that businessmen, politicians, journalists, trade unionists, advertising men and scientists, engineers and farmers, live in.

I think that the differences between John and me endeared us to each other more than the affinities. He was a Yankee; I, from Chicago, was the son of Jewish immigrants. His voice, his style, his humor, were

Eulogy read at the annual meeting of the American Academy of Arts and Letters, December 1982. Reprinted in *The New York Review of Books*, 17 February 1983.

different from mine. His manner was reticent, mine was . . . something else. It fell to John to resolve these differences. He did this without the slightest difficulty, simply by putting human essences in first place: first the persons—himself, myself—and after that the other stuff—class origins, social history. A fairly experienced observer, I have never seen the thing done as he did it—done, I mean, as if it were not done at all. It flowed directly from his nature. And although his manner was reticent, there was nothing that John would not say about himself. When he seemed to hesitate he was actually condensing his judgments, his opinions, his estimates of his own accomplishments, in order to give them greater force. He spoke of himself as he would speak of anybody else, disinterestedly and concisely. He preferred short views and practiced the same economy in speech as in writing. He might have said, as Pushkin did, "I live as I write; I write as I live."

Miss Kakutani of the *New York Times* used excellent judgment in choosing the quotation with which she began John's obituary. "The constants that I look for," he once wrote, "are a love of light and a determination to trace some moral chain of being." I'm sure that John didn't relish making statements about morals and being; that wasn't his style. I see it as a reluctant assertion, something he had at last to say to correct distortion by careless readers, book reviewers, and academic category makers. I suppose that he felt it necessary at last to try to say what he had been doing with himself for some fifty years.

There are writers whose last novels are very like the first. Having learned their trade, mastered it once and for all, they practice it with little variation to the very end. They can be very good novelists. Think of Somerset Maugham or Arnold Bennett (you can supply American names of your own), exceedingly proficient and dependable servants of the reading public. What they lack is the impulse to expand. They do not develop; they seldom surprise. John Cheever was a writer of another sort altogether. He was one of the self-transformers. The reader of his collected stories witnesses a dramatic metamorphosis. The second half of the collection is quite different from the first. Rereading him, as I have recently done, it became apparent to me, and will certainly be evident to anyone who reads him attentively, how much of his energy went into self-enlargement and transformation and how passionate the investment was. It is extraordinarily moving to find the inmost track of a man's life and to decipher the signs he has left us. Although the subjects and themes of his stories did not change much, he wrote with deepening power and feeling.

With characteristic brevity and diffidence, he only tells us, toward the end, that he loved the light and that he was determined to trace some moral chain of being—no simple matter in a world that, in his own words, lies "spread out around us like a bewildering and stupendous dream." His intention was, however, not only to find evidence of a moral life in a disorderly society but also to give us the poetry of the bewildering and stupendously dreamlike world in which we find ourselves. There are few people around who set themselves such a task, who put their souls to work in such a way. "Normal America" might ask, if it were inclined to formulate such a question, "What sense does *that* actually make?" Perhaps not much, as "sense" is commonly defined. But there are other definitions. For me no one makes more sense, no one is so interesting, as a man who engages his soul in an enterprise of this kind. I find myself, as I grow older, increasingly drawn to those who live as John did. Those who choose such an enterprise, who engage in such a struggle, make all the interest of life for us. The life John led leaves us in his debt. We are his debtors, and we are indebted to him even for the quality of the pain we feel at his death.

ALLAN BLOOM

(1992)

*T*he chapel is as full as I expected it to be. It would take a much larger hall than this—something like Grand Central Station—to hold all of Allan's students, friends, and admirers, for he attracted gifted people. The reasons for this attraction would make a fascinating study, if a man able enough to undertake it were to turn up. Allan loved company. I lured him several times to Vermont, where the trees were impressive, but when he came he never failed to quote the *Phaedrus* at me: Socrates seldom left Athens, he would say, because trees, even the most distinguished of them, couldn't talk to you. He had a great many compelling needs that could be met only in the city—in his beautiful apartment full of books and CDs, in a seminar room, or in a café on the boulevard Saint-Germain, among keen, worldly, talkative friends. At home, as if at a command post, he had intelligence coming in continually. Friends phoned from London, from Paris, from Washington, with advance information about important decisions in the making and political news soon to hit the papers. It was hard to be the first to give Allan any piece of information.

And what were the campaigns that he was running from the twelfth floor of the Cloisters—dressed in his Japanese robe, drinking powerful coffee, and smoking something like five or six packs of cigarettes daily? They were the wars of a frail civilization on the point of being shattered. In the early years of our friendship, I would kid him about this—"You're holding the whole thing together"—but it presently became clear to me that it was all most serious and most real:

Delivered at Bloom's funeral service, 9 October 1992.

that he actually did have what it took to put it all together. He was no mere armchair savior. He had also the moral courage to declare himself, to take positions, to fight. He had the nerve to show American society to itself nakedly, and for this he was denounced—he was blasted, he provoked deadly hostility and became *the* enemy, the bête noire of armies of kindly, gentle, liberal people here and abroad who held all the most desirable, advanced views on every public question: people who did good works but, through some queer inexplicable shift of psychic currents, were converted into a killer mob. You can lie and be rewarded, you can fake and be elected president, but telling people what is obviously true will not be tolerated.

His detractors made Allan out to be a rigid conservative bound to a traditional canon. In his famous (or notorious) address at Harvard in 1988, he said that he was not a conservative, adding that he was not trying to curry favor in a university setting where conservatism is anything but popular. "Any superficial reading of my book will show how I differ from both theoretical and practical conservative positions. My teachers—Socrates, Machiavelli, Rousseau, and Nietzsche—could hardly be called conservatives. All foundings are radical, and conservatism always has to be judged by the radical thought or events it intends to conserve." He went on to say that he was not in any current sense a liberal either, although the preservation of a liberal society was a central concern to him. There was an observable tendency, he went on, to suspect that every theoretical stance was covertly attached to some party or other, and, he said, it seems we have been brought to a point where the mind itself must be dominated by a spirit of party. Here Allan touched upon one of the most repulsive aspects of modern life. All theoretical speculation is made to look dishonest, a mask for secret connivance and a camouflage for partisanship.

Fully grounded in his Plato, Machiavelli, and Rousseau, Allan was an academic, but he was a literary man too—he had too much intelligence and versatility, too much humanity, to be confined to a single category. The publication of *The Closing of the American Mind* had made a public man of him, a celebrity; he had money, he was admired, he acquired enemies and detractors, and he learned what it was to cut a figure and to be attacked for it. Watching him narrowly, I saw with pleasure that he became more and more and more characteristic. Let me give you an example. When he was paralyzed by Guillain-Barré

syndrome and sent down to the intensive care unit, he was not expected to survive. I was in his hospital room when he was brought upstairs and returned to his bed. He was no sooner in it than the phone
rang—a saleswoman from Loeber Motors was calling. He indicated
that he wanted to talk to her and held the phone in his strongly trembling hand. He then began to discuss the upholstery of the Mercedes
he had ordered, trying to decide between gray leather and black.
Hardly able to speak, he went from the upholstery to the CD player.
When all this was settled, he asked my wife to buy cigarettes for him.
Some time later, when he had recovered sufficiently to go home, he
wanted to be taken in the new Mercedes, by his friend Michael Wu.
His doctor said that he couldn't yet sit up and would have to go in an
ambulance, and he agreed in the end, very reluctant to submit.

He was provided at home with a high-tech sickbed. When he was
able at last to sit, he was lifted into a chair by a hydraulic rig—the base
of a metal triangle was set under him: something like a bosun's seat—
and he was swung out and lowered into a wheelchair. The essential
Bloom was still there, intact—with never a sign of inner weakness.
The therapist came to teach him to walk again. He shuffled around
the room speaking of Jane Austen or Flaubert, of the Sviatoslav
Richter Schubert recordings he had ordered, of the season's prospects
for the Chicago Bulls. He gossiped and bantered. He was sometimes
strained but never grim.

I observed that he was bearing up like a philosopher. He didn't
like these helpful-to-the-sick clichés or conventional get-well encour-
agements, and I was rather ashamed of myself, to tell the truth. What I
was seeing, as I well knew, was the avidity for life particularly keen in
him and clearly manifest in his relations to his friends—people exceptionally close to him, like Nathan Tarcov, Werner Dannhauser,
Michael Wu, and a great many others (there was room for many a
more). On a lesser level, this avidity was apparent also in his consump-
tion of coffee and cigarettes, and in the delight he took in acquiring
Persian carpets, Chinese chests, Hermès porcelain, Ultimo cashmere
coats, and Mercedes-Benzes. In general, his attitude toward money
was that it was something to be thrown away, scattered from the rear
platform of luxury trains. With the same keenness, he was presently to
resume his tutorials on Xenophon or on Aristotle's *Politics*. Teaching
was something he could never bring himself to give up.

And then, still partially paralyzed and unable even to sign his name, he wrote a book. He dictated it over many months to Tim Spiekerman; the early chapters were devoted to *Madame Bovary, Anna Karenina, Pride and Prejudice, The Red and the Black*. He wrote also on a group of Shakespeare's plays and on Montaigne and finally on Plato's *Symposium*. I mention this because it was a remarkable thing for a sick man and a convalescent to do and because it was equally remarkable that a political theorist should choose at such a moment in his life to write about literature. I come of a generation, now largely vanished, that was passionate about literature, believing it to be an indispensable source of illumination of the present, of reflective power. Allan's friend Marc Fumaroli, in a recent number of the *Times Literary Supplement*, puts it as it should be put: "Nothing has come to replace this delicate, living, reflective organ, not the different technological media, nor the various disciplines which are described as Human Science."

This new book, to be brief about it, was Allan's sequel to *The Closing of the American Mind*. I like to think that his free and powerful intelligence, responding to great inner impulses under the stimulus of life-threatening sickness, turned to the nineteenth-century novel, to Shakespeare's love plays, and to the Platonic Eros, summoning us to the great poetry of affects and asking us to see what has happened to our own deepest feelings in this age of artificial euphorias forced upon us by managers and manipulators.

For Allan was a deeply feeling, a powerfully feeling man—a superior man. What did the people who reproached him for his elitism want him to do about his evident and—I might add—benevolent superiority? He was not a sentimental person; he was hard on many of us, hard and even cruel, but no less cruel to himself when intellectual probity demanded it.

I have known and admired many extraordinary persons in the long life I have been granted, but none more extraordinary than Allan Bloom. And I answered spontaneously when I was asked not long ago whether I had known any great men in my time. Yes, to be sure, I had indeed known some—had even loved some of them. I do believe that Allan's is a clear case of greatness. And the truth is, about those who were taught by him or who grew to be close to him, that he changed us. Nobody was ever the same again. We are here today to testify to that.

WILLIAM ARROWSMITH

(1993)

*I*n the early fifties, I landed in Princeton—I have never understood how or why this happened. I recall that Richard Blackmur, who
was taking a year's leave, had asked Delmore Schwartz to substitute for
him. Delmore, who was very generous to his troubled friends, had
wangled a job for me as his assistant. That I made no great impression
on Blackmur is hardly surprising, for I had little or nothing to say to
him. My mind was on other things; I was sleepwalking, I think. Not
quite with it. I shared an apartment with Tom Riggs, a charming, troubled man who diverted himself by giving parties. The flat smelled like
a barroom. Staid neighbors upstairs would occasionally complain. In
the end, they found Riggs's evenings diverting and watched the comings and goings. When I came down with pneumonia late in the term
and was taken away in an ambulance, the lady overhead said, "There
goes the last of the guests."

John Berryman regularly came to these parties; and R.W.B. Lewis
and his wife, Nancy, who lived across the hall; and the Monroe Engels,
who lived around the corner; and Delmore, and Elizabeth Pollet; and
Edmund Wilson, who had returned to Princeton to lecture on the Civil
War and study Hebrew. Ralph Ellison occasionally drove down from
New York, as did Theodore Roethke, on holiday from Seattle. Among
the graduate students who were part of the university community were
Robert Towers, Robert Keeley, and Bill Arrowsmith. Of this Princeton
group, Arrowsmith was the one I knew best. We had met years before,
in Minneapolis, where he was taking an army course in Japanese. I had

liked him then, and in Princeton I came to like him better and better. Riggs was a heavy drinker. His wife was divorcing him, and he was in despair. Others had reasons of their own for boozing. I tried to keep up but had no gift for it. Nor did Arrowsmith. We commented to each other on the Fitzgerald beautiful-and-damned atmosphere of Riggs's parties, which we found agreeable. Wilson, like Wordsworth's moon looking around in delight, would say, "This is what Greenwich Village was in the twenties." Bill and I often went outside to escape the noise and walked up and down, talking about the books we were then reading. He was strong on Euripides, but he was not one of those classicists who take sanctuary in the fifth century B.C. and claim immunity forever from the enormities of this present age. I was at that time winding up *Augie March*, and Bill was kind enough to say that I had hit upon a new way to write about life in the U.S.A. The *Hudson Review*, of which he was an editor, had published a chapter from my novel. He and John Berryman both saw something in my experiments with language. These experiments influenced Arrowsmith, he said, when he translated the *Satyricon*.

But it wasn't what we had in common as writers that attached me to him. I liked him first of all for his face. It was delicate and feeling, without the effect of effeminacy often produced in men by sensitivity. He had a pale, wide, strong face. His eyes have sometimes been described as small; I saw them rather as long. He had the frame of a strong man, but he was frequently ailing, and his many sicknesses brought a hint of care into his appearance—as if he were braced to defend himself. He was, moreover, highly assertive and obstinate in his opinions but very open to comic suggestion and capable of laughing at himself—a trait I value highly. We started by agreeing passionately that Silone's *Fontamara* was a wonderful book and went on from there. Agreement was not a mental matter with us, nor even an emotional coincidence, but was based, as we both understood, on an underlying human premise for which no terms are available. If I was sleepwalking when I was introduced to Blackmur, I was wide awake with Arrowsmith. I was at that time in a state of agitation, and it calmed and rested me to be with him.

I saw a good deal of Arrowsmith later in Rome. The U.S. Information Service invited me to give a talk in the embassy, on the Via Veneto, and Bill came to hear what I had to say. I had Flaubert on the brain in those days. Emma Bovary, I argued, was in a sense the mother of the art novel. But the art-novel masterpieces by Flaubert's twentieth-century successors were not accessible to the majority of readers, the great public. There was a rift, pointed out by Wyndham Lewis, between the great-public novel of Dickens and the small-public novel of the modern connoisseurs. Flaubert had assumed that the subject of *Madame Bovary* was humanly impoverished and that a reduction in human scope must be compensated or justified by brilliant workmanship—by art. My argument was only partly true, I now concede. Emma was elevated in stature by the horrors of her last state, the insupportable suffering that drove her to suicide. Flaubert himself was perhaps mistaken about her insignificance.

Still, my argument was at least partly right. Bill thought I was making a considerable point. The heavyweight intellectuals of Rome, however, didn't much care for my lecture. Nicola Chiaromonte settled his chin on his collar and sank in his auditorium seat in silent disapproval. Alberto Moravia brushed my talk aside. Yet they did the right thing afterward. Bill and I were taken by the two of them to a café on the Via Veneto, where they immediately fell into a roaring political dispute (about China, I think). I said to Bill, "Bye-bye, Bovary."

Our departure was unnoticed.

We walked back and forth on the famous *via*. Again Bill told me how wrong Chiaromonte and Moravia were to dismiss my talk. "They're a pair of dumb bastards," he said. "You're onto something they never heard before. Those lousy intellectuals are so sure they've already heard everything, they go stone deaf when something new is said."

A panhandler stopped us on a dark corner and got us into a conversation, his pitch being that he was a man of breeding and education. Bill, who took pleasure in the Roman streets, chatted him up. When the panhandler learned that Bill taught Greek and Latin literature, he was ravished, and he brought his hands together at his breast. "Listen to this," he said. He dived like a seabird into a sea of Latin, and when he surfaced, he turned his head under Bill's face, looked up, and asked, "Who was I quoting?" "Suetonius?" Bill guessed. "Suetonius!" the panhandler said, full of contempt. "You can't tell Tacitus from Suetonius? Now hear this." He spoke with gestures, and we offended him when we laughed. "A second chance for you. Who wrote those lines?" "Pliny," said Bill. "Cicero," the panhandler shouted. "Is this how professors are in America? They have no education. It's disgraceful."

We laughed again and gave him money.

"How good was he?" I said.

"I counted up to twenty errors. Those texts were neither Suetonius nor Tacitus nor Cicero nor Pliny. Just some stuff kids from a lycée memorize, probably. Well, now we've both been put down today, haven't we."

In your seventies, it becomes clear who your psychic perennials have been, the permanent characters of your dramatis personae, the persons you really reckoned with and took into your feelings, the ones you should be happy to see in the afterlife. Bill Arrowsmith is on my list. Has been for many decades.

PART SIX

Impressions
and Notions

A HALF LIFE

(1990)

*I*deas come in two different ways—conscious ideas acquired through education and reading, and things that pop into your head willy-nilly. When were you first conscious of having an idea hit you—an idea that went beyond "Let's go down and get bubble gum"? —Keith Botsford, *Bostonia* magazine

I certainly wasn't conscious of ideas as such before I was ten. I did have ideas of some sort earlier, but they were the sort of primitive metaphysical ideas a small child has. —*Saul Bellow*

Such as?

Sitting on the curbstone, looking at the sky, thinking: Where did it all come from? Why was I here? Epistemological questions. Of course, that's how many philosophers nowadays would like to handle such questions: essentially as childlike epistemology.

Were ideas much batted about in your early childhood?

I don't know that they were batted about. They were just present. At the age of about four, we began to study Hebrew and read the Old Testament, but we didn't necessarily consider the idea of creation and the present, nor where the world had come from and the explanation for its existence. I felt very cozy with God, the primal parent, and by the time I was up to the Patriarchs (I was five or six years old), I felt they were very much like members of my family. I couldn't readily distinguish between a parent and the heroic ancestors—Abraham, Isaac, and Jacob, and the sons of Jacob, especially Joseph.

So shul played a part.

It wasn't so much shul as the Torah.

Bostonia magazine, November / December 1990.

In the first stages, did you feel you were challenging these ideas, or were you largely accepting?

No; it never occurred to me that reality could be anything but what I was being offered. Not then.

When did that *notion strike you?*

Well, I had a great shock at about eight. I was hospitalized for a half year or so. A missionary lady came and gave me a New Testament for children. I read that. I was very moved by the life of Jesus, and I recognized him as a fellow Jew. I think the hospital drove a lot of that home to me. Because I'd never been away from my parents before.

But had you felt the fragility of life? Did you then?

Oh, yes. Death was something very familiar from an early age. During the great flu epidemic, my brother Sam and I used to sit in the front window, watching the procession of funerals.

This was in Montreal?

Yes. I can remember the *corbillard* [hearse], the bands, the funeral marches, and the *cortège* with its black horses.

So memory is part of the way we form ideas, isn't it? Much of our thinking does spring from remembering very specific things.

I have to think whether what I've learned is true. I never suspected that it was ever anything but true. Then it was brought home to me that other approaches were possible. I had to struggle with the charge against the Jews that they had been responsible for the crucifixion.

But that wasn't implicit in the New Testament. How did you come to that?

Oh, yes, because there were these passages in which the Pharisees especially were prominent as the enemies of Jesus. The Jews preferred Barabbas.

But in Jewish terms, Jesus was another Jew. Consequently it wasn't anti-Semitic in the modern sense of the word. It wasn't anti-Jewish.

Yes it was. It threw great blame on the Jews, which was supported by my treatment in the hospital. For the first time I was in a hospital was the first time I was aware I'd left my street and my family. I couldn't see my parents. I was allowed one visitor a week. My mother and father came on alternate weeks. I always saw them separately. This was the Royal Victoria Hospital in Montreal. The Children's Ward. Ward H. It was a Protestant hospital.

But restrictive. Was it an infectious thing? Or were they just obeying the rules? Did you read much when you were in the hospital, besides the New Testament?

I read everything I could get my hands on. There were very few books. Mostly there were funny papers, which were stacked beside the kids' beds. Piles of funny papers. Characters that disappeared long ago, like Slim Jim, Happy Hooligan, and the Katzenjammer Kids.

You were growing up in a culture, in and around Montreal, that was very French. Did that create any sense of difference?

I was aware of being *un juif.* That was driven home quite early. I don't know if it was bad, really. I got some light on it when I read the New Testament.

So in essence, as with many people, the first ideas are religious, eschatological?

Yes, and they were very keen. They were driven home very sharply. By my isolation first of all, then by the fact that I knew I was in danger of death. My reading was not so bad for a child of eight—my reading ability. I got out of bed occasionally; they used to hang your chart at the foot of the bed. I would read my chart, and I knew it was very unpromising.

So in a sense you are a survivor. You have a feeling of that?

It's fundamental, I think, with me. I felt forever after that I had been excused from death and that I was, as gamblers in Chicago used to say in those days, when I was ten or so, "playing on velvet"—ahead of the game.

One does feel strongly about survival as a child; election is added to what one is likely to have gone through, and that causes a special concentration in the mind, doesn't it?

Anyone who's faced death at that age is likely to remember something of what I felt—that it was a triumph, that I had gotten away with it. Not only was I ahead of the game. I was privileged. And there was some kind of bookkeeping going on. I did my own mental bookkeeping. I thought I owed something to some entity for the privilege of surviving.

So there was a debt as well? A debt that had to be paid off?

A duty that came with survival. Those are the primitive facts.

How did you describe that debt to yourself?

That I'd better make it worth the while of whoever it was that authorized all this. I've always had some such feeling. Overjoyed. Full of welling vitality and perhaps that I've gotten away with something but that it had been by permission of some high authority. Occasionally I talk to others about this, and I find they are dead on the subject. That they didn't have this sense for themselves. Some kind of central connection, in the telephonic sense.

So one comes out of surviving one's childhood with a sense of being privileged; then one goes home and finds the reality—one is back in a family that has proceeded without you and quite well? Did you have this feeling of imagining one's death and the tragedy it would cause to the world? Imagining your funeral and your parents weeping?

No, but what I did see was a great many kids dying in the ward. This happened regularly. A lot of fussing in the night and a screen around the kid's bed and nurses running back and forth with flashlights. And in the morning an empty bed. You just saw the bed made up for another kid. Before long there was a kid in it. You understood very well what had happened, but it wasn't discussed or explained.

So you're back home, aware you have caused grief, suffering, and anxiety to your parents. Your brothers are there. How do they behave?

At first they were sympathetic, but that wore off. Then I was just an obnoxious kid soaking up all the attention and affection and concern of the family, and I was greatly resented by my brothers. One of them was four years and the other eight years my senior. The brother who was four years older had in the meantime used and broken such toys as I had. Especially my sled.

And then came the move to Chicago?

My father left for Chicago in the winter of 1924. It was nearly summer when I rejoined the family. I didn't go back to school. That same summer, my mother brought the children to Chicago.

Did you view the world differently?

I must have. Of course, there's no such thing as thinking this through, but I certainly made decisions based on my condition. I had to decide, for instance, whether I would accept the role of convalescent sickly child or whether I would beef myself up. I decided on course two. I set myself on a very hard course of exercise. I ran a great deal.

So this is an idea in its very primitive form: I have survived. I must survive. I should survive. And the way to survive, to pay this debt, is to become good or better. When did this notion of "better" come into your life?

By the time we got to Chicago I was a confirmed reader, and so I picked up all sorts of self-improvement, self-development, books, especially physical self-improvement, at the public library. There was a famous football coach named Walter Camp, who had written a book called *How to Get Fit and How to Stay So*. This involved carrying coal scuttles at arms' length, and I did that because we had coal in the shed (this was in Chicago) and one of my jobs, which I was glad to do, was to go up and down the stairs. Up with the coal and down with the ashes. I became quite fanatical about training.

So in surviving, the mind's not really what you think about. It is the body that carries the structure of the mind. Without it, you're not going to have a mind. Had you not lived, you wouldn't have been able to develop any form of betterment, so you decide you are going to protect it in some way?

My alternatives were to remain weak and be coddled.

A delightful state for some children . . . Look at Marcel Proust: he got a cold, and it lasted a lifetime. Most people would probably think that the family that could have produced you would have been one of argumentation, dispute, rational analysis, logic, order, and violence, mental and other kinds. A picture that corresponds in any way?

Well, some of the elements are there. My father was violent, strong, authoritarian. He seemed to us as children an angel of strength, beauty, and punishment. His affections were strong too. He was a passionate person. My mother was that way also. Within the family, Jewish life is very different from life outward, facing the world. You saw your parents in two separate connections: one the domestic and internal; and the other meeting the external challenge.

Is this an idea that's formed? Is that part of the formation of an idea? The sort of double role?

I suppose so, because it was translated later in life. The contrast between strength, the strength that I felt inwardly, and the absurdity of my trying to express that strength outwardly.

There are two distinct aspects to life: in one you cope with everyone else's world, and the other you cultivate within yourself. Was there a degree of concealment involved in this?

Not concealment so much as a deep sense of strangeness in what I was doing. First I translated from the Old Testament into my inner life, then I translated from books I read at the public library, again into the inner life. In the first instance, this had the approval of Judaism—

that is, mainly from my family. In the second form, it could only be fantasy. You had to be wary of what was in truth both stirring and ennobling but at the same time dangerous to reveal.

Do you remember any of the fantasies? Did any of them approximate what you've become?

No. At first they were fairly obvious fantasies. Pioneers, frontiersmen, independent men. Going into the wilderness with your ax and gun (and your smarts). Very important.

When you arrived there, Chicago was not yet in any sense a sophisticated city—the frontier was not that far off.

No, it wasn't. We lived on an unpaved street, a dirt street with horses. Cars were few and far between. Kids used to throw themselves on the ground under a parked car to see if it had four-wheel brakes.

Was America talked about as a subject? As such? After all, back then, Montreal must have had its own flavor.

Yes, we did talk about the change. Montreal—that is, eastern Canada—was very European. I didn't realize until later in what ways the eastern seaboard is very different from the Midwest. I had a strong sense of that difference as a child. Matter seemed to me to be cruder: as if Chicago molecules were bigger or coarser. The very soil seemed different. The trees were certainly different. Chicago's trees were elms, cottonwoods. Montreal trees (maples) were bigger. The ferocious winters, boiling summers.

Did you talk about politics?

Very much so. Because my parents were following the Russian Revolution. They had a very specific interest in it. Their parents and brothers and sisters were still there. I was born in 1915. Before I was three, the Russian Revolution was fully under way.

Were you aware of it? You knew about it? That must have had an effect on your ideas.

I knew all about Lenin and Trotsky. I didn't know what the Revolution as such meant. My mother's relatives were Mensheviks. I was too young to understand that during the Kerensky period the Mensheviks and the Bolsheviks were nip and tuck.

Since it later came to have considerable meaning for you, do you recall any effect it had on your ideas back then?

I remember as quite a small kid being in the street with my father.

We met a young man called Lyova walking down the street. Lyova told my father he was going back to Russia. Lyova's father was our Hebrew teacher, and his mother, Mary, a fat lady with a huge hat, was my mother's friend. My father said, "That's a foolish thing you are doing. Don't go." He was counseling Lyova not to go, but Lyova must have had some kind of politics. He couldn't have been older than eighteen or nineteen. But things like that happened every day. Lyova went back and vanished.

How about the structure of politics? Did you have any idea how American politics were put together, how they differed from Russian or European?

In those early days your political ideas came from the papers. Al Smith was a Catholic candidate for the presidency. Newspapers were very important. There was no radio as yet. Everybody took positions based on the paper he read, whether it was the Hearst paper or the McCormick paper in Chicago. There were two Hearst papers: the *Herald Examiner* and the *Evening American*, both long since gone. And there was the Republican McCormick *Tribune*. The papers provided our daily drama. The Leopold and Loeb case, for instance. In the early twenties, the children were reading about Clarence Darrow and the Leopold and Loeb murder.

Did your fantasies ever involve such things as politics or law as ideas? Did you think about them in terms of eternal justice?

No, not really. We didn't think that way. More important to the family was Americanization and assimilation. The family was divided on this. My eldest brother pulled for total Americanization; he was ashamed of being an immigrant. He didn't want at all to be known as a back-street immigrant type. He made a beeline for the Loop.

How did you react?

I was keenly interested. I didn't have any position. It was hard not to observe my eldest brother. His histrionics had a dramatic influence on our feelings, and the fact that he was physically impressive—big and stout, aggressive, clever—simply added to the effect. By the time we got to Chicago he was a high school senior and I was in the third grade.

Were there ideas as such in the schools of those days?

"Americanism" was very strong, and there was a core program of literary patriotism. Overwhelming. Terribly important. Chicago consisted of endless strings of immigrant societies. We were in sort of a Polish-Ukrainian-Scandinavian enclave, and across Chicago Avenue (there was usually some car line that intervened) were Italians. There were also Germans, Irish, Greeks.

The "I am an American, Chicago born" with which The Adventures of Augie March *begins is a recrudescence of that in you, isn't it? You have a cosmopolitan and catholic mind, yet by far the strongest streak in you is the American.*

Well, cosmopolitanism found its point of exit from local confinement in the direction of the melting pot. But it wasn't a melting pot. It didn't melt. If you played with Polish children in the streets, you didn't also go to school with them. They went to parochial schools, where they were taught Polish only. And even until recently, the descendants of Polish immigrants, succeeding generations, spoke with an accent, a recognizable, identifiable touch of Polish.

What ideas surfaced in your mind that most subtracted from or most supported that notion of Americanism?

My father was all for Americanism. At the table, he would tell us, This really *is* the land of opportunity; you're free to do whatever you like, within the law, and you're free either to run yourself into the ground or improve your chances. The gospel of improvement came through my father, whose English was not very good as yet.

But you also felt that virtually from the time you came on the scene. The notion of progress was already built into you; it's part of your nineteenth-century heritage, Comte's idea of progress.

Comte wouldn't have liked the religious elements. The idea of the Author of Your Life (and I'm not speaking of my father here) was very powerful and received continual support from the Bible. It was a strange mixture, not an easily blending one. Let's say you went to an American school, you played baseball in cinder lots, and then you went to Hebrew school at three in the afternoon. Until five, you were studying the first five books of Moses and learning to write Yiddish in Hebrew characters—and all the rest of it. So there it was. I didn't go to a parochial school, but the religious vein was very strong and lasted until I was old enough to make a choice between Jewish life and street life. The power of street life made itself felt.

Conventionally, the next stage in the formation of ideas would be pu-

berty, schooling, reading, making oneself different from other kids, creating an identity for oneself. By then one is really conscious of ideas. You were well-read? Long past Natty Bumppo?

By the time I was in high school I was reading Dreiser, Sherwood Anderson, Mencken. Dreiser was fresh stuff, active and of the moment, right up to date. You could understand Clyde Griffiths in *An American Tragedy* if you were a kid of religious background on his way up. Full of longings and of lusts.

Did greed constitute something of an idea?

There was enough social Darwinism in the air to justify greed and a lot of other things, short of murder. It wasn't just the writers I named who had that influence, but people like Jack London and Upton Sinclair. Those two socialist apostles, who were at the same time Darwinists, taught the struggle for survival. Victory to the strong.

Two striking things about your childhood compared to most: the first is common to Jewish, Catholic, or any good religious education in general —that enormous insistence on the power of memory, on the fact that you actually had to know and be able to reproduce that. Second, you didn't read any junk.

But there *was* a certain amount of junk. And my Americanizing brother brought the *Saturday Evening Post* and *Collier's* into the house. Fannie Hurst, Edna Ferber, Peter B. Kyne, James Oliver Curwood. You read all those as well. Of course, philosophically they were usually in the Jack London vein. I imagine that even Dreiser had a good deal of it. And there were also the Horatio Alger books.

That business of memory—the retentiveness of it. How do you get it in childhood?

I didn't even think of it as memory. I always had an open channel to the past. It was accessible from the first. It was like turning around, looking backward while going down the street. You were looking behind while advancing.

Kids on the whole are not great retrospectors. They are prospectors.

Well, maybe the retrospective was strong in me because of my parents. They were both full of the notion that they were falling, falling. They had been prosperous cosmopolitans in Saint Petersburg. My mother never stopped talking about the family dacha, her privileged life, and how all of that was now gone. She was working in the kitchen. Cooking, washing, mending for a family of four children. There had been servants in Russia.

A sense of aristocracy, of a fallen aristocracy, in there?

Max Weber says the Jews are aristocratic pariahs, pariahs with a patrician streak. I suppose it's true that Jews are naturally inclined to think of themselves as such.

Surely the Jewish "aristocracy" in that sense is rather religious than social. It's not personal, it doesn't belong to the individual.

But you could always transpose from your humiliating condition with the help of a sort of embittered irony. Sufferance is the badge of all our tribe, we read at school. *The Merchant of Venice* went pretty deep. We didn't have apologetics when we did Shakespeare as high school sophomores. That's one of the curious features of American society. Everything was out in the open in those days. And while prejudice and chauvinism were almost as ugly as in Europe, they were, in real terms, ineffectual. The absence of an idea of defamation was very liberating. Everybody was exposed in the same way. Nobody could claim any protection. Of course, the respectable WASPs were somehow out of it, but even they came under attack. Nobody was immune. Not Jews, not Italians, not Greeks, not Germans, not Blacks. Everything was out in the open. Which gave an opening to freedom of opinion. Everybody took abuse. This is what's disappeared since then. Without any increase in liberty.

And certainly no increase in communication, because by papering over differences with pieties about how people differ from one another, in aptitudes and in myriad other ways, one simply reinforces prejudice. People who pretend that difference doesn't exist make a fundamental error. If you marry, you quickly realize that.

That's happened to me quite a few times. I think it's an important point to make. It's true there were unpleasant comic strips like "Abie Kabibble" with pudgy hook-nosed Jews and all the rest of that. Nobody was immune. People did strike back. But there was a kind of openness for everybody. It was a far more open society than before ethnic protectionism began.

In literature it had this grand effect, didn't it, that it allowed the writer's imagination to create characters who were larger than life. Their characteristics were so accentuated and out in the open that to be called a Jew or a Catholic or whatever just exaggerated that aspect of your life. You could write a whole book about being that. By now it's reduced to our being all absolutely identical gray specks.

Except just over the border, in the first band of the unconscious, where you know perfectly well that this isn't so. But that particular band of the unconscious somewhere in the primitive part of the brain has taken a lot of punishment.

So at thirteen or fourteen you were already aware of being in possession of unconscious feelings?

We were passing Freud from hand to hand at school. And Marx and Lenin. By the time I was fifteen, the Depression was already upon us and everybody was suffering from it. On the other hand, there was what I now recognize as an unconquerable and spontaneous adolescent spirit, which didn't recognize such things as depressions. Depression was a social fact, but it was certainly not much of a personal fact.

How does the Depression make its appearance as an idea?

It was the first time capitalism was under direct attack for its failures.

Was that the way you put it as an adolescent?

By the time I was fifteen, certainly. That was 1930. It was impossible to avoid this, you see, because the reactionary press itself introduced these terms. "We don't want any Russian revolutions here" and all the rest of it. So when they fell on their faces, they had already themselves prepared the vocabulary of accusation. And of course, immigrants were filled with revolutionary hopes, because 1917 was . . . well, so glorious.

Was there any notion in your adolescence, again as an idea, of a difference between the intelligentsia and the rest of the world?

Yes, there was that definitely. You could see it. You could go into the main Jewish streets and see people who described themselves as the intelligentsia. They dressed differently. They wore pince-nez. They smoked with curious gestures; they had a different vocabulary. They spoke of capitalism and socialism. They talked about evolution; they talked about Tolstoy. All these things were very important in my adolescence. I met a new sort of people on the main streets of the community. In making the distinction between the back streets on which you lived as a boy and the main streets on which you lived as an intellectual semi-adult, you became a grownup. In my Chicago case, it was Division Street, with its mixture of Polish, Jewish, Ukrainian, Russian, Scandinavian elements. . . .

Did you class yourself at that time as an intellectual?

It never occurred to me that I was any such thing. I was just a pair of eyes, a set of ears.

But it must have been somewhere back then that you began to see yourself as a writer, an observer. Can you remember any one moment, or was writing just part of the training of the eye? The point is, you're such a physical writer, the emanations of people, their effluvia, mean so much to you.

I don't know whether it was training at all. I think it was just spontaneous. I think that when I was a very small child it wasn't what people said, the content of what they said, so much as the look of them and their gestures, that spoke to me. That is, a nose was also a speaking member, and so were a pair of eyes. And so was the way your hair grew and the set of your ears, the condition of your teeth, the emanations of the body. All of that. Of which I seemed to have a natural grasp. That is to say, this is the way things are seen by me when they are most visible. I couldn't help but do the kind of observation that I've always done. It wasn't entirely voluntary. It wasn't based on ideas. It was the given.

But the physicality of someone or something is surely an idea. . . .

Right. It's the abstraction of a speculative principle. The abstraction came later. Actual life was always first.

What better foundation for ideas?

If you go back to the Greeks, or the Greeks *and* the Elizabethans, you may come to feel that conceptualization is a weak substitute for this sort of feeling for things and beings as they are immediately perceived.

Things are visceral. Things are real. One lives in a real world in which one sees phenomena. You have a powerful affinity to such elements. As in Michelet. That comes across in his History of the French Revolution *with such power. He understood that there are emanations from the body. And when one talks of the body politic, it really is a body; in Michelet, it isn't some metaphor of what a state should be.*

I grew up to appreciate abstraction in some forms. I was thinking about this lately because I came across a passage from a book on Kafka in which Kafka says (I'm sure I'm right in this paraphrase) that he couldn't bear to read Balzac because Balzac's novels contained too many characters. He's asked, Aren't you interested in characters? And he says, No, I'm only interested in symbols. And I could see that as a source of dramatic power. Especially when I was growing up, I found that a "personality" could also be constructed of something artificial. Something of conceptual origin. On the other hand, the number of types and roles were really limited; they soon became tiresome because they were derivative. This was confirmed when I began to go to Europe. I was already quite grown up. I soon began to understand that national character had been shaped by the classic writers. In Paris, you could identify your Balzacian or Molieresque characters in clerks and shopkeepers, in your concierge, and all the way up the scale to the intellectual and revolutionary elites. Similarly in London, with people being Dickensian or Trollopian, or Oxonian. I began to see that modern man's character is also derivative from literature or history. Or the movies, which are our equivalent of those old fictions. I won't mention television, because the psychology of that medium is in this connection of no interest whatever.

And what conclusion did you draw from Kafka's remark?

I understood it in myself. I understood that I had both tendencies in me. On the one hand, I could always count on my innate reactions to people. Baudelaire's advice: In any literary difficulty, recall what you were at the age of ten. On the other hand, those innate or early reactions weren't going to get me very far if I wasn't also prepared to think about what I was seeing.

Perhaps this goes back to the days you spent at university and afterward and to your choice of anthropology. That was a somewhat peculiar one for you, really.

The idea of anthropology is at heart a very democratic idea. Everybody is entitled to equal time. They have their culture and we have ours, and we should not get carried away by our ethnocentrism. The latter is a purely Western idea. It wouldn't occur to an Iranian to think his perspective distorted by ethnocentrism. Well, hardly ever.

On the contrary, he'd find it nefarious, as an American Indian would. It's funny that these very ancient civilizations really didn't feel their ethnocentrism as in any way slanting their vision of the world. New ones might.

I think the idea is that real culture is blinding. Because you're completely possessed by it. You don't have to think, with great difficulty and some unnatural adjustments, that the stranger coming toward you is black or white, male, female, safe, dangerous, etc. It isn't you the liberal democrat or *bien pensant* making these judgments. It's that real, sometimes embarrassingly ugly entity, your own self. Culture is prejudice in its basic (or, if you prefer, lower) forms.

The catalogue of ideas one looks back on in the years between puberty and serious study, which is universitarian, would consist of what? It's as though you drew up a mental list of what sorts of things you thought Raskolnikov had in his brain when he decided to become a murderer. What was in yours? What strange mélange?

Of course it was a mélange. It's as if the head of a modern person were sawed open and things were tumbling in from every direction. So you had the Bible and the Patriarchs cheek by jowl with Russian novelists and German philosophers and revolutionary activists and all the rest. Your mind was very much like the barrel of books at Walgreens, where you could pick up a classic for nineteen cents. I still have a copy here of the *The World as Will and Idea* by Schopenhauer, which I bought for two dimes and read when I was a high school junior—or tried to read. I think I grasped it fairly well. Those books would pass from hand to hand, and the notes in that Schopenhauer were made by my late friend Sydney Harris, a high school chum of mine. All kinds of mad scribbles in the margin. But we did read those things. On the one hand, Schopenhauer and Nietzsche, and on the other, Marx and Lenin. And then again John B. Watson, and also Theodore Dreiser and Dostoyevsky and Balzac and all the rest. You were really pitched headlong into a kind of mental chaos, and you had to make your way.

What the hell has happened to our adolescents today that this is a rare occurrence?

Well, they have their music and sex and drugs instead. And their privilege . . . compared to what we had.

It's not underprivileged to have a mind filled with books.

No, but it does create a terrible disorder, and you'd better make sense of it because the premise of the whole thing is your autonomy. You are going to govern yourself. And you don't realize what the cost of it will be. At first it fills you with pride and a sense of purpose and power, and then you begin to see that you are incapable of making the finer adjustments by yourself and life is going to be a mass of errors, that clarity is to be found only in spotting the mistakes. You are being educated by your mistakes.

Whereas today?

I suppose the objectives are simpler today. You want pleasure, you want money, you want to get ahead in the world. You want to lead a full American life.

But you don't really want anything. Everything is available, which cuts down on desire.

That's true. There's been a decline of desire. Besides, you can no longer read a contemporary book about chaste girls and wonder about the outcome, as you did then. You used to feel how impossible it was for her to choose between rival attractions. Meanwhile the girl was thinking: Which suitor shall I marry? That doesn't happen anymore.

Hence the utter impossibility of a celibate clergy, for instance, just to mention one side effect. When bishops sit around discussing whether homosexuality is acceptable sacramentally, you know there's something screwy going on.

Oh, yes, all these things have run out. When I say I had to decide between Schopenhauer and the rest, that was a sign of those times. Some or many of these burning questions have run their brief course and are no more. It's all gone. The last to be generally discredited, except in the third world and the American universities, is Marxism. I was filled with it. You couldn't read the *Communist Manifesto* when you were young without being swept away by the power of the analysis.

The studies are there, the mind is slowly filled, and there enters a strange concept in the world of ideas, which is one's own originality, one's own sense of one's difference from the stock. How does that occur to you? How does the personage Bellow emerge from this maelstrom?

He begins to see his life as a process of revision, of the correction of errors. At last you have the satisfaction of having escaped from certain tyrants. Let me make clear what I mean. I mentioned Marx— Marx and Lenin. I might have mentioned Freud. These philosophers and writers were the source of powerful metaphors, which had such a grip on you that you couldn't escape them for decades. It's not easy to get rid of the idea of history as an expression of class struggle. Nor is it easy to cast off the idea of the Oedipus complex. Those are metaphors that will have their way with you for a long time.

Yet at the same time you're working in a perfectly real world. These ideas dominate a part of your mind, but the operative part is full of its own pizzazz and ultimately goes its own way. It takes these ideas, but it moves somewhere centrally. Didn't you feel that in your pre-university late adolescence?

I suppose that more powerful than any of the books I read was my inner conviction that we were all here on a very strange contingency plan, that we didn't know how we had gotten here or what meaning our being here really had. I read many books in the hope of making some discovery of truth about these persistent intimations. At bottom the feeling was always very strange and would never be anything but strange. All of the explanations you got failed to account for the strangeness. The systems fall away one by one, and you tick them off as you pass them. *Au revoir,* Existentialism. But you never actually finish with this demand that you account for your being here.

One book after another of yours expresses the same question in different terms.

I suppose this is the highest point a modern man can hope to achieve. What do you see when you start reading Shakespeare? You begin with the early plays and you end with *The Tempest* and find just that. In *Lear* you are told "ripeness is all." We must abide our going hence even as our coming hither and all the rest of it. . . . You know, this sense of the mystery, the radical mystery of your being, everybody's being. The nature of the phenomena has changed somewhat. You're not just surrounded by nature's world, you're surrounded even more by technology's world. You don't understand it any better for having been educated. Because no matter how extensive your education, you still can't explain what happens when you enter a jet plane. You sit there, open your book, and all these strange mechanisms of which you haven't the remotest conception, really, carry you in a matter of hours to New York and you know how long it used to take on a Greyhound bus. And even the bus was a technological advance. There's something that remains barbarous in educated people, and lately I've more and more had the feeling that we are nonwondering primitives. And why is it that we no longer marvel at these technological miracles? They've become the external facts of every life. We've all been to the university, we've had introductory courses in everything, and therefore we have persuaded ourselves that if we had the time to apply ourselves to these scientific marvels, we would understand them. But of course that's an illusion. It couldn't happen. Even among people who have had careers in science. They know no more about how it all works than we do. So we are in the position of savage men who, how-

ever, have been educated into believing that they are capable of understanding everything. Not that we actually do understand, but that we
have the capacity. Since all of these objects are man-made and we are
men, we should be able to comprehend the ultimate or even the proxi-
mate mysteries.

*You're saying the sweet mystery of life is gone. And yet that particular
sort of speculative Jewish upbringing must have been one of the greatest of all
gifts. It taught you that there were miracles, that the mysterious existed—for
a Catholic, the central act of worship was something you could not understand
even if you tried, because your capacity was not equal to God's.*

Now the mysterium has passed to high tech. However, we have
all been brought up to believe that we *can* understand these things, because we are "enlightened." But in fact, we haven't a clue. We have to
be satisfied with a vocabulary, with terms like "metabolism" or "space-
time." It's a funny conjunction. . . .

*Yet we remain dismissive of mystery. We think mystery is an archaism.
Only in the Dark Ages did people wonder. There are no modern mystics except those who are spaced out—and they don't know it.*

What I am really trying to say is that we've been misled by our
education into believing there are no mysteries, and yet . . .

But, forgive me, you weren't misled by your education. Why not?

I suppose I had a radical Jewish skepticism about all the claims
that were made.

Did anthropology assume that sense of mystery in any way?

Yes, it did. But I soon realized that I was really getting a version of
primitive life produced by other people educated as I had been, giving
me nothing any newer about the Trobriand Islanders than would have
been the case if I had never heard of them. Simply because you read
Malinowski and Company didn't mean that you now knew the Trobriand Islanders. What you knew was the version of an educated civilized European. And I guess there was a kind of buried arrogance in
the whole idea of the anthropologist: in the idea that because the Tro-
brianders are simpler, their depths can be sounded. Thoroughly. With
simple peoples we can nail down the meaning of life.

Surely Malinowski understood that. That's what's good about him.

I chose one of the very best to criticize. You might entertain
doubts in the case of a Malinowski or a Radcliffe-Brown, but you

would have no confidence at all in the majority of cases. You knew when you met these scholars that they would never understand what they had been seeing in the field. To me they were suspect in part because they had no literary abilities. They wrote books, but they were not real writers. They were deficient in trained sensibilities. They brought what they called "science" to human matters, matters of human judgment, but their "science" could never replace a trained sensibility.

Which brings us back to you.

Which was what I acquired without even knowing it.

But there is no way to acquire a trained sensibility.

Not unless you take certain masterpieces into yourself as if they were communion wafers.

The Eucharist of world literature.

In a way, it is that. If you don't give literature a decisive part to play in your existence, then you haven't got anything but a show of culture. It has no reality whatever. It's an acceptable challenge to internalize all of these great things, all of this marvelous poetry. When you've done that, you've been shaped from within by these books and these writers.

While you're absorbing all this, there's one part you extract from the people you read. You extract Tolstoy's ideas, or Shakespeare's ideas. Then there's another part, which is inextricable from the way they express those ideas, which is incarnate in their style, their narrative, the characters they create. Was that distinction clear to you at university level?

It began to be clear, yes. For instance, I read all of Tolstoy when I was in college. I can agree with Natasha or with Ivan Nikolayevich even when I can't agree with Tolstoy's views on Christianity, man, and nature. So I know the difference, and so did he, evidently.

Though he would have denied it and said only, "The parables are at the heart of what I am."

Of course, there is this double, triple, or multidimensional ply in the great hawsers that attach you to life. That's why you can read Dostoyevsky without being particularly fazed by the anti-Semitism, because you know there's something at a deeper level, there's much more power at work, though many of his opinions may be trashy.

What did you make of your university education as a whole? By then you were becoming critical.

At Chicago we were educated by Hutchins, really, or by the spirit of Hutchins in which the place was saturated. You were there for four years, or for less if you were good at passing examinations. You followed at your own pace. But if you met all the requirements, you would graduate knowing everything there was to know about the physical sciences, the biological sciences, the humanities, and the social sciences. Everything. You would then be fit to stand with anybody on an equal footing and hold your own. Do more than hold your own. There was a kind of crazy, cockeyed arrogance in all this, which really appealed to young Jews from the West Side. But when I went over to Northwestern, I met just a lot of agreeable, old-fashioned WASP English professors who were eccentric, limited. They made no claims, no universal claims.

What governed the choice? Why did you go to Northwestern?

I was tired of marching with three or four hundred other students to vast lecture halls, where four days a week nobody in particular was talking to you. And on the fifth day you had a quiz section, where you actually got to see your quiz instructor for an hour and you would go over the lectures with your master tutors. And they were masters. Very good people gave those general courses. But you never got to know anybody, and nobody ever knew you. I got tired of this anonymity. I wanted a chance to distinguish myself. You took a comprehensive examination, and even if you got a good mark, you were still answering multiple-choice questions, you weren't being asked to write essays. I was in shallow waters here. So I shifted over to the other place. I suppose I wanted attention.

And got it, no doubt. Had the writing begun then?

Yes, I was already writing.

When did that fundamental idea of all writers, that this is what you are going to do with yourself, write, first strike you? In what form did it come?

It came early in my high school years, when I began to realize that I thought of myself all along as a writer. God knows there were plenty like me, so we formed a society of people with literary ambitions.

Did you think of these early texts as literary, or did you think of them as vehicles for ideas?

There were wonderful magazines available in those days. You could give yourself quite a case of ambition poisoning.

What magazines were you reading back then?

The *American Mercury*, first of all, and then the *New Republic*, *The Nation*, the *Times Literary Supplement*, the *Manchester Guardian*. You could go downtown to Monroe Street and buy all these things. There were these great shops where you could get all the English papers, the French too, if you knew how to read them. And German and Spanish.

Did you detect a visible difference between what they produced and what your local papers produced, for instance?

In Chicago, there were newspapers like the *Evening Journal* and even the *Daily News*, with people like Ben Hecht on the staff. Their book departments were flourishing, and there were reviewers on the staff like Burton Rascoe, quite good book reviewers. And Harriet Monroe was still around at *Poetry* magazine. You did get some sense that Chicago had briefly been a literary center. It was already coming apart when I was in high school. But there were still Edgar Lee Masters, who lived in Chicago, and Vachel Lindsay, who was in Springfield, and Carl Sandburg. And Sherwood Anderson had worked in Chicago. And Dreiser had been there and quite a few more. And the Hull House lady, Jane Addams, and Robert Morss Lovett and Thornton Wilder. Lots of people who had made the national literary scene. You felt this to be accessible in Chicago.

Did literature seem a career?

I never thought of it as that. I don't seem to have been aiming at a career. I never thought how will I live by it? Or how does one make a living? It never entered my mind that this was a problem. Of course I was the despair of my father.

You finished university, went to New York, and basically put together the makings of a literary career.

I reviewed books and lived from hand to mouth and was very happy. I was on the Writers' Project, the Federal Writers' Project. My special assignment was to cover Illinois writers. I suppose that on the WPA I was able to justify the idea that I was a writer.

That excursus took us away from New York just before the war. You are leading the life of poverty and literary grandeur. The idea floating about is that this is an unlimited universe; possibility and total potentiality are everywhere. What did the war bring into your life in the way of ideas?

I misunderstood the war completely. I was so much under the influence of Marxism—I took it at first to be just another imperialist war.

Had you done your Partisan Review *bit by then? Had you started?*

No. The war began in '39. I wasn't published in *Partisan* until the forties. I stood by that junky old doctrine, the Leninist line: the main enemy is at home, it's an imperialist war. I was still at that time officially sold on Marxism and revolution, but I sobered up when France fell.

You knew nothing of what was really going on in Germany then?

I began to have an idea when the Germans got to Warsaw in 1939 and began to attack Jews in the streets.

But the Kristallnacht *had made no real impression?*

Well, it had. I considered it an evil and dangerous thing. I began to have my first strong doubts when the Russians invaded Finland. But I was still in the grip of left-wing ideology. And the Trotskyists (because I was closer to the Trotskyists than any other Marxist group). The Trotsky line was that a workers' state, no matter how degenerate, could not wage an imperialist war. He also argued that though it was degenerate, it would nevertheless advance the historical cause of socialism by bringing the forms of organization of a more advanced development into Finland; the land would be nationalized, cooperatives would be established, soviets or workers' councils set up, and so on. Although Stalin had done his best to annul the Revolution, it still had been a revolution, and Trotsky told his followers they must not oppose this war, because it was a war against the whitest of white regimes, a white-guard, antirevolutionary regime. But when the Germans reached Warsaw, I began to feel differently about things. When Paris fell, of course it was devastating.

It didn't affect most Americans.

But I wasn't most Americans. I belonged to a special group of cranks that knew a little history and some Marxist doctrine and used to discuss matters on an "elevated plane."

Would you say that historical ideas played a major part, that history played a role in your development at the time?

Something like the knowledge of history. We thought that the French Communist Party was in part to blame for the defeat of France in 1940. The armies had been demoralized by the Communist line. So the word went around. *La France est pourrie.* That wasn't really enough of an explanation, no substitute for understanding. But still the people around *Partisan Review,* who then had considerable influence with me, stuck to that Marxist view. The *PR* people were the best we could do in the cosmopolitan line. They thrilled us by importing the finest European writers and familiarizing the American literary public with them. Where else would you find Malraux, Silone, Koestler, and Company but in *Partisan Review*? It's true that some of the editors had the mentality of Sixth Avenue cigar store proprietors, but they were importing good things. Some of them I liked very much. They were not only mentally influential, they charmed me personally. People like Dwight Macdonald and Philip Rahv, Delmore Schwartz and Will Barrett and Clem Greenberg. But Clem and Dwight were obstinately, rigorously orthodox in their Marxism and kept saying, "Don't kid yourself, this is just another imperialist war. Don't be seduced by propaganda as people were in World War I."

Did you feel that you were, as a young litterateur, easily influenced?

I wouldn't belong to anything. I wouldn't join any group. I was never institutionally connected with any of these people. I was the cat who walked by himself.

You look frightfully intense in the pictures of the day.

There were sexual reasons for this intense look. Then, too, the politics and literature of the period put you under great pressure. I had read all these never-again war writers like Barbusse and Remarque. There was the revolutionary myth that the masses had taken things into their own hands in 1917 and destroyed the power of capitalist imperialism. It took me a long time to get over that. It was probably the most potent political mixture in the twentieth century.

What caused the myth to collapse?

Stalin himself did a great deal to discredit it. I knew about the purges. I knew the Moscow trials were a put-on and a hoax. All of that was quite clear. And like everybody else who invests in doctrines at a young age, I couldn't give them up.

Does the adult Bellow criticize himself for this?

No, I don't see how I can. To avoid every temptation of modern life, every pitfall, one would need a distinct genius. No one could be so many kinds of genius.

At what point does it become impossible to forgive people for holding ideas that are patently false?

It depends on the weight of the evidence available. People who clung to Stalinism after the Hitler-Stalin pact deserve harsh criticism, of course. But then most people somehow failed to—they were reluctant to—grasp the meaning of the concentration camps, both the German and the Russian kind.

Could you tell us something about your circle of affinities, about close friends like Isaac Rosenfeld and Delmore Schwartz and John Berryman? The forming of ideas with one's close friends at a critical age between eighteen and thirty is absolutely fundamental. What was the energy flow of those ideas, and how would you describe the people and the ideas they represented?

After some years full of love and admiration, I began to suspect Isaac of having a weakness for orthodoxies. He was in many ways an orthodox left-winger. Which I found curious. He couldn't relinquish some of these fixed convictions. But even some of the best people I knew, and I include Isaac among the best, were unable to divest themselves of their Marxism.

Did you know anybody contrary to that flow?

Jewish friends who had a more American orientation, yes. They didn't drift leftward. Mostly schoolmates of mine in Chicago. I use the word "intellectual" nowadays in a much more pejorative sense. I never did like the idea of being an intellectual, because I felt that the intellectuals had no power to resist the great orthodoxies and were very easily caught up in Marxism and Stalinism.

Did they lack the penetration, or did they fall for the romance?

They were intellectuals. I think they saw there was an advantage for them in following a certain line. One of the things that was very clear to me when I went to Paris on a Guggenheim grant was that *Temps Modernes* understood less about Marxism and left-wing politics than I had understood as a high school boy. I strongly suspected they expected the West to fall to communism and they would be advantageously placed when this happened. I don't know how else to explain some of Sartre's positions and those of the people around *Temps Modernes*. Why was it they were unable to criticize the Russians in 1956? To behave as they did, you had to be attracted by more than doctrine. You had to have some idea of possible advantages. One saw so much of this, especially in France and Italy.

What were you doing during the war?

When I was called up, I was rejected because I had a hernia. Immediately I went into the hospital to have surgery. The operation was not successful. I didn't recover for about a year and a half. The war in Europe was then coming to an end. So I went into the Merchant Marine. I was in Merchant Marine training when the bomb fell on Hiroshima. I had recognized Hitler for "what he was." I knew most of the story, and not only did I feel that my Jewish Marxist friends were wrong in theory, but I was horrified by the positions they—we—had taken. That was the end of that. And I felt that I should do something in the war.

Did the break with these people hurt?

No. By this time I was estranged from them. I was still going through an educational self-wrestling routine. I do it all the time. Trying continually to correct, correct, correct. And I also find that the more isolated you are, the more you develop a terrible book-dependency; you begin to see how you protected yourself from what you thought to be brutal, vulgar, and squalid. Building a fortress of high-mindedness. Really bad stuff. I don't mean to say books are bad. I mean to say that I have used them like a dope addict. I still catch myself doing that. I'm not accusing myself of anything. I'm just saying that this has been the case. Zola wrote *J'accuse* over the Dreyfus case, but our mighty book is *Je m'accuse*. On the other hand, silence is enriching. The more you keep your mouth shut, the more fertile you become.

Would you say you had any mentors between eighteen and thirty? Did they play a role in the formation of ideas?

I would like to have had some, and some people came forward in that role; but I had trouble accepting them. In fact, I was always looking for guidance. A leading art critic of the day offered to take me in hand. He was strangely persuaded that a young man needed to be formed by an older woman, preferably a European woman, who would civilize him, teach him something about sex, and introduce him to a higher social sphere—smooth his rough edges. Somehow I didn't take to that, especially not when I saw whom he had in mind for me—his castoffs. Another senior intellectual who took an interest in me was Dwight Macdonald, but he was himself nervous and unfocused. I suppose Isaac had really a great influence on me. After Isaac, Delmore Schwartz was really an important guide and, later, John Berryman. But these were friends, not shapers of my character.

When did you first know Berryman?

In the Village, around the *Partisan Review*, and then I went down to Princeton for one year when Delmore and I replaced Blackmur. That was about 1952.

Tell us something about your first contact with Europe.

My first trip over (to Spain) was in 1947, when I was in charge of a student group from the University of Minnesota. I was an assistant professor there in 1946. *That* promotion came thanks to Red [Robert Penn] Warren, because I was brought in as an instructor and he twisted Joseph Warren Beach's arm and got him to advance me. He rescued me from freshman comp papers. Madrid in 1947 was a great eye-opener for me. In Spain, I felt as if I was returning to some kind of ancestral homeland. I felt that I was among people very much like myself, and I even had notions that in an earlier incarnation I might have been in the Mediterranean. I was absolutely charmed by it, by everything. The air seemed to be different. Something especially nourishing. And then, of course, I had followed the Spanish Civil War and knew as much about what had gone on in Spain between 1936 and 1938 as a young American of that time could learn.

The place was still shot up. Virtually as it had been during the war. The buildings were all pockmarked. Madrid itself was like a throwback to a much earlier time. The streetcars, for instance, were strictly Toonerville trolleys. I wrote a piece about all this for *Partisan Review*. I met a great many Spaniards; it was my first prolonged contact with Europeans and the European intelligentsia. At least the members of a *tertulia* in the café near my pension, which was in the middle of Puerta del Sol. I had a letter to some people—Germans, who had been journalists during the Civil War. They received me and introduced me to people like Jiménez Caballero, a fascist and a literary man in the Cortes, with whom I had a few dinners. People were curious. They hadn't seen many Americans. Spain had been completely sealed off for years. They felt so isolated that even a trifling instructor from Minnesota was eagerly taken up by them.

I met the papal nuncio in Madrid. Since when does a kid from Chicago get to meet a papal nuncio? And had dinner at the Nunciatura. And had one of his assistants say to me that these Spaniards were not Europeans—*son moros*, they are Moors. They don't really belong to the European community. I also spent a lot of time in the Prado, which was then empty and soiled-looking. I brooded for hours over Goya and Velázquez and Bosch. I banged around Spain in antique railroad cars. I went to Málaga. We had come by way of Paris, so I spent a preliminary week there and, on the way out, a second week. London in '47 was absolutely miserable. All those vacant lots, flowers growing everywhere in bomb craters. There was nothing to eat in the restaurants, and you strongly suspected they were serving you horse meat.

When did you finally hit the heart of the matter, Germany, and what had happened there?

I went to Salzburg in 1949 and then to Vienna. The Russians were still in occupation. I had been invited to the Salzburg Seminar, but I took a trip to Vienna. I was fascinated, of course. I went to see the monuments. I didn't like Vienna much. I knew a lot of Central European literature. My favorites were Kafka and Rilke. In Rilke, the poetry meant less to me than the *Brigge* book, which I loved. It had a great effect on me. Thomas Mann I always viewed with some mistrust.

You are then in your early thirties. You are on the verge of writing The Adventures of Augie March. *Would you have called yourself a formed man by then? Or is this really a half life that doesn't conclude?*

No, I don't really think I was formed. There were lots of things I hadn't been able to incorporate. Things that got away from me. The Holocaust, for one. I was really very incompletely informed. I may even have been partly sealed off from it, because I had certainly met lots of people in Paris when I lived there who had been through it. I understood what had happened. Somehow I couldn't tear myself away from my American life.

That's what I see now when I look back at the writing of *The Adventures of Augie March*. That I was still focused on the American portion of my life. Jewish criticism has been harsh on this score. People charge me with being an assimilationist in that book. They say I was really still showing how the Jews might make it and that I used my best colors to paint America. As if I were arguing that what happened in Europe happened because Europe was corrupt and faulty. Thus clearing the U.S.A. of all blame.

For a Jew to say that is like saying to be a Jew is to be condemned.

That's right. That's as much as to say the West has nothing to offer Jews. But I wasn't considering that question when I wrote the book. I wasn't thinking about it at all. There's no shadow of it in *Augie March*. It was later, when I myself went to Auschwitz in 1959, that the Holocaust landed its full weight on me. I never considered it a duty to write about the fate of the Jews. I didn't need to make that my obligation. I felt no obligation except to write what I was really moved to write. It is nevertheless quite extraordinary that I was still so absorbed by my American life that I couldn't turn away from it. I wasn't ready to think about Jewish history. I don't know why. There it is.

Perhaps your mind didn't want to be limited.

Perhaps. At the same time, I can't interpret it creditably to myself. I'm still wondering at it. I lost close relatives.

Perhaps such things can only become central at an appropriate time. The time wasn't yet.

Yes, but even then, what would writing about it have altered? You wouldn't know when you're reading Kafka's letters that a world war was raging in France and in the East. There's no mention of war in *Ulysses*, which was written in the worst hours of World War I. Proust took it in, but that's because Proust accepted his assignment as a historian of French life. He knew how to combine the aesthetic question with the historical one. This doesn't often happen. Very few writers are able to keep the balance, because they feel they have to create a special aesthetic condition for themselves, which allows only as much present actuality as they can reconcile with their art. So Proust was not destroyed by the Dreyfus case and the war; he mastered them aesthetically. A great thing.

You said the Holocaust was missing. What else do you feel was missing in your formation?

Somehow I managed to miss the significance of some very great events. I didn't take hold of them as I now see I might have done. Not until *The Bellarosa Connection*. So I have lived long enough to satisfy a few neglected demands.

A SECOND HALF LIFE

(1991)

*W*e left you in New York. We pick you up at Princeton. What part does the academy play in your life?

At first Princeton was a relief from hack writing. I was supporting a wife and a small child. I took a few jobs at NYU, teaching evening courses in creative writing and literature. This was an amusing interlude. I was living in Queens then, and I was glad of the opportunity to bum around in the streets near Washington Square. The Village was jumping at the time. The jumpers who attracted me were Isaac Rosenfeld, Harold Rosenberg, Delmore Schwartz, Philip Rahv, Dwight Macdonald, William Barrett.

So the intellectual life in New York is where we were . . .

Entrenched? I wasn't entrenched.

And you just got into the Partisan Review *office. The critics were taking over and . . .*

Oh, they were *well* entrenched.

Why is that?

The critics, the "thinkers," were the organizers and promoters. *Partisan Review* in those days brought current European intellectual life to literate Americans and the university public. Rahv and Phillips were successful entrepreneurs in this line. As well as they could, they followed the example of *The Dial*, a magazine with a much higher literary standard. Of course, *The Dial* took little interest in the political crises of the twenties. The people attracted by *Partisan Review* were radicals who had been associated until the mid-thirties with the communist movement. They had literary tastes. They were, however, operators. Naturally, they cleaned up on both sides of the Atlantic. But they also performed an important cultural service here.

The European stars of those decades were glad to contribute to an American magazine: George Orwell, Arthur Koestler, T. S. Eliot, Ignazio Silone, André Malraux, et al. If you were an American, a putative writer, you were lucky to be published in *Partisan Review*. You appeared in very good company. It was terribly exciting for a boy of twenty-three or -four, who had only seen Eliot, Silone, and André Gide on library tables. During the Spanish Civil War, even Picasso appeared in *Partisan Review*. Mighty exciting to sophomoric Midwesterners.

Whence came the despite of what neither of us likes to call the "creative" figure? What turned people against creation, against literature?

Well, the editors were interested in creative figures only insofar as they had some political interest. *Partisan Review* wanted the political glamour that surrounded these writers.

Did they think that you were a potential political figure?

They thought that I was a kid from the sticks, from Chicago, who showed some promise and might develop into something. They were very encouraging, especially Philip Rahv. I don't think William Phillips had high expectations.

Was Dangling Man *the first manuscript of fiction that they had of yours?*

No. I had published some things earlier in *PR*. Sketches . . .

So you became one of their stable. . . .

Yes, a young highbrow Midwestern Jew.

Did you enjoy your first serious teaching?

By "serious" do you refer to my year of teaching at Princeton? I met my classes and taught my pupils. Some of them seemed likable. I wasn't overwhelmed by the Ivy League. I was curious about it. I had heard of these Ivy-college compounds for class and privilege. I didn't assume a posture of slum-bred disaffection. Princeton was partly entertaining, partly touching, partly a scene of gloomy bravado. The Fitzgeraldian boozing was not associated with literary distinction. Except in the case of John Berryman, whose talent was genuine and powerful. Booze was not a primer of geniuses. Delmore became my friend there. R. P. Blackmur was and was not around. He was absent for most of that year. I never got to know him at all well. I observed that he liked to have an entourage sitting on the floor listening to his labyrinthine muttered monologues. I listed him as a brilliant court-holder.

Many people were attracted by the gathering of intellectuals and writers at Princeton in 1952. Ted Roethke turned up, and Ralph Ellison came down regularly to attend our parties. I had reviewed Ralph's *Invisible Man* for *Commentary* in 1949 or '50, but Ralph was not entirely satisfied with my highly favorable review. He complained gently that I had failed to find the mythic substructure of his novel. I took Ralph very seriously. He had the subject, the rhetoric—all the gifts.

I lived in Princeton with a man named Thomas Riggs, an assistant professor of English, whom I loved dearly. He was a heavy drinker—multiple personal defeats, a despairing character. He died in the next year—the year following—when I was no longer at Princeton. I was laid low by his death—by the circumstances of his life, leading to his death. I knew him well. In his big Princeton flat, he threw open-house parties in the old-fashioned Greenwich Village style. People in large numbers tramped in and out, noisily eating and drinking and smoking, looking for useful contacts, gabbing, putting on the make. R.W.B. Lewis lived across the hall from Riggs. In Riggs's apartment I slept on a cot, stuffed bookcases towering over me.

Edmund Wilson was absolutely delighted by this Village revival; he adored Riggs's parties. Wilson was wonderful, if you could interest him. If you failed to interest, you didn't exist. You were wiped out—nothing. He was always in pursuit of particular items of knowledge. When he discovered that I knew some Hebrew, he was enthusiastic. He would come to my office with hard texts. And when I was stumped and said that I needed a Hebrew dictionary, he was off and away. He was a bit like Mr. Magoo. I don't mean that he was literally short-sighted, but he had eyes only for what was useful in his projects. He also had the same gruff Magoo strained way of speaking. Partly colloquial, partly highbrow.

Was he the representative intellectual for those times?

He ranked very high. Aspirants like me were usually put down in those circles. But those who had made it stood very high. Like Matthew Arnold on Shakespeare: "Others abide our question. Thou art free." Certain people were above criticism, like Wilson. Meyer

Schapiro was another unchallenged eminence. Sidney Hook too, though Sidney confined himself entirely to politics. No literature for Sidney Hook. Lionel Trilling, in those days, carried himself like an Olympian. That was beautifully done. And you wanted to be one of those people no one could lay a glove on. Some managed to arrange this. Wilson was one who did not. He didn't have to.

Were you one of the unassailables?

Me? Oh, no! I was boundlessly assailable!

But not often assailed.

I made no great impression on the *Partisan Review* heavy hitters.

Not all of the people were really seriously at work, were they?

Schwartz was and Berryman was. William Barrett was mastering existentialism—about to begin his book on the subject. In the early fifties, Berryman was writing the Bradstreet poem. I was finishing *The Adventures of Augie March*.

Where had the writing of that started?

I began it in Paris, on the Guggenheim grant. You leave the U.S.A. and from abroad you think of nothing else. I wrote in Paris, and later in Rome, at the Casino Valadier, in the Borghese Gardens. I went every morning with a notebook, drank Roman coffee, and poured out the words. Around noon, my friend Paolo Milano would appear—would mosey up. We'd go down to the Caffè Greco for more coffee.

Did you stay in Princeton?

I went up to New York as often as I could. I had an apartment in Forest Hills and kept a room in MacDougal Alley. In those days you could rent one for three or four dollars a week.

You must have felt on writing Augie *that you were on some quite major departure.*

I knew it was major for me. I couldn't judge what it might be for anybody else. What I found was the relief of turning away from mandarin English and putting my own accents into the language. My earlier books had been straight and respectable. As if I had to satisfy the demands of H. W. Fowler. But in *Augie March* I wanted to invent a new sort of American sentence. Something like a fusion of colloquialism and elegance. What you find in the best English writing of the twentieth century—in Joyce or E. E. Cummings. Street language

combined with a high style. I don't today take rhetorical effects so seriously, but at the time I was driven by a passion to *invent*.

I felt that American writing had enslaved itself without sufficient
reason to English models—everybody trying to meet the dominant
English standard. This was undoubtedly a very good thing, but not for
me. It meant that one's own habits of speech, daily speech, had to be
abandoned. Leading the "correct" grammatical forces was *The New
Yorker*. I used to say about Shawn that at *The New Yorker* he had traded
the Talmud for Fowler's *Modern English Usage*. . . . I'd like to mention,
before we leave the subject of Princeton, that in 1952 Bill Arrowsmith
was there, finishing his degree in Classics. I was very happy in his
company. I had met him in Minneapolis when he was a GI studying
Japanese. He's even splendider now than he had been then.

This use of language you were talking about in Augie . . . *It always
seemed an inner necessity.*

Paris in 1948 was a good year for this *grisaille*. Paris was depressed;
I was depressed. I became aware that the book I had gone there to write
had taken a stranglehold on me. Then I became aware one morning
that I might break its grip, outwit depression, by writing about something for which I had a great deal of feeling—namely, life in Chicago as
I had known it in my earliest years. And there was only one way to do
that—reckless spontaneity.

Didn't the book take off once you decided to do that?

It did. I *took* the opening I had found and immediately fell into an
enthusiastic state. I began to write in all places, in all postures, at all
times of the day and night. It rushed out of me. I was turned on like a
hydrant in summer. The simile is not entirely satisfactory. Hydrants
are not sexually excited. I was wildly excited.

Externally, I led the life of a good little bourgeois. Not that anybody was noticing. Once, I ran into Arthur Koestler on the boulevard
Saint-Germain. I was leading my small son by the hand—Koestler and
I had met briefly in Chicago. He said, "Is this your *child*?" I said,
"Yes." I was then reprimanded: a writer had no business to beget children. Hostages to fortune . . . the whole bit. I said, "Well, he's *here*." It
wasn't that I didn't admire Koestler. I did. But he was as well furnished
with platitudes as the next man, evidently.

The one thing that really shines out is your sheer prodigious energy.

I hadn't read Blake then. I read him later. Coming upon "energy is delight," I remembered how I had overcome the Parisian depression of 1948. *That* spoke to me.

When did it become fashionable that there should be an etiolation of this energy?

Writers in the 1950s arranged themselves, it seems to me, along the lines laid down by Yeats: the worst were full of passionate intensity. Such was the demand of history. Well, the Célines had the passionate intensity. The demonic figures on the right were all energy. The *bien pensants* were pallid. *La vie quotidienne* was something that prostrated and exhausted "good men," "men of good will." It put you in an honorific category to be able to display the ravages of this wasting disease of civilization. There was a nasty mournfulness in books written by the well-intentioned and the "ideologically correct" in the fifties. On the left, Sartre had great energy, but he was even more depressing than the *bien pensants*. I thought when he wrote his sponsoring essay on Frantz Fanon that Sartre was trying to do on the left what Céline had been doing on the right—Kill! Kill! Kill! With all his desperate outlawry, Sartre made me think of Peck's Bad Boy.

Your inner nature is basically optimistic.

Well, what you call optimism may be nothing more than a mismanaged, misunderstood vitality.

We arrive at Annandale-on-Hudson and Bard College. A really curious place. It had already been celebrated in a novel by the then wife of a rather famous husband.

Mary McCarthy and *The Groves of Academe*. There was also Randall Jarrell's *Pictures from an Institution*, which I thought much more amusing. Mary was unquestionably a witty writer, but she had a taste for low sadism. She would brutally work over people it wasn't really necessary to attack. She was by temperament combative and pugnacious. We were curious about her because she was, in her earlier years, a most beautiful woman, terribly attractive and apparently the repository of great sexual gifts. I never dreamed of sampling those—you might as well have been looking at sweets in Rumpelmayer's window. They were there, but you didn't want to eat them. I can remember her at *Partisan Review* parties. She was very elegant, the only elegant woman present. Her face was done up in a kind of porcelain makeup. Her look was dark—arched brows, a clear skin under the makeup. You'd run into her on the street, as Nicola Chiaromonte once told me

he did. She was blooming, he said, and he asked, "Why are you looking so well, Mary?" She said, "I just finished a piece against So-and-so,
and now I'm writing another, about such and such. Next, I'm going to
tear You-know-who to pieces." She was our tiger lady.

What brought you to Bard?

Princeton had only given me a one-year contract. I needed a
place to lay my head. At the time, the Bard job sounded easy. Low pay,
but the country air and pleasant surroundings would compensate me. I
could entertain my little boy there—take him out of the city, keep him
with me on holidays and long weekends. Much nicer than dragging
him around to museums and zoos in New York. Nothing is more
killing. To the divorced, the zoo can be a Via Crucis.

But then, I've had more metamorphoses than I can count. It was a
time of plunging into things, attractive-looking things, which quickly
became unattractive. I went through a period of psychiatry. Everybody
was immersed in "personal" difficulties. Later, all this would fall away,
and you would feel you'd squandered your time in "relationships" and
that there was no way in which you could understand your contemporaries and their sexual or therapeutic ideas. Seeking stability, you
hunted for clues, looked them over, cast them aside. I would read up on
a subject, discard it, and try again. I let myself in for a course of Reichian
therapy. Curious. A violent attack upon the physical symptoms of your
character neuroses.

To what degree was Henderson *under way then?*

I started to write *Henderson* after I left Bard. I had bought a house
in Tivoli, New York, a few miles north of Bard. I poured my life's
blood into that place: hammering and sawing, scraping and painting,
digging and planting and weeding until I felt like a caretaker in my
own cemetery. So that as I mowed the grass I would think: Here I will
be buried by the fall. At this rate. Under that tree. But Bard wasn't entirely a negative experience. I learned certain things there. Don't forget I'd gone from an Ivy League environment to a progressive one, to
Bard, where there were numerous castaways from ships that had
foundered en route to Harvard or characters who had fallen from
grace at Yale. Some of the faculty were still refining the airs they had
acquired in the great Ivy League centers. Bard was like Greenwich-
Village-in-the-Pines. The students came from small, wealthy New
York families. Many of the kids were troubled, some were being psy-

choanalyzed. Then there were the "great" families of the locality. It was useful to get to know them. Not at first hand, because they wouldn't invite me for drinks. Indirectly, however, I learned a lot about them.

My neighbors and acquaintances were Dick Rovere, Fred Dupee, Gore Vidal. My colleagues, *some* of them friends, were Keith Botsford, Ted Hoffman, made up to resemble a cocky Brechtian, and Tony Hecht. I loved the company of Heinrich Blücher. Occasionally I met his wife, Hannah Arendt, in New York, and she would set me straight about William Faulkner—tell me what I needed to know about American literature. I remember her in red dancing shoes.

There wasn't much humility in the Bellow of that period. It was understandable. You had made it. Most of them hadn't.

I made a point of speaking down to people (the nobs) who believed that I should look up to them. My lack of humility was aggravated by the rejections I met or expected to meet. Those confrontations were a part of my education. Five minutes of friendly clarity would have spared me this, but there was no one to assist my poor, slow mind. At that time, I was under tremendous emotional pressure. I had married into a New York bohemian family, and before long my wife began to say that my mind had been formed in the Middle Ages. She might have gone back even further—to antiquity, to the Patriarchs. My childhood lay under the radiance (or gloom) of the archaic family, the family of which God is the ultimate father and your own father is the representative of divinity. An American (immigrant plus WASP) version of the most ancient of myths: the creation, the garden, the fall, Genesis, Exodus, Joshua, Judges. The Old Testament became part of your life, if you had had that kind of upbringing. Imagine how well this fundamentalism would equip you to face the world I was entering—bohemianism, avant-garde art, the sexual revolution. I took to saying that in the sexual revolution there was no 1789. It was all 1793—all Terror.

My wife's father was a painter, a Marxian-Freudian-Jungian theorist, and the genius of a group of disciples for whom he was *the* artist. My wife had *had* it with artists. . . . This flamboyant Svengali circle was fun—in a hateful way. But my young wife and I should have agreed to jettison all "formative experiences" and, to the extent possible, make a new start, shelve our respective fathers. . . .

322 » Saul Bellow

I had an additional burden—my "higher education." That counts for a great deal. When that higher education was put to the test, it didn't work. I began to understand the irrelevancy of it, to recoil in disappointment from it. Then one day I saw the comedy of it. Herzog says, "What do you propose to do now that your wife has taken a lover? Pull Spinoza from the shelf and look into what he says about adultery? About human bondage?" You discover, in other words, the inapplicability of your higher learning, the absurdity of the culture it cost you so much to acquire. True devotion to Spinoza et al. would have left you no time for neurotic attachments and bad marriages. *That* would have been a way out for you.

What the above argues is not that higher education is a bad thing but that our conception of it is ridiculous.

One of the things you have to learn, which is never clear to you until an advanced age, is how many of the people you have to deal with are cut off from their first soul. This is in itself a revelation. And it never ceases to be a surprise to you that other people have a personal history so very different from your own. And have completely lost sight of that first soul, if indeed it ever existed for them. They may have turned away from it at a young age. In the earlier Greenwich Village generation, there was still some memory of it, even among the most anarchic and revolutionary. A person like Paul Goodman had a grip on it—on that first soul of his, as curious as it was, and as disfigured by psychoanalytic examination and the eccentric ideas he elaborated or fabricated. Still, it was there somewhere, a core of the self from first to last. It need not be—often it is not—a good or desirable core.

To many, the notion of an original center is alien and preposterous. Experience shows us more reproductions than originals. Zarathustra on the Last Man is hard for us to take. But Nietzsche didn't describe the Last Man *for* Last Men, any more than Marx described the alienated proletarian *for* proletarians. Marx was certainly addressing a new historical protagonist who was expected to survive the grinding forces of depersonalization. But who can deny that we are confronted daily with a mass of artificially constructed egos? And even relatively enlightened people prefer a Fabergé to a real egg.

Why would one marry a Fabergé?

Because of the attraction of art. And because you may feel (or wish to feel) that somewhere within the Fabergé you see before you there is a real egg with a rich yolk, a hidden residual first soul. Remember the E.T.A. Hoffmann story of the woman of springs, cushions, and wires invented by a mad Italian, and of the inflammable student who falls in love with her. She comes apart in his arms. In short, your own passion in some cases makes you think the power to reciprocate is there. And then we are not dealing with out-and-out automata—the object of your affections may know what it is that you want and have the talent to simulate it. A marvelous skill in deception often lies within "constructed" personalities.

To learn all this requires time, and you must wait long before you are ready to deal with human nature *telle qu'elle est*. Finally, we are unwilling for ideological reasons to think such things. They do not suit the liberal vision of human nature instilled by our *bien pensant* education. We shrink from cruelty and sadism. We hate to discover scheming, cunning, sharp practice. The ideology referred to is our middle-class legacy.

The high comedy of the intellectual in the never-never land of the "heart." I refer to men and women who love painting or poetry or philosophy and who are surrounded and nurtured by fictions. Perhaps they rely on crisis, war, revolution, to bring them to "reality" again. Hitler, Stalin, death camps, terrorist operations—these were the "real life" antidote to the "fiction" opiates.

We apparently have concentration camps of our own: in neighborhoods that are a vision of some future hell.

The actual urban environment of fear and caution. What I like to call the Fort Dearborn complex.

Except the cavalry is not riding up. . . .

The cavalry is not riding up, and your comrades inside the fort have no intention of fighting the Indians.

The Nobel Prize seemed as much a burden as a pleasure.

Yes, I didn't really like the volume of attention it brought. I wanted *some* recognition, of course, but I didn't need, or expect, supercertification.

The tone of your acceptance speech seemed to indicate that the times were slipping into a posture antagonistic to serious thought, anti-intellectual; literature was taking a beating; it was no longer taken seriously.

Literature in my early days was still something you lived by; you absorbed it, you took it into your system. Not as a connoisseur, aesthete, lover of literature. No, it was something on which you formed your life, which you ingested, so that it became part of your substance, your path to liberation and full freedom. All that began to disappear, was already disappearing, when I was young.

Under the influence of politics?

Partly under the influence of the world crisis, yes. I often try to fathom the feelings, attitudes, and strategies of a Joyce during the Great War when he concentrated on the writing of *Ulysses.* Could the fury of such a war be ignored? There's hardly a trace of it in *Ulysses.* But the war claimed the attention of most of mankind. Like the army mule struck between the eyes: an infallible way to get the critter's attention. I understand that Rilke, sick at heart, wrote almost nothing between 1914 and 1918.

In the first session, you acknowledged that you consistently ignored certain major events.

I was late in catching up. It wasn't that I wasn't interested. I was deafened by imperious noises close by.

American culture can isolate, it can muffle. . . .

The immediate American surroundings are so absorbing, so overwhelming. Because our minds are all over the place, we tend to forget that America, like Russia, is not a country, merely, but a world unto itself.

It has always been difficult for us to imagine life on premises different from our own. We take foreigners to be incomplete Americans—convinced that we must help and hasten their evolution.

But if literature is something to be lived and absorbed, Americans generally represented that as "ego."

Important American writing after the Great War was avant-garde writing. Young Americans took as their models the great figures of Symbolist and postwar European literature. That was, after all, small-public literature. It was not meant to be offered broadly to a democratic public.

It was something of a paradox for writers whose background, whose vital substance, was American to adopt these imported attitudes. The truth is that they weren't entirely imported. You had here a great public utterly devoid of interest in your literary plans. And in fact, you didn't wish to approach this public on *its* terms.

Wyndham Lewis, in a book called *Rude Assignment*, his intellectual biography, examines this question with exemplary clarity. He makes a distinction between small-public art and great-public art. The great-public writers of the nineteenth century were the Victor Hugos, the Dickenses, the Tolstoys, the Balzacs. They wrote for a national public. With the appearance of a Baudelaire, a Flaubert, you had an art that was intended for a limited public of connoisseurs. As the indifference of the great public to this dusk art increased, it became, perhaps from defiance, less and less accessible to the generality of readers.

I think this happened on both sides of the Atlantic. The Americans, of course, closely following the best European models, produced their own kind of small-public art. It was one of the achievements of Hemingway to reach a vast public with small-public stories and novels. What you had in America subsequently was a generation of writers who, with an esoteric outlook, presented themselves to a large public.

A doomed enterprise.

An odd one at best. Also increasingly associated with the universities, which gave shelter to small-public artists.

Did you feel it yourself?

Of course I felt it myself. I was schooled, as others were, in this art of choice means. Or refined instruments. I think *The Adventures of Augie March* represented a rebellion against small-public art and the inhibitions it imposed. My real desire was to reach "everybody." I had found—or believed I had found—a new way to *flow*. For better or for worse, this set me apart. Or so I wished to think. It may not have been a good thing to stand apart, but my character demanded it. It was inevitable—and the best way to treat the inevitable is to regard it as a good thing.

That might account for some of the petty rancor the American literary establishment does feel toward you at times: that you've tried to occupy a stage, take literature seriously, and deal with public issues. They really don't like that, do they?

They don't take it kindly. But let's remove me from this for the moment. The question has a wider interest, which ought to be addressed.

I think the mood of enthusiasm and love for literature, widespread in the twenties, began to evaporate in the thirties. Not only in America but in England, France, and Italy. Not in the Soviet Union.

There the Stalin dictatorship generated a spiritual need for it. In the United States, and even in France, it became nugatory. In the United States you had a brand of intellectuals who presented themselves at the beginning of their careers as literary people. But they quickly abandoned literature. Didn't really much care for it. They made their reputations on the ground between literature and politics, with diminishing attention to literature. Not large-scale politics, because they were ineffectual there. They were literary highbrows who continued the work of Orwell and Koestler. They moved from literature to political journalism. The "literary" screen, a stage property, was hoisted away into the flies.

Here's my recollection of an exchange between William Phillips and Philip Rahv. I heard it in the Astor Place office of *Partisan Review* nearly fifty years ago.

I have come to deliver the manuscript of a story. Rahv enters and asks Phillips, "Has anything for the next number come in?" Phillips says, "None of the important stuff [i.e., political, critical, academic] is here yet."

Though half of his preoccupations were political, Rahv was genuinely a literary man. But the repositories of vast power in my day never were art lovers. Stalin telephoned Pasternak to get a reference for Mandelstam: not because he was thinking of reading his poems but because he had Mandelstam on his hit list. Party leaders, heads of state, generalissimos, board chairmen, etc.—down to junk-bond scammers—have no time for belles lettres. Nor do the once literary intellectuals who buzz about them as (largely unheeded) advisers, rooters, and *besserwisser*—know-betters.

These intellectuals, now totally political, have gone over to junk culture. High-level junk culture, to be sure, but junk is what they genuinely prefer. After a day of unremitting crisis, they want pleasant entertainment. They're not rushing home to read Act Three of *The Tempest* or to get in a few pages of Proust before bedtime, are they? And much of junk culture has a core of crisis—shoot-outs, conflagrations, bodies weltering in blood, naked embracers or rapist-stranglers. The sounds of junk culture are heard over a ground bass of extremism. Our entertainments swarm with specters of world crisis. Nothing moderate can have any claim to our attention.

The prospect of his soon being hung will concentrate a man's thoughts wonderfully, Dr. Johnson has told us. For us, perhaps, thrillers are aids to such concentration and help us to stay braced through our dark night. Nothing "normal" holds the slightest interest. Spare us the maiden joys of Tolstoy's Natasha. Give us only his spinning minié balls, about to explode. We use the greater suffering to expel the lesser. The top ratings are permanently assigned to Auschwitz, Treblinka, and the gulag. The Vélo d'Hiver is somewhat lower. Famine makes Ethiopia eligible. And North America, if you except Mexico, isn't even in it.

This continent is the Kingdom of Frivolity, while all the "towering figures" are in Eastern Europe. This is how literary-political intellectuals view the present world. It isn't contemporary literature alone that is threatened by this. The classics themselves are shooting, not drifting, Letheward. We may lose everything at this rate.

Is this a note of despair I hear?

Do I look or sound despairing? My spirits are as high as ever. Not despair—anger. Contempt and rage. For this latest and longest betrayal by putty-headed academics and intellectuals.

Copyright Acknowledgments

FOR THE BEST IN PAPERBACKS, LOOK FOR THE

In every corner of the world, on every subject under the sun, Penguin represents quality and variety—the very best in publishing today.

For complete information about books available from Penguin—including Pelicans, Puffins, Peregrines, and Penguin Classics—and how to order them, write to us at the appropriate address below. Please note that for copyright reasons the selection of books varies from country to country.

In the United Kingdom: For a complete list of books available from Penguin in the U.K., please write to *Dept E.P., Penguin Books Ltd, Harmondsworth, Middlesex, UB7 0DA.*

In the United States: For a complete list of books available from Penguin in the U.S., please write to *Consumer Sales, Penguin USA, P.O. Box 999—Dept. 17109, Bergenfield, New Jersey 07621-0120.* VISA and MasterCard holders call 1-800-253-6476 to order all Penguin titles.

In Canada: For a complete list of books available from Penguin in Canada, please write to *Penguin Books Canada Ltd, 10 Alcorn Avenue, Suite 300, Toronto, Ontario, Canada M4V 3B2.*

In Australia: For a complete list of books available from Penguin in Australia, please write to the *Marketing Department, Penguin Books Ltd, P.O. Box 257, Ringwood, Victoria 3134.*

In New Zealand: For a complete list of books available from Penguin in New Zealand, please write to the *Marketing Department, Penguin Books (NZ) Ltd, Private Bag, Takapuna, Auckland 9.*

In India: For a complete list of books available from Penguin, please write to *Penguin Overseas Ltd, 706 Eros Apartments, 56 Nehru Place, New Delhi, 110019.*

In Holland: For a complete list of books available from Penguin in Holland, please write to *Penguin Books Nederland B.V., Postbus 195, NL-1380AD Weesp, Netherlands.*

In Germany: For a complete list of books available from Penguin, please write to *Penguin Books Ltd, Friedrichstrasse 10-12, D-6000 Frankfurt Main 1, Federal Republic of Germany.*

In Spain: For a complete list of books available from Penguin in Spain, please write to *Longman, Penguin España, Calle San Nicolas 15, E-28013 Madrid, Spain.*

In Japan: For a complete list of books available from Penguin in Japan, please write to *Longman Penguin Japan Co Ltd, Yamaguchi Building, 2-12-9 Kanda Jimbocho, Chiyoda-Ku, Tokyo 101, Japan.*